Supervision and Authority in Industry

International Studies in Social History
General Editor: Marcel van der Linden,
International Institute of Social History, Amsterdam

SUPERVISION AND AUTHORITY IN INDUSTRY

Western European Experiences, 1830–1939

Edited by

Patricia Van den Eeckhout

Berghahn Books

NEW YORK • OXFORD

Published in 2009 by
Berghahn Books

www.berghahnbooks.com

© 2009 Patricia Van den Eeckhout

Library of Congress Cataloging-in-Publication Data

Supervision and authority in industry : Western European experiences,
    1830–1939 / edited by Patricia Van den Eeckhout.
        p. cm. — (International studies in social history ; v. 15)
    Includes bibliographical references and index.
    ISBN 978-1-84545-600-9 (alk. paper)
        1. Labor supply—Europe—History—Case studies. 2. Supervision of
    employees—Europe—History—Case studies. 3. Industrial management—
    Europe—History—Case studies. I. Eeckhout, Patricia Van den, 1953–.
    HD5706.S847 2009
    331.25—dc22

                                                    2009015698

British Library Cataloguing in Publication Data

A catalogue record for this book is available
from the British Library.

Printed in the United States on acid-free paper

CONTENTS

ILLUSTRATIONS

ABBREVIATIONS

AEU	Amalgamated Engineering Union
AGM	Annual General Meeting
ASE	Amalgamated Society of Engineers
Ct	centime
CVM	Centrale der Vrije Mijnwerkers
DCRO	Durham County Record Office
EC	Executive Committee
EEA	Engineering Employers' Association
EEF	Engineering Employers' Federation
ESEA	East of Scotland Engineering Employers' Association
FED	Glasgow West of Scotland Association of Foremen Engineers and Draughtsmen
FMBS	Foremen's Mutual Benefit Society
FMWS	Foremen's Mutual Welfare Society
Fr	franc
GCA	Glasgow City Archives
INSEE	Institut National de la Statistique et des Etudes Economiques
MC	Mijnwerkerscentrale
MRC	Modern Records Centre
NCL	Newcastle Central Library
NFA	National Foremen's Association
NGA	National Graphical Association
NRO	Northumberland Record Office
NWETEA	North West Engineering Trades Employers' Association
OCL	Oxford City Library
PAH	Provinciaal Archief Hasselt
RH	Rijksarchief Hasselt
VLM	Verzameling Luc Minten
VMM	Archief Vlaams Mijnmuseum

ACKNOWLEDGEMENTS

I wish to thank the participants in the conference 'Supervision and Authority in Nineteenth-Century Industry', which was held at the Vrije Universiteit Brussel in December 2005 and was funded by FWO-Vlaanderen. Apart from the authors represented in this volume, those who participated in the discussions included Yves Cohen, Ad Knotter, Philippe Lefebvre, Sven Steffens and Lex Heerma Van Voss. I also would like to thank Frank Winter, who corrected the contributions of Bart Delbroek, Peter Scholliers and myself.

– Patricia Van den Eeckhout

CHAPTER 1

FOREMEN IN AMERICAN AND WESTERN EUROPEAN INDUSTRY BEFORE THE FIRST WORLD WAR

Patricia Van den Eeckhout

In Sydney Pollard's inexhaustible *The Genesis of Modern Management*, first published in 1965, the emergence of management structures in large-scale industrial enterprises is explored, but foremen are hardly mentioned. Pollard asserts that the division of labour and the increasing size of British plants between 1750 and 1830 'made the introduction of wage-earning foremen and managers essential',[1] but in his discussion of these emerging management structures, he largely ignores the role of foremen. In the twenty-five years that followed, foremen appeared unable to attract historians' attention to any significant extent. 'A strategically vital, if largely unstudied figure in the history of labour', is Patrick Joyce's assessment of the foreman in English social history.[2] 'Etre contremaître est bien un métier, même si celui-ci est rarement décrit', argues Sylvie Vandecasteele-Schweitzer, on the basis of her experience of French social history.[3]

The Invisible Foreman

More than ten years after Patrick Joyce and Sylvie Vandecasteele-Schweitzer wrote down their impressions, our knowledge of the role and function of foremen before the First World War remains extremely fragmented. Contributions dealing with the history of management, the bureaucratization of work and the history of labour relations often devote some passing attention to foremen, but these are seldom their main preoccupation. Monographs about the history of a firm or industrial sector often contain

Notes for this chapter begin on page 29.

some paragraphs about foremen, but it is hardly feasible to collect all this scattered information.

Since a nuanced answer to the question 'What is a foreman and what does he do?' is part of our investigation, I start with a very broad and open working definition: a foreman is a salaried or wage-earning person in charge of a group of workers. This definition implies that there is a hierarchical relationship between the foreman and the crew he is in charge of, but leaves open what the exact content of this hierarchical relationship is. The fact that we focus on foremen will not prevent us from exploring supervisory functions performed by persons who did not belong to the salaried or wage-earning personnel as such. Since our study is limited to the industrial sector, the foremen whom we investigate are in charge of manual workers, but it remains to be seen whether foremen are considered manual workers themselves.

Why should we be interested at all in the history of foremen? The number of studies discussing the labour relationship under industrial capitalism is overwhelming, but the literature on labour and the labour process as concrete, day-to-day shop-floor practices seems much less abundant. The labour process is frequently dealt with as if it were an abstraction. In business histories it is often merely implicitly present; in histories of industrial relations it is frequently reduced to a matter of discussion between unions, employers and governments. In quite a few working-class histories, theoretical and ideological assumptions and debates have obscured the view of the labour process as a lived relationship between creatures of flesh and blood.

Ideally, studying foremen is a good antidote to a history of labour based on simple dichotomies and caricatures as historical actors: on the one hand employers devoured by the ambition to deskill and subordinate the working class, on the other hand proud workers who bemoan the world of self regulation and autonomy that they have lost. Commonly portrayed as an intermediary between capital and labour, the foreman embodies the complexity of the labour relationship and the ambiguous boundaries of class. Confronted with both workers' and employers' diverging expectations, hopes, fears, representations of self and assumptions of what is fair and reasonable, the foreman has to be a tacit negotiator if he wants to survive. Watching the foreman operate can tell us more about the stuff that relations of authority are made of and how these are influenced by changing technologies, conceptions of skill, labour market conditions and social relations outside the workshop.

As will be shown in the following survey of American and Western European literature, the representation of craft workers' status on the shop floor often functions as a watershed in the assessment of the foreman's role. In contributions emphasizing craft workers' relative control of the labour process, the foreman is either hardly visible or he is presented as the *primus inter pares* whose authority was based on a combination of personality and a superior command of his craft. This type of foreman was a mediator who took the sensibilities of both workers and employers to heart. His relationship with his subordinates appeared to be one of reciprocity and mutual respect, but this did not necessarily prevent violent clashes and strong language. More difficult to assess is the foreman's role in the contributions combining an emphasis on craft workers' control of the labour process and minimal or no mention of foremen. How is the reader supposed to interpret this: as an indication that the role of foremen was marginal, or as the result of a sort of authors' 'blindness'? Overemphasizing workers' autonomy can indeed lead to an unjustified neglect of hierarchical relations on the shop floor.

Authors who do not underscore craft workers' autonomy tend to present the foreman as a tyrannical figure who let loose his driving methods on his hapless collaborators. In the latter case coercion and the threat of being fired were brought into play. This contrasting picture suggests that relations of reciprocity can exist only if power relations are more or less balanced. In this respect the literature on supervisory functions in India, Japan and China is relevant. Even if the relationship between foremen or contractors and their subordinates had an exploitative character, both parties had the impression of benefiting from it. While keeping in mind the different contexts, the study of foremen in the Unites States and Western Europe could gain from the acknowledgement that even in strikingly unequal power relations, the 'weak' did not necessarily negotiate empty-handed.

Class Struggle on the (American) Shop Floor?

When we examine the emergence, the role and the function of foremen before the First World War, we are in fact studying why and how industrial labour was managed. The 1970s and 1980s witnessed the publication of some very influential American contributions carrying the message that class struggle (and not technological reasons or the quest for efficiency) is the major driving force in the organization of the labour process and the development of structures of control.

The publication in 1974 of Stephen Marglin's allegedly provocative article 'What Do Bosses Do?' launched the debate. The 'radical' economist Marglin challenges the view that the rise of the factory was due to its technological superiority. He claims the putting-out system had to give way to the factory because the latter allowed a closer supervision of work-ers by capitalists, who could then extract a greater output and further increase their 'share of the pie'. In this 'factory debate' the supervision of workers is at the heart of the discussion.[4] However, despite the centrality of supervision in his argument, Marglin hardly discusses it. 'Under the watchful eye of the foreman, the worker was no longer free to pace him-self according to his own standards', is about the only sentence in Marg-lin's article where the concept of supervision is actually linked to concrete persons and practices. Authors participating in and commenting on the 'factory debate' acknowledge that the question of supervision played a role in the rise of the factory, albeit a minor one compared to technology. However, supervision is treated cursorily, as if there were common agree-ment on what it consisted of and how and by whom it was implemented.[5] Although the question of supervision is not expanded, it is clear that it is interpreted as being mainly disciplinary. Is that all there is to supervision: imposing discipline? And was it a foreman who took care of that in the early days of the factory or is Marglin merely referring to an archetypical figure, a shorthand symbol for an unspecified shop-floor hierarchy?

The idea of the factory as a system of control aiming to extract labour from workers is shared by other 'radical' economists and sociologists.[6] While Marglin focuses on the emergence of the factory system in Eng-land at the end of the eighteenth and the beginning of the nineteenth centuries, the latter contributions focus on the American craft system, its gradual demise around the turn of the twentieth century, deskilling, and workers' loss of control over the labour process.

Katherine Stone, David Montgomery and Dan Clawson deal with the 'golden age' of the American craft system, a system in which skilled work-ers allegedly controlled many details of the work process and more par-ticularly output. Workers in the skilled trades appeared to have their own collective definition of a reasonable day's work. The employers' struggle to undermine workers' control is seen as an attempt to circumvent these output restrictions.[7]

In Montgomery's and Stone's description of the craft system, fore-men play only a marginal role.[8] According to Stone, who studied labour relations in the American steel industry between 1890 and 1920, author-ity on the shop floor was in the hands of teams of skilled workers who contracted with the steel companies, largely controlled production, set their own pace and workload, shared in the profits via the sliding scale for wages and hired their own helpers. Foremen had authority only over the pools of unskilled workers engaged by the steel company itself.

David Montgomery's account equally emphasizes skilled workers' 'managerial' role. In fact these workers managed themselves, as well as the helpers they hired. In the iron and steel industry, skilled workers sub-contracted jobs as a group, exercised a substantial degree of control over productive tasks and imposed their collective ethical code. In the chapter 'The manager's brain under the workman's cap', foremen, supervisors or overseers are not mentioned and thus we cannot but conclude that they played a rather marginal role in these skilled workers' lives. In the machine-building sector as well, skilled workers often imposed their collective control, ethical code and work culture.[9] On the basis of the attention devoted to foremen, one gets the impression that only in the world of 'the common labourer' and the operative did foremen play a role of importance. The nineteenth-century operative is described as a specialist doing repetitive work that could be easily defined and measured. Operatives were supervised by foremen who hired and fired, assigned tasks, set the pay rate, decided who had to quit and who had to do overtime, resolved disputes and who were able to favour or punish as they liked.[10]

However, Montgomery signals that there was trouble in the craft workers' paradise. When the leader of a crew, rather than a group of workers, subcontracted, then the system served not the collective self-imposed craft discipline but the individual material advantage of the 'Yankee contractor', who derived his income from the margin between the payment he received from the company and the wages he paid to his crew.[11] This hierarchically structured form of contracting spread substantially between 1860 and 1890.[12] As a result more and more workers became the employers of other workers, using the firm's infrastructure.

Dan Clawson's discussion of developments in American industry between 1860 and 1920 (and more particularly in the machine-building sector) deals extensively with the hierarchically structured, rather than the collective form of inside contracting.[13] In Clawson's account contractors and foremen are presented as more or less interchangeable figures who were both part of the craft system.[14] Clawson devotes several pages to the undermining of Stone's and Montgomery's romanticized vision of the craft workers' world.[15] His argument, however, that skilled workers were not 'really' in control is aimed at demonstrating that these cases 'cannot be regarded as a socialist model of workers' control'.[16] This rather self-evident acknowledgement does not in fact contradict Stone's and Montgomery's account. For Clawson too, skilled workers and not their foremen or internal contractors controlled the details of the work process: a lot of decisions that were formally the responsibility of contractors and foremen, were in fact made by workers.[17]

It goes without saying that this emphasis on skilled workers' predominant position on the work floor enables authors to contrast labour relations under the American craft system with its gradual demise as a result of management and Taylorist practices. It was Harry Braverman who wrote the canonical account of that process.[18] Braverman's argument hardly needs presenting: by means of mechanization, division of labour and the implementation of Taylorist techniques, capitalist management actively promoted the loss of craft skills, the de-qualification of the workforce, the separation of conception and execution of tasks, and the transfer of knowledge and control of the labour process from workers to management. Braverman's thesis on deskilling met with a lot of approbation but even more criticism.[19] Idealization of the craft worker's past, neglect of workers' resistance, exaggeration of the impact of Taylorism and overestimation of the purposefulness and coherence of management's actions are among the most cited points of critique. Anyway, for a student of the role and function of foremen, Braverman has not much to offer. In his work we meet managers, engineers, workers and so on, but foremen remain invisible.

Stone's article does not contain any references to Harry Braverman's book, published in the same year as her paper. Montgomery's *The Fall of the House of Labor* carries only two minor references to Braverman's classic. This does not prevent Stone and Montgomery sharing the thesis of deskilling. Dan Clawson presents himself as a critical admirer of Braverman and he emphasizes that it was this craft system, in which workers both planned and executed production, had to use their judgement and insight and largely controlled their work pace, that Frederick Taylor wanted to destroy.[20] As Jean Monds stated in a critical survey of this line of history writing: the craft workers' world is presented as a lost paradise and Frederick Taylor is cast in the role of the serpent.[21]

Another authority in American labour relations, Richard Edwards, can also be counted among the 'workers' control school' of labour history, but several points distinguish him from the authors already mentioned. Edwards is rather critical of Braverman and in contrast with Stone, Montgomery and Clawson he does not idealize the craft workers' past, while he is also convinced that Taylorism was an outright failure.[22] As a result, Edwards has no need to emphasize the contrast between these two episodes. He does stress, however, that the workplace is a battlefield and that control is the weapon capitalists and managers use to obtain the work behaviour required, so as to extract an increasing amount of labour.[23]

According to Edwards there are basically three forms of control on the shop floor: simple control based on direct supervision, technical control where control is embodied in the machine, and bureaucratic control when control is achieved by a host of organizational rules. Each form of control corresponds to a phase in the history of the capitalist firm.[24] Bureaucratic control developed essentially in the post-1945 period, at least according to Edwards. Edwards's book is constructed round this theory of three successive stages and this gives his account a somewhat ahistorical flavour. The British labour historian Craig Littler (see below) does not mince his words in his discussion of Edwards's thesis: he reproaches him with being a linear theorist, with presenting an idealized historical analysis and with underestimating the complexity of control relations.[25]

When firms were small it was the capitalist himself (assisted by a growing number of foremen as firms grew bigger) who controlled the workforce. Edwards does not go in for nostalgia. He characterizes the 'personal touch' of the capitalist and his foremen as harsh, arbitrary and despotic, although he also points to the fact that the charisma of the owner and the personal ties he established with his workers could have motivated the latter.[26] Near the end of the nineteenth century, the consolidation of industry produced larger workforces which were increasingly difficult to control. The regime of foremen hardened, totally lacked positive incentives and triggered violent reactions from workers. With the disappearance of personal ties between the capitalist, foremen and workers, class conflict surfaced in all its rawness. Since ties between foremen and capitalists also weakened, doubts rose as to whether those in subordinate management positions defended their own interests rather than their employer's. Taylorism, so Edwards argues, was an attempt to solve the crisis of control through scientific study, but it failed. It failed for the simple reason that it was hardly implemented, and when it was, workers succeeded in fighting it. However, it was an interesting failure, because capitalists learned from it.[27] On the terrain, the introduction of technical control changed the struggle between bosses and workers, since a form of structural control emerged that was built into the design and functioning of the machines. While machine pacing was already known in the textile industries, continuous flow spread to meatpacking, electrical products and automobile manufacturing. From now on pace was dictated by the assembly line or other machinery and not by foremen. Speed was thus checked in an impersonal way, but the inspection and evaluation of the worker's performance were still the foreman's prerogative.[28]

The views of the 'workers' control school' of labour history are not shared by authors such as Daniel Nelson, Ernest Englander and Sanford Jacoby, who have also studied the role of contractors and foremen in American industry.[29] Nelson and Jacoby deal with different industrial sectors, while Englander focuses on firms assembling interchangeable parts, such as the firearms, machine-tool and sewing-machine industries.

When in 1995 Daniel Nelson published the second edition of his 1975 classic, *Managers and Workers*, he omitted references to the work of Braverman, Stone and Edwards (numerously cited in other literature on labour relations) although he announced in his preface that he would include important literature not included in the first edition.[30] In other contributions Nelson has been more explicit in his criticism of the 'group of scholars associated directly or indirectly with the Marxist journalist Harry Braverman'.[31] He characterizes the work of Bravermann, Stone, Edwards, Montgomery and Clawson as 'suggestive and impressionistic' and as 'a series of provocative hypotheses rather than a description of Taylorism in the workplace'. While Nelson appreciates Montgomery's use of primary sources (a contrast with the other authors voicing the 'radical critique'), he criticizes him for relying 'almost exclusively on anecdotal evidence'.[32]

Reading the chapters 'The Foreman's Empire' and 'The Rise of Scientific Management' we can see why Nelson distances himself from these neo-Marxist perspectives. In his account we find neither the idealization of craft workers' past, nor the conviction that management's primary concern was to end craft workers' control of the labour process.[33] Ernest Englander in his turn argues that a variety of reasons – not class-conflict arguments alone – explain changes in the organization of the labour process.[34] Jacoby challenges the view that bureaucracy was consciously designed by employers in order to increase their control of the labour force and he emphasizes that unions and workers also derived benefit from it. He reproaches Braverman and Stone with wanting to return to the craft system and with being insensitive to the plight of the less-skilled worker.[35]

But do these differing ideological perspectives have implications for what we learn about contractors and foremen? Jacoby and Clawson mention its existence,[36] but none of the other authors discuss the craft workers' more 'egalitarian' form of subcontracting, cherished by Montgomery and Stone. This might lead to the conclusion that a labour process where skilled workers managed themselves and supervision played a minimal role was quite marginal. A hierarchical relationship between supervisor (contractor or foreman) and workers seemed to have been the rule, even in the craft workers' world.

These four authors have similar views on the role and function of foremen and contractors, but there are some differences as well. Englander, Nelson and Clawson agree that inside contracting was an important system of production in American industry until the beginning of the twentieth century, but according to Jacoby's unsubstantiated observation it was not very common.[37] In contrast with the other three, Clawson emphasizes craft workers' control of all the details of the work process. There is disagreement also on the question of why internal contractors had to give way to foremen and why systematic management methods were introduced.

What do these authors tell us about internal contracting? The inside contractor had a contractual relationship with his 'employer'. The former agreed to produce a certain quantity of objects or components at a certain cost. While the firm provided him with machinery, raw materials and working capital, the contractor (who was a skilled worker) bore complete responsibility for the production process. That included the hiring, firing, rate setting and supervision of labour. One of the major advantages of internal contracting for entrepreneurs was the fact that internal contractors provided the know-how the capitalist lacked, freed the latter from worrying about technological improvements and labour supervision, and kept production costs low. The system could be beneficial for skilled workers as well. As subcontractors, they retained some independence and they could still use their craft skills without having to worry about capital, marketing and sales.[38]

Daniel Nelson and Dan Clawson point to the difference between internal contracting and the helper system.[39] In the textile, pottery, glass and iron industries skilled workers hired women and boys who assisted them in their work and who were paid from the skilled worker's earnings. In contrast to 'true' contractors, these skilled workers had fewer managerial responsibilities and they saw themselves as workers, not as managers.

Why was the internal contractor gradually replaced by a salaried foreman? Dan Clawson mentions several reasons why, from the 1870s on, inside contracting began to decline in American industry. By liquidating contractors, firms could shift income from contractor to company because foremen earned much less than contractors. Moreover, when technological improvement led to cost reduction, the company benefited from this immediately and did not have to wait for the adjustment of the contractors' contract price. The contractor's high earnings and the social status that went with it, also provoked the envy of company officials who preferred a more modest foreman.[40] According to Ernest Englander and Daniel Nelson, owners got rid of contractors because they wanted to have their say in hiring procedures and were looking to avoid labour unrest resulting from contractors' cuts in wage rates, while their salaried managers wanted to apply their new management techniques.[41]

Andrew Dawson recently proposed an alternative view of inside contracting, which has repercussions for our interpretation of the position of the foreman.[42] He challenges the vision that the form of contracting described in the literature as inside contracting spread from New England where it was initially introduced, to other machine-building centres and continued to exist until the beginning of the twentieth century. He claims there was no continuity between the semi-independent entrepreneurs operating in mid-century New England and the contractors of the Philadelphia engineering shops of the 1870s and 1880s. While the former corresponded to the rather powerful figure described above, the contractors of the end of the nineteenth century received only contracts of short duration, had to recruit their labour from the existing personnel of the company, did not earn high incomes but a premium for supervising labour and did not pay their workers themselves, because the company did. In other words: the Philadelphia contractors were not small capitalists, but craft workers who were given a position of responsibility and who formed a layer of overseers between the foremen and the workers. Dawson proposes to call the system 'piece contracting' instead of inside contracting. In the system of piece contracting not the inside contractor led the game, but the company foreman who invited contractors to bid for a job. The piece contractor checked machines, material and quality and maintained discipline. Agreeing with Andrew Dawson's alternative framework means challenging the received view that the foreman was the successor to the internal contractor. Further research will have to bring clarification. Meanwhile we continue with our exploration of the existing literature.

The foreman is often characterized as a supervisor with similar responsibilities to those of the internal contractor, but without his degree of independence. Depending on the industry and production process, management interfered and made sure the foreman had less power than the internal contractor. However, where workers were concerned, the foreman was still the undisputed ruler. He hired, trained, motivated and disciplined the workforce, set wage rates and 'got the work out' by a combination of threats, abuse and physical compulsion. The practice became known as the drive system: pressure and fear were supposed to enhance efficiency.[43] Clawson emphasizes, however, that not the foreman, but the workers' controlled the details of the work process and he characterizes the atmosphere on the shop floor as one of rough egalitarianism. Despite their powers (they are referred to as the 'tsars' of production), Clawson's foremen are not pictured as tyrannical figures: they were craft workers like their subordinates, the best workmen of the department, chosen for their skills and experience and often working side by side with those they supervised.[44] According to David Montgomery, one could even speak of a form of complicity between workers and foremen in the deception of higher management. Foremen kept their production standards rather lax so as to make the crew's output look good, while it also created a sense of goodwill among the workers.[45]

Nelson and Jacoby confirm that foremen were chosen for their know-how and experience.[46] But Jacoby underlines the arbitrariness of the foremen's rule. Often the foreman hired his friends or relatives, while he accepted bribes in exchange for a job. Craig Heron reports that foremen even succeeded in getting invited to workers' weddings and other celebrations.[47] Favouritism also occurred in wage setting and promotions. Foremen ran their shops autonomously and this resulted in very different rates for similar jobs. Since the 1880s the increasing power of skilled workers' unions succeeded in gradually curbing the foremen's prerogatives in the realm of hiring, wage setting, output quota and layoffs.[48] As I mentioned earlier, Richard Edwards too emphasizes the despotic character of the foreman's power: skill and experience did not even seem to be part of his job description. According to Jürgen Kocka, American foremen were white-collar workers.[49] It remains to be seen whether earning a salary instead of a wage, wearing a suit and tie and giving orders is sufficient to define a white-collar worker. One can even wonder whether the polarity blue collar/white collar was relevant in the context of exercising shop-floor authority.

Gunther Peck stresses that the foreman's power as regards hiring and firing was one of the pillars on which the abusive *padrone* system rested.[50] *Padrone* was the nickname for the Italian, Greek, Mexican and Japanese labour contractors who provided industrial and agricultural firms in the North American West with cheap and seasonally disposable unskilled labour. These middlemen recruited immigrant workers in North American cities and in their home countries. They advanced their clients' passage fares, cashed in commissions for the procurement of a job and provisioned them with high-priced food and sometimes lodgings. Foremen and gang bosses 'appointed' by the *padrone* or on his pay list made sure the *padrone*'s clients were hired and that job fees and debts were deducted from workers' wages. The rise of personnel departments after the First World War eroded the foreman's authority over hiring and subsequently undermined the *padrone* system.

How did pre-war management and Taylorist practices change the role of the foremen? It was Frederick Taylor's ambition to eliminate the traditional foreman altogether. The idea was to replace him by functional foremen while a planning office would take care of the direction and coordination of work, thus doing all the 'brainwork' that was once the responsibility of the traditional foreman.[51] Functional foremen would each perform one of the eight different functions which (according to Taylor's analysis) belonged to the job description of the traditional foreman: training, controlling machines, preventing breakdowns, maintaining quality, determining the order in which work had to be done, maintaining discipline, controlling time and cost, and giving instructions.[52] Each functional foreman would command workers in the area of his particular expertise.

According to Clawson, piecework, improved record keeping, division of labour, new machinery and eventually Taylorism were part of capitalists' efforts to undermine workers' autonomy and to speed up work, but we do not learn how all this changed the role of the foreman.[53] In Stone's account, the foremen's new and more important role is presented as part of a policy that had to solve the disciplinary problems caused by the dismantling of the collective internal contract system. As a result of increasing mechanization and the undermining of skilled workers' control over the labour process, workers no longer had a stake in the production process. This engendered problems of labour discipline. Meanwhile the homogenization of the workforce (downgrading of the skilled, upgrading of the unskilled) de-motivated the men, stuck in dead-end jobs. The introduction of wage incentives and the creation of strictly demarcated job ladders, with differentiated status and pay, were supposed to solve the problem of discipline and worker motivation. This policy also included a different role for the foremen. While under the contract system their role seemed to be quite marginal, they now became management's representatives on the shop floor. They were recruited from the ranks of skilled workers but subsequently retrained because they had to learn to limit themselves to supervision and not to intervene in the manual work as such. Foremen were to become the lowest-ranking 'mind' workers, but they were not the beneficiaries of the expropriation of workers' skills and knowledge: management was.

However, Stone's views are not uncontested. Craig Heron, who studied the Canadian steel sector, challenges Stone's thesis of deskilling, the stripping away of workers' shop-floor discretion, foremen's loss of conceptual responsibility and the impact of Taylorist principles on day-to-day operations. He emphasizes the continuity in foremen's practices, but he also acknowledges that the pressure from cost-conscious managers to increase daily output intensified. A combination of the 'drive system' with the carrot of wage incentives had to prevent men from restricting their output as they did in the nineteenth century.[54]

Montgomery and Nelson agree that functional foremanship was not a success.[55] Very few firms adopted it, because employers were not keen on paying an army of supervisors, while commands by eight different foremen tended to be confusing. In the Ford Motor Company where Taylorite principles were applied although this was officially denied,[56] a variant of functional foremanship was introduced. The driving was done by a 'working' sub-foreman or straw boss who mediated between the foreman and the increasing number of immigrant workers who did not speak English.[57]

If we measure the success of Taylorism in the pre-war period by the acceptance of the total package of Taylorist principles and the implementation of functional foremanship, then its impact can hardly be called impressive. However, since the 1880s, the rise of systematic management quietly influenced the foreman's role. Nelson and Jacoby point to the fact that trained engineers, eager to solve the problems caused by increased mechanization and reacting against the improvised nature of factory administration, the lack of control and coordination and the animosity provoked by the foremen's driving methods, tried to integrate and control different steps in the process of manufacturing. As a result, the foreman's responsibilities regarding production and costs were reduced, since certain tasks (assembling raw materials for production, keeping stock of tools and materials, routing of orders, scheduling of jobs, movement and storage of finished parts, recording of production costs) were allocated to other employees.[58] Nelson concludes that the foreman ceased to be the all-round manager that he had been in the past. After 1910 the foreman's responsibilities regarding employment matters were often transferred to the personnel department.[59] William Lazonick, who presents a more nuanced version of the thesis of the 'workers' control school', argues that one of the goals of this transfer was the attenuation of the negative impact on productivity of foremen's arbitrary practices. Having a personnel department attending to workers' grievances was supposed to put an end to adversarial shop-floor relations.[60] In his history of the Canadian steel sector, Craig Heron claims that the creation of such a department did not change so much in practice: through quiet instructions to this department foremen seemed to hold to their authority.[61]

With the growth of mass production, the numbers of supervisors multiplied because one 'recalcitrant' operative sufficed to interrupt even the most routinized flow of work. Lazonick notes a more than threefold increase in the number of foremen in American manufacturing between 1900 and 1920, while the ratio of foremen to operatives rose by 15 per cent between 1900 and 1910.[62] As in the past, foremen were recruited among skilled workers but in the subdivided production process their place was taken up by cheaper help.[63]

The History of the Industrial Firm with Labour Left Out

The writings of Stephen Marglin and Katherine Stone not only provoked reactions from labour and business historians, but they also inspired the New Institutional Economist Oliver Williamson to reflect on the history of hierarchy.[64] Williamson is challenged by the view of the 'workers' control school' that hierarchy operates in the service of power and not of efficiency. According to Williamson, hierarchy economizes on transaction costs and results in more efficiency. The quest for more efficiency was the reason why putting out was supplanted by factory production and why inside contracting gave way to the hierarchically organized factory, based on authority relations. Williamson avoids the simplistic dichotomy

putting out/factory and discusses six different ways of organizing production. However, references to historical experiences are superficial and
scarce and therefore his remains a merely theoretical exercise, performed
in a chronological no-man's land.

Williamson evaluates the efficiency of six different organizational modes
using eleven criteria. Philippe Lefebvre made a devastating critique of this
attempt.[65] Williamson's de-contextualized approach fails to acknowledge
the historicity and the dynamics of the transformation of the different
ways of organizing production. Implicitly the reader is led to believe that
the six organizational modes co-existed since the beginning of industrialization and that their characteristics did not change over time. Given the
ahistorical character of this approach, it is no surprise that in Williamson's
text we fail to meet real people. One can but wonder how the desired
outcomes of organizational modes (preventing embezzlement, an optimal assignment of tasks, work intensity and equipment utilization, the
ability to respond to 'local shocks' such as machine breakdown or illness
of workers) were to be achieved and by whom.

For the student of shop-floor hierarchy, so Philippe Lefebvre argues, the
work of business historian Alfred Chandler has not much to offer either. In
Chandler's account, middle and upper management appear to have a history, but shop-floor management does not.[66] His criticism is in line with
the reproach that in Chandler's firm the fate of labour is neglected.[67]

Craft Workers' Managerial Role

In the 1970s American 'radicals' put the historical development of the
labour process on the agenda, and quite a few contributions to labour
history in these years are reactions to Braverman's thesis. Some British
labour historians are quick to denounce the 'historical romanticism' of
the 'workers' control school'.[68] The comparison between the American
and British trajectories figures on the research agenda, either explicitly or
implicitly. The claims of the 'workers' control school' are verified, such
as the capitalists' striving to suppress craft workers' control of the work
process, the bureaucratization of work and deskilling.

Richard Price uses the Marxist concepts of formal and real subordination for the analysis of the British trajectory. The distinction between
formal and real subordination consists in the degree of labour's discretion in the execution of work. Due to the limited and fractured impact of
mechanization on British industry, the subordination of the British worker
remained formal rather than real.[69] Division of labour did not prevent
skilled workers from transposing their control of the labour process onto

the new work organization. The boundaries between worker independence and employer authority were a matter of constant negotiation. A combination of relative independence of labour in the work process with relations of paternalism, family loyalty and reciprocity shaped the social relations of production.[70] From the 1880s on, increased competition and falling profit margins led to the striving to increase efficiency and to lower labour costs. However, the reorganization of the labour process in a Taylorite fashion met with managers' scepticism and reluctance to confront skilled workers' autonomy.[71] Instead a combination of old (e.g. piecework and overtime) and new devices (new machinery and premium bonuses) were used to intensify work. Employers now interfered in the work process itself so as to limit the discretionary power of the workers and the effect that their restrictive practices had on output. Both old and new work-intensifying devices led to deeper intrusion by management in the work sphere, bureaucratization of supervision and an undermining of relations of reciprocity and paternal loyalty.[72] The role of the traditional foreman, described as a fatherly ruler and natural leader who hated interference, was redefined. Loyalty to management rather than independent autonomy became part of his job description, as he was assigned a place in the hierarchy of command and control. The foreman lost some of his traditional responsibilities such as hiring, control of the work flow, distribution of tools and rate fixing to other members of the supervisory hierarchy.[73]

If we compare Price's account of the British world of labour *prior* to the 1880s with Craig Littler's, we have the impression of dealing with descriptions of two different countries. Price emphasizes the Victorian skilled workers' relative autonomy, while Littler underscores the importance of internal contracting. By pointing to the significance in Great Britain (but also in the United States) of inside contracting, Littler seems anxious to demystify the idealization of the craft workers' world. He emphasizes the petty capitalist character of internal contracting and the fact that it served the interests of capitalists in the first place.[74]

Littler describes how British inside contracting, well entrenched in textiles, mining, iron works and shipbuilding, was gradually undermined from the 1870s on, just like its American counterpart. The internal contractor was replaced by a directly employed foreman and there was a shift to a directly employed and directly controlled labour force. In his book and in a chapter of an edited volume (focusing on the inter-war period, however), Craig Littler provides a comparative perspective by dealing with managerial structures in Great Britain, the United States and Japan.[75]

The demise of the British internal contract system, so Littler argues, was an indirect result of the employers' attempt during the Great Depression to use labour more intensively, so as to reduce labour costs. Under this pressure, contractors turned to cheaper, less-skilled labour and speeded up workers with the result that the system became associated with sweated labour. This provoked reactions from the unions, while employers increasingly resented the contractors' profits and their own ignorance and lack of control.[76] British foremen had barely gained in importance, when their power started to be modified. Littler and Price give a similar description of the whittling down of foremen's responsibilities in the period 1890–1914 and they both downplay the influence of Taylorism in Britain before the First World War.[77] While in the United States the bureaucratization of the labour process occurred in the period 1900–1920, in Great Britain it took place in the 1920s and 1930s. In both cases foremen constituted a major source of resistance.[78]

Both in Price's and Littler's account, foremen appear to play a rather limited role before the 1880s. Perhaps that is the unintended effect of these authors' emphasis on other forms of supervision (internal contract) or craft workers' autonomy. In Price's history of labour relations in the building trade in the 1830s and 1840s, however, we find some interesting paragraphs on the '"marginal" situation foremen occupied between employers and men' as well as a complaint that historians are not in the least interested in this professional category.[79] Price stresses the foreman's dilemma: he was an agent of the employers' authority, but in order to ensure the effectiveness of that authority he had to maintain good relations with the men.

The theme of the 'man in the middle' is further developed by Joseph Melling. He asserts that Victorian foremen were pivotal figures in many of the staple industries.[80] He discusses the position of foremen in the engineering and shipbuilding trades in the period 1880–1914, characterized by increasing mechanization, rationalization and changing management techniques. Despite their differences (the pace of mechanization was much greater in engineering), both industries witnessed a struggle between workers and employers for control of the labour process.[81] Foremen were caught in between, and employers and unions competed for the foremen's loyalty. Unions tried to appeal to the craftsman in the supervisor, while employers attempted to gain foremen's undivided devotion by offering advantages such as greater job security, bonuses and premiums, a limited period of sick leave with full wages, subsidized meals, and company housing, neatly separated from the workers' dwellings. Since foremen in engineering and shipbuilding were promoted from the ranks of skilled workers, they often held union cards. In order to provoke their departure from trade societies, employers patronized supervisory associations but they were not very successful in prying foremen away from their unions.[82] Alastair Reid even goes so far as to characterize the foremen in the shipbuilding industry as unreliable tools of supervisory control, since they sided with the workers under them.[83]

In this survey we observed more than once that authors emphasizing craft workers' autonomy, tend to neglect the role of the foremen. That skilled workers' autonomy and foremen can be addressed simultaneously, is illustrated by Alan McKinlay's account of labour relations in the ship-building industry.[84] In this sector the need to join specialization and adaptability, as well as the harsh and permanently changing conditions under which work was performed, required skilled workers who were capable of organizing the work process autonomously. Crews of skilled workers operated as collective subcontractors who managed themselves as well as the unskilled labour they hired. Employers sought a balance between what they considered to be the limits of this flexible autonomy and the advantages it offered them. That is where the foremen came in. The latter coordinated work and had to reconcile management's techno-cratic directives and craft workers' practices.

The association of the British world of labour with craft workers' mana-gerial role on the shop floor is confirmed by William Lazonick's discus-sion of labour management in Lancashire cotton spinning. In a chapter that 'provides some support for the Marglin thesis', Lazonick describes a system which he designates as an internal subcontract system, but which is called the helper system by Clawson and Nelson (see above).[85] Anyway, in Lancashire cotton spinning, shop-floor authority was largely in the hands of adult male spinners, known as minders. They took care of the recruit-ing, training, supervision and firing of their assistants, named piecers. Although Lancashire cotton-spinning employers made attempts to under-mine the system, shop-floor power remained in the hands of craft workers: the divided employers were no match for the united minders while some employers still saw the minder-piecer hierarchy as an efficient method of shop-floor management.[86] In this constellation the role of the foreman seemed to be more technical than supervisory. The latter was essentially a mule mechanic who had to set the mules up and keep them in good repair. He was often recruited from the ranks of the minders. The foreman hired and fired the minder, but his right to fire was substantially constrained by the potential protest and strikes of the strong minders' unions.[87]

For William Lazonick, leaving shop-floor authority in the hands of skilled workers was a major problem for British industry. It not only shaped social relations of production in cotton spinning and in other old staple industries, but also in new branches such as the automobile sector. The fact that British employers were not willing to invest in technology and managerial structures but relied on the experience of skilled work-ers to keep imperfect machinery running, guaranteed low fixed costs but resulted also in declining competitive advantage on the international market. The structures of shop-floor control established in the nineteenth century proved to be very resistant to change.[88]

Although Price and Littler also downplay the influence of American management techniques on pre-war British industry, I have the impression that Lazonick, Jonathan Zeitlin and Steven Tolliday emphasize even more strongly the craft-based structures of shop-floor control. They underline the contrast with American managerial capitalism. In the United States vast national markets, abundant unskilled immigrant labour, relatively weak craft unionism, the growing number of horizontally concentrated and vertically integrated firms and the development of mass production encouraged the use of labour-saving technologies, the rise of systematic management, bureaucratic personnel policies and elaborate managerial hierarchies.[89] British industry, however, relied on craft production and relatively cheap and abundant skilled workers until the twentieth century. The latter operated autonomously, combined skill-intensive technologies and manual methods and were managed by craft-trained foremen. The cost-conscious employers used traditional methods to cheapen and intensify labour. This constellation was the result of the pattern of demand for British products, strong occupational unions who protected the market value of their members' skills and the limited size of family-owned firms which developed less elaborate supervisory hierarchies.[90]

Differences between countries regarding practices of shop-floor control are usually explained by referring to a combination of the above economic variables. Richard Biernacki's approach, however, emphasizes cultural differences and more precisely how diverging views of labour as a commodity influenced shop-floor practices. Comparing the weaving sector in Britain and Germany at the end of the nineteenth and the beginning of the twentieth centuries, he concludes that differing cultural constructions of labour led to substantially different relations between overseers and their subordinates. These overseers were not foremen, however, although the difference seems not always clear. Overseers were responsible for the supervision of a certain number of looms and weavers, and they stood between the weavers and the foreman, about whom we do not learn anything. Overseers hired and fired workers, maintained discipline and adjusted the machinery.[91] Even if we must not confuse overseers with foremen, Biernacki's findings are important. It appears that in the British weaving sector the technical aspect of the overseer's function was emphasized while his authority position was much less pronounced than in Germany. In contrast with Germany, the relations between British overseers and their weavers were characterized by familiarity, expressions of reciprocity and even solidarity, and when workers criticized them for their rudeness they targeted the person as such and not the figure endowed with authority.[92] This might lead to the conclusion that in pre-war Britain not only overseers but also foremen and others in supervisory functions stood in a closer, more equal relation to their subordinates than, for instance, in Germany or the United States.

'Les Rois de l'Usine'

The American and British literature on foremen and shop-floor hierar-chies focuses mostly on the end of the nineteenth and the beginning of the twentieth centuries, the period associated with the struggle for shop-floor control between workers and employers to determine 'les rois de l'usine'.[93] Philippe Lefebvre's quest for the emergence of shop-floor hierarchies in France covers the entire nineteenth century. Inspired by the above American and British literature and using secondary sources himself, Lefebvre questions the seemingly self-evident character of these hierarchies by exploring the organization of production in the textile, mining and metal trades.

Lefebvre is struck by the limited role of hierarchy in French industry until the 1870s. Using the studies of Claude Fohlen, G. Dufresne-Seurre, Serge Chassagne and William Reddy on the French textile sector, he concludes that foremen were far from numerous and that their role was hardly disciplinary. They trained workers, assisted in delicate operations and repaired and adapted machinery. In other words: foremen were highly qualified workers who ensured that quality standards of production were maintained. Forms of internal contracting reigned and as a result disci-pline was largely self-imposed.[94] The studies of Alain Leménorel, Donald Reid, Rolande Trempé and M. Sutet provide information on mining, and here as well hierarchy was limited and far from dependable. Direct super-vision of production was in the hands of contractors who hired individual workers or whole crews, but whose authority was limited if workers were not dependent on the mine for their income. *Maitres-mineurs* functioned as intermediaries between management and contractors. They negotiated the tariffs of the contracts and they assisted the engineers in maintaining the infrastructure.[95] In the metal trade, hierarchy was equally underde-veloped, concludes Lefebvre on the basis of the findings of Patrick Bour-delais. The limited number of foremen per worker suggests that labour operated with a substantial autonomy while supervision was exercised by fellow workers, known as *chefs-ouvriers* or *chefs d'équipes*.[96]

Lefebvre concludes that in the French skilled worker's world the func-tion of shop-floor hierarchy was not to supervise the familiar routines of craft labour, but that it did play a crucial role when procedures were modified. In other words, foremen (possibly recruited outside the firm, sometimes even abroad)[97] came to the fore when production processes were innovated, technology changed and workers were to be trained in the new *savoir faire*. Ensuring that production could take place in optimal technical conditions was another responsibility of foremen. They also took care of the hiring, firing, training, promotion and payment of workers, although internal contractors shared some of these responsibilities. Foremen were less suitable for imposing discipline and intensification of work. They were merely imperfect replacements of the real boss and as a result the above objectives could be reached far more efficiently by *l'incitation marchande*: using some form of internal contract, workers were turned into small entrepreneurs.[98]

Given their role as initiators and guardians of technological and other know-how, it is no surprise that in France too, foremen were chosen for their craft skills and experience, qualities which were often but not necessarily linked to age.[99] However, there were many ways of being a *contremaître*, depending on the industrial sector and the size of the firm.[100] Often, as Sylvie Vandecasteele-Schweitzer remarks, the foreman was a man of many talents (an assessment confirmed by Alain Dewerpe's description of the *capo mastro* in the Genovese machine and shipbuilding industries).[101] Both Vandecasteele-Schweitzer and Patrice Bourdelais point to the fact that a docile attitude towards the employer could also be a reason for being promoted *contremaître*, but these men had difficulties in gaining the respect of their subordinates.[102] Anyway, foremen were most often recruited in the internal labour market of the firm. Although a diploma of technical education could be an asset, it did not lead automatically to a job in the hierarchy. While technical education provided potential foremen with the technological know-how that the job required, it fell short where personnel management was concerned. Besides that, the conviction existed that strength of character and experience could not be learnt at school.[103] Those who secured promotion to foreman had to be prepared to break with their working-class background and suffer the envy of their former co-workers: in the Schneider company in Le Creusot, for instance, foremen earned twice as much as a skilled worker and received free lodgings and heating.[104]

As in the United States and Great Britain, the period of the Great Depression constituted the background to changes in shop-floor management. The combination of technological innovation, increased competition, declining prices and a reversal of the French labour market unfavourable to workers, culminated in an increase in the foreman's responsibilities. Since labour was no longer scarce, there was less need to

delegate recruitment to internal contractors, and so personnel management, the allocation of work and supervision became entirely the responsibility of the foremen. The striving to enhance productivity, to intensify
work and to control costs and consumption of material also contributed
to an increased workload for the latter, because foremen retained their
original more technical duties.[105] It would appear that before the First
World War French foremen experienced a more limited erosion of their
powers than their American and British counterparts. As a reaction to
increasing social tension, matters of personnel management were sometimes centralized.[106] Before the Great War, Taylorism and other rationalization doctrines had but little impact on French industry and foremen
did not seem to have reasons to feel threatened.[107] In 1917 they were still
called 'les rois de l'usine'. Higher management sometimes even contributed to the strengthening of their shop-floor authority by emphasizing
the social cleavage between workers and their immediate superior. In this
perspective, firms' housing policies directed at foremen were a means of
assuring that both workers and foremen remembered on whose side the
latter belonged.[108]

Meister and *Steiger*: Monarchs in Their Domains

Jürgen Kocka's description of supervisors (*Werkmeister* or *Werkführer*)
– characterized by Anderson as monarchs in their domains[109] – in the
Siemens mechanics workshop during the third quarter of the nineteenth
century presents a figure with by now familiar traits. The supervisor was
recruited among skilled workers, chosen because of his experience and
know-how, and he often had a keen sense for technological innovation.
He supervised craft workers who operated with relative independence and
with whom he collaborated in a fairly harmonious atmosphere. He trained
newcomers and had the final say over hiring and firing. However, as the
quest for profitability and efficiency became stronger, workshop relations
became harsher and discipline was imposed with greater vigour.[110]

Neither Kocka nor Elaine Glovka Spencer, who worked on supervisory
personnel in the Ruhr heavy industry, use the word 'foremen' but speak of
'supervisors'. However, the function they describe corresponds to the job
description of foremen in other literature, while *Werkmeister* (or *Steiger* in
mining) is usually translated as 'foreman'. In Glovka Spencer's account,
focussing on the mid-1890s to 1914, it is the harsher regime already
evocated by Kocka, which is described.[111] There is no mention of worker
autonomy and the only actors on the shop floor to use their own discretion
seemed to be the foremen who assigned work, supervised its execution,

hired and fired, and decided on wage rates, fines and other punishments. Again we find that foremen were upwardly mobile workers, but their promotion to foreman was to be their ultimate professional achievement because it proved difficult to advance into middle management.[112] This corresponds to what Patrice Bourdelais observed in Le Creusot: he speaks of 'une promotion "cul-de-sac"' and 'petits chefs sans avenir'.[113] It contrasts with Kocka's assessment of the earlier period: apparently, foremen could move on and become branch managers or shop directors.[114] In the mining sector, training in the *Bergschule* became almost compulsory for promotion to foreman.[115] In other sectors training was less formal, despite the existence of special schools for foremen created by the Prussian government at the end of the nineteenth century. Apparently their name was misleading: they offered a more comprehensive technical training and were not adapted to foremen's actual practices.[116]

The description of labour relations in France and Great Britain revealed that employers and higher management made efforts to secure the loyalty of their foremen. Company housing and other benefits were provided, while foreman's wages were substantially higher than those of skilled workers. In the Ruhr area similar policies were developed.[117] I have the impression, however, that in Germany foremen were expected to deliver much more in return. It is no surprise that they were not supposed to side with workers in social conflicts, but there was not much comprehension either for the fact that a good relationship with the crew might be a precondition for an efficient exercise of authority. There was more tolerance towards a tyrannical supervisor than a lenient one.[118] Glovka Spencer's description of the functioning of foremen echoes the American literature on tyrannical overseers. Moreover, foremen had to be prepared to act as spies and to inform on workers who participated in strikes.[119] Margaret Anderson reports that foremen were also requested to put pressure on workers in voting matters.[120] In contrast with Britain, social democrats and unionists could abandon any hope of being promoted foreman.[121] If the foreman fraternizing with his workers was condemned, so was the abusive and arbitrary one. The striving for rationalization required supervisors who observed company regulations and declined bribes and illegitimate privileges. An increasing number of company officials became responsible for the surveillance of the supervisors, while there was also a tendency to shift responsibility for matters of hiring, firing and wage setting from foremen to centralized offices.[122]

Richard Biernacki's assessment of the perception of German supervisors in the weaving sector confirms this impression of supervisory functions in Germany. In comparison with Great Britain there was much more emphasis on the fact that the supervisor represented the authority of the owner. Offending the supervisor meant insulting the latter and as a result manifestations of insubordination were not taken lightly. The social cleavage between weavers and their overseers was consolidated because it was inconceivable that the two groups would socialize. While British workers visited the same pubs as their supervisors and presented them with gifts when they left, no friendly gestures were exchanged in the German case. Whereas German workers took if for granted that their supervisors would inform higher management of their errors, British workers were furious when they learnt the supervisor had been talking, thus expressing their assumption that supervisors were basically on their side.[123]

An Overview of the Present Volume

If we reduce the types of foremen we encountered in our survey of the Western European and American literature to two archetypical figures, two contrasting pictures emerge. On the one hand we have the foreman as the *primus inter pares*, the most experienced craft worker, with a superior know-how and technical knowledge, whose disciplinary functions were rather limited, given craft workers' autonomy and self regulation. Since the end of the nineteenth century another type of foreman became more predominant: although he is still recruited among craft workers, his craftsmanship is overshadowed by his ability to discipline workers and to realize 'the economies of speed'. He is the tyrannical character with the driving methods. The contributions to this book, dealing mostly with the role, function and careers of foremen up to the First World War, do not aim to confirm or contradict these archetypical portrayals of the foreman. Rather do they illustrate S. Vandecasteele-Schweitzer's remark that there is no such thing as a typical foreman's job and that there are different kinds of foremen, depending on the exigencies of a sector, firm or department in question. Interesting as the articles collected in this volume are, they will thus not settle the question of whether in the foreman's job description, the disciplinary function rather than, for instance, excellence in a craft predominated. Far more cases would have to be studied in order to verify whether the patterns suggested in the postscript can be confirmed. Future research would also have to address the question of the supervision of labourers whose jobs required hardly any skill at all. In the cases at hand the supervised workers were either craftsmen or trained workers, such as spinners, weavers and miners. The foreman's job profile undoubtedly reflected to a certain degree the characteristics of the labour force he was supervising. Skilled workers, trained workers and unskilled workers probably required different styles of supervision.

Even if the final word on foremen is not pronounced in this collection of articles, they have the advantage of placing the foreman at the centre of attention. Numerous publications on factory life and labour relations treat supervisors as walk-on parts. As a result, the act of supervising and exercising authority is not seldom reduced to an abstraction or made into a caricature. The articles in this volume also exploit a wide range of primary source material (diaries, oral history, company archives, wage books, judicial proceedings, statistical surveys, union archives, management literature of the period in question, etc.), thus avoiding the tendency of some of the older contributions to the history of labour relations to rely on standard secondary sources and published material. However, despite their firm determination to grasp as completely as possible the complexity of the foreman's role, the authors of these chapters are aware of the fact that the insights they have gained relate to some aspects of the foreman's job, while neglecting other facets not dealt with in the available sources. We still know far too little about the foreman's daily routines: a 'thick description' of the latter would certainly enrich our knowledge of how relations of authority were constructed on a day-to-day basis.

Cristina Borderías's study of a vertically integrated Catalan cotton mill (1849–1888) illustrates the variation in foremen's job profiles. In the dyeing and printing workshop where technical expertise had to be combined with artistic creativity, foremen were highly qualified technicians who were attracted from abroad. In the other sections foremen were recruited locally, and although they were qualified technicians as well, their expertise had less scarcity value than that of the dyeing and printing foremen. This Spanish cotton mill had a rather complex hierarchy, populated by foremen with varying qualifications, functions, salaries and status. Although the role of supervisors was determined by the specific hierarchical structure and the activities within each section, technical expertise and the ability to train and guide workers was part of the job profile of all supervisory functions. However, the more creative handling of technology was the realm of highly trained technical experts, while the solving of coordination and organizational problems also seemed to be the terrain of a more limited number of supervisors. The complaints of unions notwithstanding, the coercive role of foremen comes to the fore only in the weaving section. The foremen's wages of this department were linked to weavers' output and the former therefore benefited directly from pressuring the workers.

In Peter Scholliers's article on the Ghent cotton and weaving mill Voortman (1830–1914), the difference between the profiles of weaving and spinning foremen is emphasized. They also had something in common though: they were all recruited locally and in this respect they did not differ from other Ghent cotton workers. Wage differentials were the expression of the differences between spinners' and weavers' foremen and, as such, wages reflected the difficulty of the problems the respective foremen had to solve. When the weaving department received new machinery in the 1830s, its foremen began to earn higher wages than their colleagues in spinning. However, when the spinning section was modernized in the 1850s the situation was reversed. This could be an indication of the fact that the employer rewarded the technical expertise that a foreman had to offer. Discrepancies in wages could also be linked, however, to the foreman's alleged efforts in recruiting and disciplining labour. The wages of the weavers' foremen were higher than their colleagues' in spinning in the years characterized by increasing weaver militancy. Weavers' foremen started to earn less when adult weavers had to make way for women and youngsters. Disciplining the labour force might have become easier then, and its recruitment was certainly less difficult. That Ghent foremen in the cotton trade were key figures in the recruitment of labour is also illustrated by the fact that during the temporary closure of the factory, foremen were kept on. When activity resumed several months later, a substantial number of the newly hired spinners and weavers appeared to have worked for Voortman before. Foremen may have played an important role in keeping in touch with the labour force.

That nineteenth-century Ghent was the Belgian textile centre is hardly apparent in Patricia Van den Eeckhout's chapter, which focuses on foremen in the artisanal sector (1885–1913). Since the foremen studied in this article had been fired before their contract ended, their files tell us about their employers' expectations and complaints. Some of these foremen were regarded as keepers of trade secrets, whose know-how and technical expertise were not readily available in the company and who could thus contribute to the advancement of the firm. Sometimes these specialists were recruited abroad. However, a foreman had to offer more than specialized knowledge. He also had to be dependable and trustworthy and he had to look after his employer's interests. Crucial for both employer and worker were the foreman's qualities as a good organizer. A foreman had to guarantee a fluid workflow and distribution of tasks, ensuring that workers were able to earn a 'normal' wage and were not sent home or kept idle as a result of poor organization. In none of these disputes do we meet the foreman as the embodiment of the 'driving' of labour.

Neither is this the case in James Jaffe's account of the role of supervisors in the mining and printing sectors of the 1830s. The shop-floor managers of northern England's coal industry were less involved in disciplining the labour force than in negotiating the delicate balance between effort and pay. The viewers (who conducted the wage negotiations with the miners) had to propose a balance between earnings and effort which was perceived as fair and predictable, if they wished to obtain workers' wholehearted collaboration. The overmen, who monitored production and imposed fines, appeared to be reluctant to enforce new work practices if they threatened to disrupt this balance. Neither viewers nor overmen were thus simply carrying out orders, but rather they were using their own discretion in order to establish a viable work relationship with their subordinates. In the London printing trade, foremen went to great lengths to secure a workable relationship with their men, rather than imposing their authority and compromising future output.

In these four articles studying foremanship before the advent of scientific management, supervisors figure as technical experts, craft workers with a superior command of their trade, privileged observers of the labour market, dependable collaborators, capable organizers and coordinators or as negotiators who tried to reconcile employers' and workers' expectations. The foreman's coercive role is not very prominent. In the cases of the cotton factories of Ghent and Barcelona this might come as a surprise. However, where the spinning teams of these factories were concerned, the 'driver' was not the foreman but the spinner (female in the case of Barcelona) who received a piece wage and paid his or her collaborators a time wage. It was in the spinner's interest to put his or her helpers under pressure. The weavers' foremen in Barcelona were in a similar situation. One might conclude that in these two companies supervisors (spinners or foremen) played their coercive role with gusto only when they benefited from it directly. That coercion was not the foremen's major concern may perhaps be illustrated by the fact that in the Ghent cotton factories, fines (the foreman's territory *par excellence*) amounted to only 0.01 per cent of the weekly wage earned by 1,919 workers around the turn of the century.[124] The suggestion that disciplining the workforce was only one of the foreman's duties (and sometimes not even the most important one), does not mean, however, that coercion was absent while training workers, coordinating the work flow or demonstrating technical expertise.

Gilles Postel-Vinay and Jérôme Bourdieu investigate the importance of the foreman's coercive role on the basis of French labour statistics of the 1890s. A stratified sample of some 3,000 firms allows them to investigate the relationship between the presence of foremen and the size, composition and wage form of the labour force, the type of industry, location of the plant and capital intensity (represented by steam engines and horse power). Postel-Vinay and Bourdieu conclude that foremen were hired less to solve coordination problems than to impose discipline. The mere size of the plant was not indicative of the presence of foremen: large plants, which undoubtedly encountered more coordination problems, were proportionally not more provided with foremen than smaller ones. Plants with incentive wage systems were less in need of foremen than those with time wages, and the same goes for towns (Paris in particular) characterized by the presence of a workforce with plenty of experience in industrial wage labour. All this suggests that disciplining the workforce was the foreman's main function. On the other hand, more capital-intensive technology meant more foremen, and there the foreman as a technical expert comes in. I do not think it makes any sense to try to reconcile these findings based on aggregate figures with the conclusions based on four case studies. Again, I am struck by the difficulty in establishing where coordination, technical expertise and training end and coercion begins.

The contributions by Jo Melling and by Richard Coopey and Alan McKinlay discuss the role of foremen during the years when scientific management was introduced, albeit rather hesitantly, on the British shop floor. Jo Melling describes the foreman in mid-Victorian engineering as an experienced craft worker, whose superior command of his trade gained him the respect of his subordinates. By the First World War these qualities were still cited as the main asset of the foreman in engineering. Melling sees little signs of a decisive shift towards a Taylorist organization of the shop floor, although discourses in technical and professional circles promoted a more systematic approach to management. However, British employers preferred fairly simple and direct hierarchies of command. They therefore continued to rely on the experienced and well-respected foreman rather than on trained technicians such as timekeepers, draftsmen and rate-fixers. While these technical employees grew in number, their responsibilities were largely restricted to a supporting role. The introduction of premium bonus systems seemed to increase rather than to diminish the role of the foreman. The question of whether foremen embodied expertise rather than coercion seems rather superfluous in this case. It seems that the foreman's continuing authority was based on the perfect intertwining of both.

The chapter by Richard Coopey and Alan McKinlay on foremen in the heavy manufacturing and car industries (1890–1939) confirms the view of the foreman as a craft worker whose authority was based on his superior knowledge of production techniques and of the abilities of individual workers. By the 1920s and despite the introduction of more systematic forms of management, the foreman was still perceived (even by employers and managers) as the vital link in the organization and distribution of work and the control of its quality and quantity. In the car industry, production planning, rate fixing, and quality control gradually became the preserve of specialized staff, but the power of these technicians varied markedly between firms. Both in heavy engineering and the car industry, the introduction of payment-by-results systems and rate-fixers did not necessarily undermine the foreman's personal powers. Neither did the development of personnel departments diminish the foreman's command in hiring and firing. But the appearance on the shop floor of rate-fixers and quality inspectors certainly added to the complexity of authority relations. An important source of the foreman's continuing authority seemed to be his ability to create a space where tacit compromises could be negotiated without loss of face. A foreman's authority in the heavy manufacturing and car industry was not based on the brutal exercise of power, but on the establishment of a fragile balance between tacit indulgence and repression. This chapter (as well as the contributions by Peter Scholliers and Cristina Borderías) suggests that the basis for a foreman's authority could also lie in the intertwining of work and family networks. Foremen introduced and sponsored relatives and sometimes sons stepped into their fathers' shoes and became foremen. Undoubtedly this contributed to the construction of the foreman as a fatherly figure.

In Bart Delbroek's account of foremen in the coal mines of Belgian Limburg (1917–1939), we meet foremen who often resorted to harsher, even violent, methods and who were far more apt to impose fines. This can be explained by the high rates of labour turnover and absenteeism. Also significant was the fact that supervisors' yearly Saint Barbara bonus was linked to output, so that a *porion* had a direct interest in 'driving' his workers. A prerequisite for becoming a *porion* was an all-round work experience in mining, by the 1930s supplemented perhaps with some evening classes in the mining school. Miners in Beringen were about thirty years old when they reached the first step on the hierarchical ladder and became *porion*. A sample of supervisors of the same mine indicates that most supervisors were recruited locally but that they had had previous work experience in the Walloon mines. That gave them the advantage of being able to communicate with the miners in Flemish, and in French with the engineers. Besides 'driving' and disciplining their crew, these mining foremen controlled attendance, composed work crews, distributed work, maintained machinery, cared for safe working conditions and reported daily on work done. Although *porions* were required to be impartial, a good relationship with the foremen could ensure better working conditions or a place in a highly productive work-team for the miners and probably saved on fines.

Notes

1. S. Pollard, *The Genesis of Modern Management: A Study of the Industrial Revolution in Great Britain* (Harmondsworth, 1968), 308.
2. P. Joyce, 'Work', in *The Cambridge Social History of Britain 1750–1950,* vol. 2: *People and Their Environment,* ed. F. M. Thompson (Cambridge, 1992), 131–193; here 158.
3. 'Being a foreman is definitely an occupation, although it is seldom described': S. Vandecasteele-Schweitzer, 'Comment peut-on être contremaître?' in *L'usine et le bureau. Itinéraires sociaux et professionnels dans l'entreprise XIXe et XXe siècles,* ed. Y. Lequin and S. Vandecasteele (Lyon, 1990), 93–108, here 93.
4. S. Marglin, 'What Do Bosses Do? The Origins and Functions of Hierarchy in Capitalist Production', *Review of Radical Political Economy* 6, no. 2 (1974): 60–112.
5. D. Landes, 'What Do Bosses Really Do?' *Journal of Economic History* 46, no. 3 (1986): 585–623, here 610; M. Berg, 'On the Origins of Capitalist Hierarchy', in *Power and Economic Institutions: Reinterpretations in Economic History,* ed. B. Gustafsson (Aldershot, 1991), 173–194, here 182; S. R. H. Jones, 'The Rise of the Factory System in Britain: Efficiency or Exploitation?' in *Authority and Control in Modern Industry: Theoretical and Empirical Perspectives,* ed. P. L. Robertson (London, 1999), 17–44, here 29–30, 34.
6. G. C. Hamilton and R. C. Feenstra, 'Varieties of Hierarchies and Markets: An Introduction', in *Technology, Organisation, and Competitiveness: Perspectives on Industrial and Corporate Change,* ed. D. Teece, J. Chytry and G. Dosi (Oxford, 1998), 105–146, here 109.
7. Patrick Fridenson tries to validate Montgomery's and Stone's views for France: P. Fridenson, 'France – Etats Unis: Genèse de l'usine nouvelle', in *Le soldat du travail: Guerre, fascisme et Taylorisme,* ed. L. Murard and P. Zylberman (Paris, 1978), 375–388.
8. K. Stone, 'The Origins of Job Structures in the Steel Industry', *Review of Radical Political Economics* 6, no. 2 (1974): 113–173; D. Montgomery, 'Workers' Control of Machine Production in the Nineteenth Century', *Labor History* 17 (1976): 486–509; D. Montgomery, *The Fall of the House of Labor: The Workplace, the State, and American Labor Activism, 1865–1925* (Cambridge, 1987), 9–57.
9. Montgomery, *Fall of the House of Labor,* 9–20, 191–192, 204–205, 213.
10. Ibid., 115.
11. Ibid., 11, 20–21.
12. Ibid., 187–188.
13. D. Clawson, *Bureaucracy and the Labor Process: The Transformation of U.S. Industry, 1860–1920* (New York, 1980), 71–125.
14. Ibid., 126.
15. Ibid., 160–166.
16. Ibid., 165.
17. Ibid., 130–132.
18. H. Braverman, *Labor and Monopoly Capital: The Degradation of Work in the Twentieth Century* (New York, 1974).
19. M. Wardell, 'Labor Processes: Moving beyond Braverman and the Deskilling Debate', in *Rethinking the Labor Process,* ed. M. Wardell, T. L. Steiger and P. Meiksins (Albany, 1999), 1–16.
20. Clawson, *Bureaucracy and the Labor Process,* 168.
21. J. Monds, 'Workers' Control and the Historians: A New Economism', *New Left Review* (May–June 1976): 81–100, here 85.
22. R. Edwards, *Contested Terrain: The Transformation of the Workplace in the Twentieth Century* (New York, 1979); R. Edwards, 'The Social Relations of Production at the Point of Production', *Insurgent Sociologist* 8 (1978): 109–125.
23. Edwards, *Contested Terrain,* 16–17.
24. Ibid., 18–21, 131.

25. C. Littler, 'The Labour Process Debate: A Theoretical Review 1974–1988', in *Labour Process Theory*, ed. D. Knights and H. Wilmott (London, 1990), 46–95, here 59–61. This article (and the other contributions in this collection) also discusses other authors of the 'workers' control school'. See also P. Thompson, *The Nature of Work: An Introduction to Debates on the Labour Process* (London, 1983).

26. Edwards, *Contested Terrain*, 23–36; Edwards, 'Social Relations of Production', 112–114.

27. Edwards, *Contested Terrain*, 48–65, 97–104.

28. Ibid., 111–122.

29. D. Nelson, *Managers and Workers: Origins of the New Factory System in the United States, 1880–1920* (Madison, 1975); E. Englander, 'The Inside Contract System of Production and Organisation: A Neglected Aspect of the History of the Firm', *Labor History* 28, no. 4 (1987): 429–446; S. Jacoby, *Employing Bureaucracy: Managers, Unions, and the Transformation of Work in American Industry, 1900–1945* (New York, 1985).

30. D. Nelson, *Managers and Workers: Origins of the Twentieth-Century Factory System in the United States, 1880–1920* (Madison, 1995). Further references are to the edition of 1975.

31. D. Nelson, 'Mass Production and the U.S. Tire Industry', *Journal of Economic History* 47, no. 2 (1987): 329–337, here 329.

32. D. Nelson, 'Scientific Management and the Workplace, 1920–1935', in *Masters to Managers: Historical and Comparative Perspectives on American Employers*, ed. S. Jacoby (New York, 1991), 74–89, here 75–76.

33. Nelson, *Managers and Workers*, 34–78.

34. Englander, 'Inside Contract System', 445–446.

35. Jacoby, *Employing Bureaucracy*, 3, 96.

36. Ibid., 15; Clawson, *Bureaucracy and the Labor Process*, 92–93.

37. Jacoby, *Employing Bureaucracy*, 15.

38. Nelson, *Managers and Workers*, 36–39; Englander, 'Inside Contract System', 431, 435, 438; Clawson, *Bureaucracy and the Labor Process*, 71–125.

39. Nelson, *Managers and Workers*, 38–40; Clawson, *Bureaucracy and the Labor Process*, 94–97.

40. Clawson, *Bureaucracy and the Labor Process*, 119–123.

41. Nelson, *Managers and Workers*, 38; Englander, 'Inside Contract System', 445–446.

42. A. Dawson, 'A New Framework for Workshop Contracting: Philadelphia Machine Building, 1870–1914', *Labor History* 47, no. 3 (2006): 343–359.

43. Nelson, *Managers and Workers*, 40–45; Jacoby, *Employing Bureaucracy*, 16–23.

44. Clawson, *Bureaucracy and the Labor Process*, 126–156.

45. D. Montgomery, 'Immigrant Workers and Managerial Reform', in *Workers' Control in America: Studies in the History of Work, Technology, and Labor Struggles*, ed. D. Montgomery (Cambridge, 1979), 32–47, here 42.

46. Nelson, *Managers and Workers*, 42.

47. C. Heron, *Working in Steel: The Early Years in Canada, 1883–1935* (Toronto, 1988), 93–96.

48. Jacoby, *Employing Bureaucracy*, 17–30.

49. J. Kocka, *White Collar Workers in America 1890–1940: A Social-Political History in International Perspective* (London, 1980), 24, 93, 96–97.

50. G. Peck, *Reinventing Free Labor: Padrones and Immigrant Workers in the North American West 1880–1930* (Cambridge, 2000), 49–81.

51. Nelson, *Managers and Workers*, 57; Jacoby, *Employing Bureaucracy*, 46.

52. Montgomery, *Fall of the House of Labor*, 222–225.

53. Clawson, *Bureaucracy and the Labor Process*, 167–253.

54. Heron, *Working in Steel*, 53–54, 71–72, 90–93.

55. Nelson, *Managers and Workers*, 72–73; Montgomery, *Fall of the House of Labor*, 225.

56. D. Hounshell, *From the American System to Mass Production 1800–1932: The Development of Manufacturing Technology in the United States* (Baltimore, 1984), 251.

57. S. Meyer III, *The Five Dollar Day: Labor Management and Social Control in the Ford Motor Company, 1908–1921* (Albany, 1981), 53–56.

58. Nelson, *Managers and Workers*, 48–51; Jacoby, *Employing Bureaucracy*, 39–44.

59. Jacoby, *Employing Bureaucracy*, 47–49, 161–163.

60. W. Lazonick, *Competitive Advantage on the Shop Floor* (Cambridge, 1990), 245–246.

61. Heron, *Working in Steel*, 94.

62. Lazonick, *Competitive Advantage on the Shop Floor*, 229, 235.

63. Montgomery, *Fall of the House of Labor*, 223, 233.

64. See the chapter titled 'The Organisation of Work' in O. Williamson, *The Economic Institutions of Capitalism* (New York, 1985), 206–239.

65. P. Lefebvre, *L'invention de la grande entreprise: Travail, hiérarchie, marché. France, fin XVIIIe–début XXe siècle* (Paris, 2003), 141–156. See also Jones, 'Rise of the Factory System', 35–39.

66. Lefebvre, *L'invention de la grande entreprise*, 8–16.

67. D. Nelson, 'Western Business History: Experience and Comparative Perspectives', in *Chinese Business History: Interpretative Trends and Priorities for the Future*, ed. A. McElderry, J. Leonard and R. Gardella, Armonk, 1999, 151–170, here 159.

68. Monds, 'Workers' Control and the Historians'; C. Littler, 'Understanding Taylorism', *British Journal of Sociology* 29, no. 2 (1978): 194–195.

69. R. Price, 'Structures of Subordination in Nineteenth-Century British Industry', in *The Power of the Past: Essays for Eric Hobsbawm*, ed. P. Thane, G. Crossick and R. Floud (Cambridge, 1984), 119–142, here 120–123.

70. R. Price, *Labour in British Society: An Interpretative History* (London, 1986), 73–83; Price, 'Structures of Subordination', 124–125.

71. Price, *Labour in British Society*, 97–99.

72. Price, 'Structures of Subordination', 127–137.

73. Price, *Labour in British Society*, 108–109.

74. C. Littler, *The Development of the Labour Process in Capitalist Societies* (London, 1982).

75. Ibid., 64–67; C. Littler, 'A Comparative Analysis of Managerial Structures and Strategies', in *Managerial Strategies and Industrial Relations: An Historical and Comparative Study*, ed. H. Gospel and C. Littler (London, 1983), 171–196.

76. Littler, *Development of the Labour Process*, 64–79.

77. Ibid., 84–90, 92–98.

78. Ibid., 184.

79. R. Price, *Masters, Unions and Men: Work Control in Building and the Rise of Labour 1830–1914* (Cambridge, 1980), 38–39.

80. J. Melling, '"Non-Commissioned Officers": British Employers and Their Supervisory Workers, 1880–1920', *Social History* 5, no. 2 (1980): 183–221, here 191; J. Melling, 'Men in the Middle or Men on the Margin? The Historical Development of Relations between Employers and Supervisors in British Industry', in *International Yearbook of Organisational Studies*, ed. G. Salaman and D. Dunkerley (London, 1982), 242–264.

81. Melling, '"Non-Commissioned Officers"', 201–205.

82. Ibid., 206–210; J. Melling, 'Employers, Industrial Welfare, and the Struggle for Work-Place Control in British Industry, 1880–1920', in *Managerial Strategies and Industrial Relations: An Historical and Comparative Study*, ed. H. Gospel and C. Littler (London, 1983), 55–81, here 70–75.

83. A. Reid, 'Employers' Strategies and Craft Production: The British Shipbuilding Industry 1870–1950', in *The Power to Manage? Employers and Industrial Relations in Comparative-Historical Perspective*, ed. S. Tolliday and J. Zeitlin (London, 1991), 35–51, here 44.

84. A. McKinlay, 'Maîtres ou employeurs? Travail et rapports d'autorité dans la construction navale: L'exemple des chantiers de la Clyde (1900–1939)', *Le Mouvement Social* (1989): 75–94, here 76–89.

85. Lazonick, *Competitive Advantage on the Shop Floor*, 79–114, 119.
86. Ibid., 109.
87. Ibid., 119.
88. Ibid., 182–201.
89. S. Tolliday and J. Zeitlin, 'National Models and International Variations in Labour Management and Employer Organisation', in *The Power to Manage? Employers and Industrial Relations in Comparative-Historical Perspective*, ed. S. Tolliday and J. Zeitlin (London, 1991), 273–343, here 286–289; Lazonick, *Competitive Advantage on the Shop Floor*, 212–236, 301–303.
90. Tolliday and Zeitlin, 'National Models', 279–281.
91. R. Biernacki, *The Fabrication of Labor: Germany and Britain, 1640–1914* (Berkeley, 1995), 148–150, 167–168, 171–173.
92. Ibid., 181–196, 461–464.
93. 'The rulers of the factory': assessment of the foreman's position in 1917 by Henry Le Chatelier, a promoter of Taylorism in France. See Lefebvre, *L'invention de la grande entreprise*, 275.
94. Lefebvre, *L'invention de la grande entreprise*, 56–68.
95. Ibid., 68–81.
96. Ibid., 81–91.
97. See also A. Dewerpe, 'Les pouvoirs du sens pratique: Carrières professionnelles et trajectoires des chefs d'atelier de l'Ansaldo (Gênes, 1900–1920)', in *L'usine et le bureau: Itinéraires sociaux et professionnels dans l'entreprise XIXe et XXe siècles*, ed. Y. Lequin and S. Vandecasteele (Lyon, 1990), 109–150, here 124–125, 126–128.
98. Lefebvre, *L'invention de la grande entreprise*, 102–137.
99. Ibid., 220–224.
100. Vandecasteele-Schweitzer, 'Comment peut-on être contremaître', 95.
101. Dewerpe, 'Les pouvoirs du sens pratique', 113–114.
102. Vandecasteele-Schweitzer, 'Comment peut-on être contremaître', 97; P. Bourdelais, 'Des représentations aux réalités, les contremaîtres du Creusot (1850–1900)', in *L'usine et le bureau: Itinéraires sociaux et professionnels dans l'entreprise XIXe et XXe siècles*, ed. Y. Lequin and S. Vandecasteele, Lyon, 1990, 151–165, here 163.
103. Lefebvre, *L'invention de la grande entreprise*, 220–230; Vandecasteele-Schweitzer, 'Comment peut-on être contremaître', 98–99.
104. Vandecasteele-Schweitzer, 'Comment peut-on être contremaître', 97; Bourdelais, 'Des représentations aux réalités', 163.
105. Lefebvre, *L'invention de la grande entreprise*, 182–207.
106. Ibid., 231–237.
107. Ibid., 272–275.
108. Ibid., 238–240.
109. M. Anderson, *Practicing Democracy: Elections and Political Culture in Imperial Germany* (Princeton, 2000), 216.
110. J. Kocka, *Industrial Culture and Bourgeois Society: Business, Labor, and Bureaucracy in Modern Germany* (New York, 1999), 10–13; J. Kocka, *Les employés en Allemagne 1850–1980: Histoire d'un groupe social* (Paris, 1989), 30–38.
111. E. Glovka Spencer, 'Between Capital and Labor: Supervisory Personnel in Ruhr Heavy Industry before 1914', *Journal of Social History* 9, no. 2 (1975): 178–192.
112. Ibid., 181.
113. 'Dead-end promotions' and 'Petty bosses without future': Bourdelais, 'Des représentations aux réalités', 163.
114. Kocka, *Industrial Culture and Bourgeois Society*, 10.
115. Glovka Spencer, 'Between Capital and Labor', 183.
116. K. Gispen, *New Profession, Old Order: Engineers and German Society 1815–1914* (Cambridge, 2002), 176–177.

117. Glovka Spencer, 'Between Capital and Labor', 184.

118. Ibid., 187–188.

119. Ibid., 182.

120. Anderson, *Practicing Democracy*, 216–218.

121. Glovka Spencer, 'Between Capital and Labor', 183.

122. Ibid., 185–189; for the motor car trade, see P. Fridenson, 'L'autorité dans l'entreprise en France et en Allemagne 1880–1914', in *Les bourgeoisies européennes au XIXe siècle*, ed. J. Kocka (Paris, 1997), 307–332, here 326.

123. Biernacki, *Fabrication of Labor*, 185–193.

124. P. Scholliers, *Wages, Manufacturers and Workers in the Nineteenth-Century Factory: The Voortman Cotton Mill in Ghent* (Oxford, 1996), 126.

CHAPTER 2

WORK ORGANIZATION AND SUPERVISION IN THE TEXTILE INDUSTRY

The Case of La España Industrial, Barcelona (1849–1888)

Cristina Borderías

In Spain, as in many other European countries, the histories of work and business have tended to follow separate paths. In the history of shop-floor management the two themes meet, but this has received very little attention from Spanish scholars, especially for the period of the first industrial revolution. Although a lot has been written on Catalan textile industry, the history of shop-floor management has been neglected. Labour management sparked a great deal of historical debate. Marxist ideas about direct forms of supervision and labour control have been challenged.[1] The first industrial revolution is now recognized as a much more uneven and complex process, in which traditional modes of work organization and control persisted in tandem with emerging modern models of management. It has been emphasized that during this period most textile factories were still marked by a relatively simple division of labour, a lack of coordination and control over working conditions, and a weak hierarchy.[2]

As the country's largest textile factory by 1849, La España Industrial constitutes an excellent example of the modernization of Spain's cotton industry in the nineteenth century.[3] This chapter re-examines the existing literature and provides new data and insights regarding models of supervision and shop-floor management during the first industrial revolution. Data come from the firm's wage books, contracts and other records as well as from cotton industry statistics and workers' press.[4]

The first section gives an overview of the firm, including its capital, technology and product line. The second section explores the structure of its internal hierarchy and places it within the context of the management debates of the

Notes for this chapter begin on page 57.

time. The third section addresses the changing patterns of labour organization and supervision in the firm's various textile-production processes. The final section provides additional information on professional profiles and status of foremen and explores workers' resistance to the new forms of management.

La España Industrial

The cotton textile company known as La España Industrial (1847–1978) was founded by a group of Spanish industrialists, bankers and politicians. As the first Spanish joint stock company in the field, the group sought to establish a nationwide, modern cotton textile complex, which would benefit from the experience of Catalonia's leading cotton industrialists. Originally it was the project of the Instituto Industrial de España, but the latter suspended its activity.[5]

La España Industrial's shareholders, a ten-member advisory board, jointly controlled the company and a board of directors governed by six Muntadas brothers. The brothers, who played a central role in the foundation of the firm, were the sons of a woollen-cloth producer who in 1812 had set up shop in the town of Igualada, some seventy kilometres from the city of Barcelona. Between 1828 and 1841, the family had extended its industrial activities into other areas of Catalonia, where it established up to nine mills and two merchant houses in Reus (Tarragona) and Madrid, all of which would merge in 1840 to form the Muntadas and Brothers Company. In 1847 the family integrated its industrial activities into the new firm.

Although the latter boasted a start-up capital of 50 million *reales*, in the end only 16,000 shares of 2,000 *reales* apiece were sold, including 15,000 within the city of Barcelona, of which 2,122 went to the Muntadas family. Although the initial aim of the new corporation was to 'set up a wide range of mills along the Spanish territory', the economic crisis forced the company to suspend this plan and to concentrate all of its industrial activities within a single factory complex.

The location chosen for the new factory was Sants, an industrial district that was incorporated into the nearby city of Barcelona in 1897. As a result of the move to Sants, the firm's central offices were transferred to Barcelona in 1851. The new factory was envisioned as the starting-point for a more ambitious project, as revealed by the corporation statutes:

> [The Sants mill] will provide the model for other establishments, which will gradually spread into other areas of the Iberian Peninsula on the basis of the funds obtained from the initial investment, or else by means of the social capital that will be reserved for use in opportune moments. [The Sants mill] will generate young men who have been scientifically trained to take on the most delicate industrial

combinations, and practical *contramaestros*, those skilled workers who are able to produce, through training, other, equally excellent workers.

The new mill was a large, steam-powered factory that vertically integrated the processes of cotton spinning, weaving, dyeing, printing, machinery repairs and wholesale distribution. It strived to adopt 'the latest and most advanced technology and production methods developed in foreign countries'. The most prestigious French and English textile factories and machinery firms were visited, and the advice of other Spanish manufacturers and highly specialized French and English technicians was sought.

The new mill began operations with two new steam-powered machines (75 hp. each); 2,560 throstle mules (H. Platt) and 18,036 self-acting mules (Sharp) of about 320 to 340 spindles each, and 500 mechanical looms (Platt & Oldham). By the late 1850s, the firm had acquired 42,000 spinning bobbins and 1,000 looms.[6] In 1857, with 1,250 workers (34 per cent of whom were women), the company employed 7 per cent of Barcelona's overall cotton workforce. This made La España Industrial the most important cotton manufacturer in Spain, as measured in terms of capital, technology, production and employment.[7] By 1880, in response to the competition brought on by the new commercial trade treaties, declining domestic market demand, and the emergence of the new riverside factories, the firm had entered into a new phase of technological modernization. The installation of a new steam engine, the replacement of mules by ring-frames and the modernization of the printing process considerably reduced the firm's combustible expenses and helped shrink its workforce, reducing costs by about 25 per cent. Nevertheless, with nearly a thousand workers it continued to be the third largest firm of Catalonia.

La España Industrial had initially specialized in the so-called white fabrics, including specialized cotton fabrics such as elephants, hamburgs and guineas, as well as percale, ticking, broadcloth and eventually printed calicos. Later on, it diversified its product range to include cretonne and velveteen for furniture and draperies, printed flannels, cotton piques, crepes, fine linens, bindery cloths, imitation wools and silks, and finally, in the twentieth century, artificial leather, felts, velvet silks, rayon, mohair and goat fur. This wide product range sought to strengthen the firm's position within a context of fierce competition and low domestic market demand.[8] The constraints on the latter also account for its decision to specialize in coarse and medium-grade yarns and its preference for self-acting technology.

In most Barcelona-city textile mills spinning underwent a feminization process during the mid-1800s, and La España Industrial was a pioneer in this respect. But in the case of the latter, the female spinners worked under an internal subcontracting system and the mules they operated were predominantly self-acting ones. These conditions made the firm unique within the Catalan textile industry as a whole.[9]

Women also worked as fibre rowers, warpers, piecers and pin operators, fly-frame tenters, roving-frame tenters, pluckers, stitchers, darners, cylinder painters, curlers, fibre pickers and, to a lesser degree, bleaching and carding-machine assistants. Fifty per cent of the mill's male workers served as piecework weavers, and the rest worked in the lapping, carding, bleaching, flax-preparing, printing, dyeing and machinery-repair sections. Around 1856, at the height of its activity, the firm's overall female workforce represented between 33 per cent and 35 per cent of the mill total. This situation was to last until 1888, before which changes in the sexual division of labour within the company were minimal. With the feminization of the weaving staff in 1888, the percentage of female workers within the factory rose to represent nearly two-thirds of all employees.

Firm Structure and Supervision

In the mid-nineteenth century, labour organization and management within the textile industry were the subjects of widespread debate among European and American industrialists. Oger's *Traité élémentaire de la filature du coton* (Elementary Treatise on Cotton Spinning), translated into Spanish in 1847, carefully addressed these issues and stressed their critical importance for the establishment of an efficient production process ('Knowledge is not enough: one must also know how to lead', he wrote). Among other things, he discussed which types of organizational hierarchies were most appropriate for the spinning and weaving sections, and observed the potential risks and conflicts that could result from a sloppily organized hierarchy; for example, he warned that 'when more than one foreman is appointed for each section, the situation can lead to confusion as to who must be held accountable for mistakes'. To remedy this, Oger suggested subdividing each section into various sub-sections, each of which would be managed by one overseer who reported directly to the section manager.

In 1885 Leslie C. Marshall considered this form of management as the most appropriate for big establishments, which he considered to be 'happily the exception and not the rule':

> Objections can be advanced against the founding of those mammoth spinning mills, which owe their origin chiefly to the speculative enterprise of joint stock options. In these establishments (which are happily the exception and not the rule) the various departments, likewise of abnormal extent, have to be sub-divided into rooms or sections, each of these being placed under the charge of an overlooker, and these overlookers being responsible to one who is head over the particular

department. These headmen receive their orders from the sub-manager, and he from the general manager. The general manager must consult and be guided by the managing director, and the latter has to work in conjunction with the head director. In such an establishment the broth is, no doubt, often spoiled, but even this is preferable to its entire disappearance from the inadequate utensil. Thus is the acquiring of a spinning mill of fair proportions, say of from 10,000 to 25,000 spindles, only second in importance to the securing of the best possible intelligence for its proper conducting.[10]

These were precisely the characteristics of La España Industrial in terms of capital, technology, management and labour hierarchy. Their frequent visits to the main European textile mills must have kept the Muntadas directors quite up-to-date. Evidence from the company archive, containing several foreign books and treatises on the subject of mill management, suggests that the company directors followed the ongoing debates.

A number of variables may have influenced the complex hierarchy (comprised of numerous sub-hierarchies) that developed at La España Industrial. First, this was a large-scale, vertically integrated mill with conditions unlike those to be found in most other textile mills during the first industrial revolution, where even the workshops had an unusually high number of production stages. This increased the management of flows between the mill's various sections. Second, the firm's investment in the latest innovative technology increased the need for employee supervision, since the installation and adjustment of the new machines required careful control and, at the same time, gave rise to new production tasks involving the application of new technical skills and knowledge, all of which had to be closely monitored. Third, the mill's constant innovations in production demanded a smooth coordination between the different sections and a continual re-adjustment of the various production tasks. Finally, the flow of activity within and between the various sections was significantly increased by the physical characteristics of the factory building itself (see Figure 2.1).

In 1852 the mill had seven sections, each corresponding to key textile production processes: (1) steam engine, (2) spinning, (3) weaving, (4) bleaching, (5) dyeing and printing, (6) carpentry and locksmith workshops, and (7) doormen, night watchmen and porters. Over the course of the next five years, during which construction of the mill complex was completed, these seven sections were subdivided into twenty sub-sections, a number that coincided with the spatial distribution of the various buildings and mill rooms. By 1860 the mill, a walled complex of some 17,000 square meters on the ground, boasted several independent buildings. In addition to the mill director's private residence, there were two buildings housing the steam-powered looms, a three-story building dedicated to carding and other yarn prep work (first floor), spinning on the mules (two rooms on the second floor), and

Figure 2.1 *La España Industrial in 1847–1853. Source:* Historical Archive of the Municipality of Barcelona. Photograph by Heribert Mariezcurrena.

weaving prep work (third floor), two three-story buildings where the cloth was lapped, two buildings for weaving and two buildings housing the printing and the repairing workshops. The bleaching, calico- and percale-dyeing, and drying sections also had their own buildings, as did the carpentry and moulding workshops, dye kitchen and porters' hall.

The fact that each section had its own director meant that when the number of mill sections increased in 1860, the number of section directors rose from six to twenty. Section management was also entrusted to the foremen, who occupied a range of intermediate posts of varying scope and authority. While the hierarchical organization of labour within the firm established clear lines of authority and control, each associated with a different managerial category, not all of these categories could be found in all of the sections, as we shall see. The following functions appear in the firm's wage books and foremen contracts:

1. Manager of the section. Various denominatives, such as director, first *contremaître*, supervisor or *majordomo*, were used to identify these foremen in the different sections.
2. *Majordomo*'s assistant or second *majordomo*
3. Second *contremaître* of section
4. Assistant of the second *contremaître* of section
5. *Vigilant*
6. *Contremaîtres* of work-groups (carding, lapping, flax preparers, etc.). These were under the manager of the section, although in some cases they could be more qualified.
7. *Contremaîtres* of weaver brigades
8. Master craftsman

While the majority of workers were hired on the basis of oral contracts, the most qualified technicians, and *contremaîtres* had written contracts, which stipulated roles and responsibilities, tasks, apprenticeships, hiring period, salary, compensations, fines, etc. The level and form of their wages (Table 2.1) reflected these differences, with section directors and technicians generally receiving a monthly wage and other types of foremen receiving a weekly or daily wage, depending on the section to which they were assigned. In addition, the hierarchical organization within the craft workshops varied considerably.

Work Organization and Hierarchy

Hierarchy varied considerably according to the sections and types of work. Such differences corresponded to a number of interrelated factors, including the degree of technological innovation, the division of labour in a given

Table 2.1 *Daily Wages of Directors, Foremen and Workers in 1865 (in reales)*

Section	A	B	C	D	E	F	G	H
Director	38	51	64	35	45	35	77	38
Other foremen		18	20	20	31	21		
Adult male workers	13	8	9	14	12	11	12	11
Adult female workers		6	7	6		6		

Section	I	J	K	L	M	N	O	P
Director	51	83	21	58	23	33	26	45
Other foremen			15					
Adult male workers	10	27	11	10	15	17	9	13
Adult female workers			6					

Sections: A: Steam power; B: Yarn preparation; C: Spinning; D: Weaving preparation; E: Weaving; F: Bleaching; G: Colors kitchen; H: Calico dyeing; I: Percale dyeing; J: Designers, moulders and engravers; K: Printing preparation; L: Printing; M: Carpenters; N: Locksmiths; O: Porters; P: Accounting.

Note: The daily wages of directors and foremen were calculated on the basis of their monthly and weekly wages.

Source: Contracts and wage books, La España Industrial.

section which multiplied the number of tasks and work-groups, the spatial distribution of work activities among these groups (that is, whether they took place within a single room or were spread over different rooms), the flow of activity within and between the different sections, the presence of trades and teams, and the form of salaries.

Preparation and Spinning Sections: Teams, Wages, Organization and Hierarchy

In the mid-1800s, spinning was the most technologically advanced sector of the cotton industry, thanks to the development of new lapping, carding and drawing machines, slubbing frames and spinning mules. In the case of La España Industrial, the firm's specialization in medium- and coarse-grade yarns influenced its decision to acquire self-acting mules. The majority of this machinery was purchased in England. Bruno Vidal and Manuel de Castro, the company's two original spinning masters, personally supervised the construction of this new machinery. They stayed on in England to ensure that the modifications to the carding and drawing machines were carried out according to J. A. Muntadas's specifications, but left the firm once the purchase was completed.

It seems clear that the skills and knowledge demanded of spinning masters after the mid-nineteenth century must have been greater than those of their predecessors, since the installation, adjustment and maintenance of this new machinery required a specialized technical education as well as extensive hands-on experience. In 1852 Oger, spinning master in Mulhouse, described this situation as follows:

> In earlier times, when the industry was less advanced, a certain level of practical knowledge of the various spinning machines was enough to make a worker into a foreman or even a master. But nowadays, this art has reached such an advanced state of perfection that workers are required to have a background in calculus and a precise knowledge of machinery construction and output.[11]

In 1847 the firm hired Angel Martorell as first spinning and weaving mechanical *contremaître* to monitor both the installation of the spinning and weaving machinery,[12] and Muntadas sent him to Manchester to perfect his education and to learn about the new technologies, particularly the corduroy production machines developed by the Sharp & Brothers Company. Martorell's father was a cotton manufacturer, and he himself had taken courses in the *cathedra* at the Barcelona Chamber of Commerce. He visited a number of factories and oversaw the functioning of different machines advising Muntadas about the most convenient purchase.[13] He was a highly skilled technician with both practical experience and theoretical knowledge. His contract was one of the first formal and written contracts of the company. It was brief and concise, compared with those signed in the years that followed. His position and function were stipulated as well as the term of the contract (one year) and his annual salary (14,000 *reales*).[14] Nevertheless, he left the firm in 1855 to work with Joan Güell, a textile manufacturer who had a monopoly for the production of corduroy in Spain. His premature departure might have influenced the content of the foremen's contracts that followed, since from then on five years was the minimum term of engagement, while high mutual compensations for breach of contract and clauses of exclusivity and confidentiality were stipulated.

In 1856, after the new machinery had been installed, the yarn preparation and spinning activities were divided into two separate sections, each with its own work organization, wage form, and hierarchy. But since the quality of the yarn depended largely on the skill with which it was handled during the preparatory stages (especially during carding), the activities in the yarn-prep and -spinning sections had to be carefully coordinated by the foremen, for whom this was one of the most demanding tasks. Yarn preparation involved four basic processes: (a) lapping, (b) carding, (c) fibre draughting on the drawing machines and (d) fibre-draught finishing on the slubbing frames. These four processes took place in two buildings, one of which was dedicated exclusively to lapping.

The yarn-preparation section was run by a *majordomo*, who mainly resolved technical issues, and by three or four assistants or *sub-majordomos*, whose basic role was to assist the *majordomo* in coordinating the different work-groups and to help direct the flow of work activity between the yarn-preparation and -spinning sections. The lapping and carding groups also had a *contremaître* each, who responded to technical and organizational issues and oversaw the training of highly skilled workers and one or two assistants, who oriented the workers and oversaw the activities of the group as a whole. According to several technical manuals of the time, the lapping *contremaître* had to 'calculate and adjust the correct speed of the lapping's flying, to avoid high temperatures on the bearings, to control the accuracy of the operatives' work and to guarantee the finished lapping veil is correctly weighted'.[15]

Carding was 'the most important stage in the yarn preparing process to the point that bad carding results in the ruin of spinning'.[16] Indeed, the contract of Pierre J. Croisin (Tessy, France), hired in 1847 as the first carding mechanical *contremaître*, shows that he was a highly trained technician. According to his initial five-year contract, his main responsibility was to 'properly run and adjust the new machines no matter what their number might be' although if they increased 'the company had to provide him with more assistants'. Additionally, he was required to take an apprentice 'to instruct him in all the secrets of his art'. His annual salary rose to 12,492 *reales de vellón* (85 per cent of the section's director). The contract also contained a long list of other clauses regarding dismissal and compensations, health insurance, travel expenses, etc.

Croisin was the only foreign *contremaître* in the yarn-preparation section, where – as was the case throughout the mill – management posts tended to pass from fathers to sons, once the latter had acquired several years of experience as workers and assistant *majordomos*. Thus, members of the Sirvent, Ventura, Garriga, Jover and Armengol families, among others, worked for generations as the section and sub-section foremen, eventually expanding into the spinning and other sections of the mill.

The sexual division of labour was very strict: men lapped and carded while women ran the drawing machines and the slubbing frames always under the supervision of a group leader who, like the foremen, was invariably male. All of the foremen and workers in this section, except for the *majordomo*, received a daily wage.

In sum, the yarn-preparation section had a relatively high number of foremen (Table 2.2) and a hierarchy that was well defined in terms of roles, status and wages (Table 2.1), just as the technical manuals of the time recommended. This was due to the fact that workers had to be taught how to use the new machinery, the running of which had to be carefully monitored. The new technology also increased the division of labour within the section. The number of foremen multiplied with the number of production-related tasks, since each foreman was charged with monitoring one of the many working groups active in different buildings and rooms.

Table 2.2 *Number of Foremen and Workers in La España Industrial, 1857–1905*

Selected Sections	1855 F	W	W/F	1860 F	W	W/F	1877 F	W	W/F	1905 F	W	W/F
Preparation of yarn	11	308	28	8	138	17	5	157	31	2	107	54
Spinning				4	218	55	3	221	74	2	121	61
Prep. weaving	24	518	22	6	151	25	4	141	35	4	70	18
Weaving				26	490	19	25	516	21	13	331	25
Bleaching	2	18	9	1	27	27	3	64	21	1	24	24
Prep. printing	10	160	16	2	59	30	2	65	33	1	32	64
Printing				1	30	30	1	48	48		32	
Designers, engravers, moulders				1	27	27	1	32	32			
Dyeing				1	32	32	1	21	21	1	12	12
Locksmith	1	18	18	1	25	25	2	32	16	1	15	19
Tinsmiths	1	4	4	1	7	7	1	7	7		4	
Carpenters	1	10	10	1	14	14	1	9	9	1	5	5
Steam machine	3	23	8	1	27	27	1	35	35	1	22	22
All	53	1,059	20	54	1,245	23	50	1,348	27	27	775	29

F: Foremen (Directors of sections, *contremaîtres* and *majordomos*); W: Workers.

Source: Wage books of La España Industrial.

Overall, hierarchy within the spinning section was weaker than in the yarn-preparation section. Moreover, different labour systems and hierarchies coexisted within the spinning section. This section was subdivided into various work-groups: (a) throstle spinners, (b) self-acting spinners, (c) twisters, (d) height-of-yarn and bundlers operatives, and (e) sweepers. The last three groups were very small with less than six workers each.

Between 1855 and 1888, control of the spinning section fell to *majordomo* Francisco Ventura and one or two assistants (listed in the wage-books as either *sub-majordomos* or assistant *contremaîtres*), who also enjoyed long-term appointments and who received a monthly wage, as did Ventura himself. The throstle-spinner work-group, comprised of female spinners who received a fixed daily wage, also had a *contremaître* and an assistant *contremaître*, both of whom were also paid a fixed daily wage. The fact that the assistant *contremaître*'s salary was only half that of the *contremaître* denotes a clearly established management hierarchy, as expressed through differences in title and wages (Table 2.1).

The ratio of foremen to workers in the throstle-spinning group was about 1:20 for the duration of the period under study, while in the section as a whole this ratio ranged from 1:57 to 1:88 (Table 2.2). This discrepancy can be explained by reference to the alternative model of work organization among the self-acting spinners.

In 1856 the factory had around ninety self-acting mules of 320–340 spindles each. Self-acting spinning was organized in teams working on a piece-system. Each team consisted of one spinner, two piecers and one creel-filler, all of which were women. Each of the teams tended two machines while in most Catalan textile factories the male teams operated a single self-actor of about 400 to 500 spindles. This means that female teams' earnings could be higher since the running of more spindles allowed an increased output, but this was the result of a greater effort.[17] This system was established by 1852 after different systems had been attempted in previous years. At first, the company itself recruited the piecers and creel-fillers and paid them a time-wage directly, just as it did with the spinners. Shortly thereafter, however, it decided to try out a team-based piecework system, which co-existed with the time-wage system until it was eliminated in 1851. Thus, just a few months after the opening of the factory, the female spinning teams were functioning like the male teams in most other cotton factories. The company paid the piecework rate to the spinner, and she distributed it among the members of her team. When the time-wage was replaced by a piecework system, the skill level of the team increased: instead of one spinner, one piecer and two creel-fillers, its composition changed to one spinner, two piecers and one creel-filler. The role of the spinner was reappraised: the piecer's wage fell from 75 per cent to 50 per cent of the spinner's wage. At the same time, the spinner's authority and responsibility within the teams was reinforced, and her job was given a higher status. A recent study has shown that where spinners teams were male the introduction of mules did not imply a deskilling of work, internal subcontracting prevailed and piece wages were high. When teams were female, it was considered an unskilled activity since the jobs performed by female spinners and piecers were so similar that the spinner was really nothing more than a 'piecing-up machine', while the organization of spinning work and the tending of mules were foremen's tasks.[18] However, at La España Industrial the spinner incomes almost doubled that of piecers of their teams and the average of adult women workers. Until 1875 their wages were even very similar to or even higher than the average for adult male workers (Figure 2.2). If wage is a good proxy for status, then spinners at La España Industrial certainly cannot be viewed as unqualified workers and their role is by no means comparable to that of the piecers.

In companies where spinners were male, the teams were under the supervision of *contremaîtres* – at a ratio of foremen to spinners of about 1:14. Their role was to take care of coordination and the adjustment and reparation of machines, a task performed by the spinners in the case of the mule-jennies. At La España Industrial this task was probably in the hands of a group called

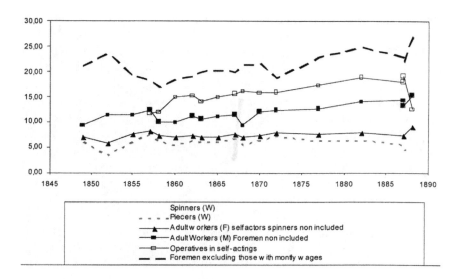

Figure 2.2 *Daily Earnings of Workers at La España Industrial, 1849–1888 (in reales).*
Source: Archive of La España Industrial.

'operatives employed in self actors', whose ratio in relation with spinners varied between 1:14 to 1:30. This ratio makes it rather unlikely that they would have been able to monitor the rise of the faller and the wire used to guide the yarn during the last stages of the inward run, which were motions that at that time still required manual assistance and close attention.[19] Consequently, even if the spinners had to help their piecers, they also had to tend the mules.

From 1872 on, spinners' income dropped steadily, approaching the average for female workers by 1888. This was not due to any reduction in yarn tariffs, productivity or work time, but rather to a general company drift towards producing thicker yarns and coarser fabrics, which were paid at a lower rate. Modern ring-frames replaced self-acting mules in 1888, and none of the spinners working on the old self-acting mules remained in the firm. Until then, however, their careers had lasted longer than that of the average worker, whether male or female, and this is another possible indicator of their high status (Figure 2.3).

To sum up, the spinning teams working on the self-actors were the only teams in the mill doing piecework under an internal contract system. This explains the lower ratio of foremen to workers to be found in the spinning section, in comparison with that of other sections. But spinning outputs were very similar among all the teams, indicating that the rhythm of production was extremely intense and also highly standardized – in contrast, for example, to that of French textile mills.[20] The hiring of piecers and creel-fillers – a

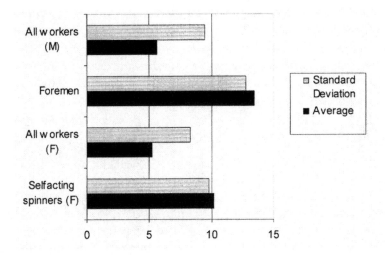

Figure 2.3 *Years in the Firm. Source:* Archive of La España Industrial.

traditional emblem of the autonomy and status of the spinners – is a topic that requires further investigation. We know that in some other Barcelona mills, even when the spinners were men, such hiring responsibilities fell to the masters and foremen, who also determined the wages the spinners had to pay to their piecers.

Transition to New Forms of Supervision in the Weaving Sections: The Undermining of Weavers' Autonomy

Under the direction of Angel Martorell, who was responsible for the acquisition and installation of the new mechanical looms, the weaving-preparation and weaving sections were merged into a single unit between 1849 and 1855. Thereafter, the two were separated again and placed under the supervision of Joaquín Oller and Theodoro Flores, managers of the weaving-preparation and weaving sections respectively, until 1888. As in the case of the manager of spinning and other sections, they founded their own familial networks. Thus, Oller's son eventually became a foreman in the weaving section, as did Flores's son in the tinsmith section.

The weaving-preparation hierarchy was very similar to that of the yarn-preparation section. It consisted of four working groups: (a) winders, (b) beam warpers, (c) doffers and loom threaders, and (d) flax preparers. In this section the *majordomo* was aided by up to three assistants whose wages increased on a sliding scale, with the highest wage being equal to half that of the *majordomo*. In addition, each of the four groups – even those of the winders, beam warpers and doffers, whose workers were exclusively female – was assigned a specific male supervisor.

The existence of these intermediate posts within the work hierarchy suggests that supervision in the section was not weak, which would have been the case if the section managers and their assistants had assumed this duty. In fact, the role and status of these 'intermediate supervisors' differed significantly from that of the managers and assistants. The fact that the leader of the female winder working group was the only post listed in the wage-book as a *vigilant* (overseer) suggests that this position in the management hierarchy was predominantly geared towards ensuring worker compliance. By contrast, the lead of the flax-preparer working group must have played a more technical role, since his category was *contremaître* and the group's incentive-based wage system ensured an intense production pace. The high status of the flax-prep group leader in comparison with that of other working group *vigilants* also accounts for the fact that his daily wage was double that of his peers. His was a high status indeed, for his salary exceeded even that of the assistant *majordomos*.

As for the weaving section, it was divided in two sub-groups consisting of weavers on the one hand, and a group of operatives responsible for weighing the fabric and cleaning the section quarters on the other. The hierarchy for this section was a complex one. An assistant *majordomo* and two 'second' *contremaîtres*, whose status was graded on an upward scale, aided the manager of the section or *majordomo*. This may be deduced from the salaries for this group, which ranged from 80 per cent to 65 per cent of the section manager's salary (Table 2.1).

As late as 1900, manufacturers complained of weavers' restrictions on output. However, at La España Industrial the weaver's traditional autonomy and his ability to control pace was undermined since in 1849 a new work and wage system and closer supervision replaced the internal subcontract system. Although weavers were paid a piece wage, they were not able to control the pace of their work. Their working hours were fixed by collective agreements and they were required to meet minimum weekly production quotas, with premiums being awarded to those who exceeded the quota.

The weavers were organized into brigades of some twenty workers apiece, headed by brigade *contremaîtres*. The intense pace of work in this section was reinforced by the brigade *contremaîtres*, who closely supervised the weavers and whose salary was intimately linked to the unit's productivity thanks to an incentive system that paid a bonus to the *contremaître* whenever his brigade realized 'production excess'. This bonus represented up to 25 per cent of the *contremaître*'s daily wage, which could become up to 75 per cent higher than the weaver's wage after bonuses were added. The difference between the weaver's salary and that of the *contremaître* exceeded the wage differential between adult workers and foremen of other sections. The brigade *contremaîtres* enjoyed one of the highest salaries of all the section foremen of their kind, and the salary of the section director also compared favourably to that of his peers at the mill. The social and economic polarity between the weavers and their direct superiors became more marked after 1888, when the weaving brigades were completely feminized.

The salaries among this group depended as much on the competitiveness and skill of the weavers as on the *contremaître*'s ability to control the smooth functioning of the looms as well as to monitor the productivity of the workers under his charge. In short, the quality and productivity of work in the weaving section was strictly controlled through a specific form of payment as well as through close supervision of the weavers themselves.

This organizational structure suggests that it was the brigade leaders who directly monitored the continuous adjustment of the looms required by the wide variety of fabrics produced at the mill, and who personally supervised the work of the weavers, while the section managers coordinated the activities of the section as a whole and resolved technical issues. A smooth coordination between the weaving, spinning and printing sections was vital to the quality of the finished cloth, as was the foreman's correct installation and maintenance of the looms (something that most weaving manuals pointed out), which was also necessary to ensure an efficient rhythm of production.

Printing and Workshop Sections: Crafts and Trades as Alternatives for Hierarchy?

The printing sections were seen as the 'heart' of the firm, since the ability to offer a wide variety of textile designs, in addition to the quality and innovative nature of the cloth itself, could bolster the firm's competitiveness in a domestic market in which Alsatian fabrics predominated.

The dearth of local skilled workers with training in the new dyeing and printing technologies forced the company, as well as many of the most important firms (Rull & Cia; Achon, Puigmartí & Cia; Achon, Germans & Cia; Ricart and Manoury, etc.) to seek out the services of foreign (mainly French – particularly Alsatian – but also some English) chemists, dyers, designers, moulders, engravers, etchers and printers. To this end, the manager of the mill, Josep Antoni Muntadas, travelled to Paris and Mulhouse, where he sought advice from André Koechlin and Henry Schlumberger with regard to the hiring of a new chemist. At their recommendation, the firm hired Martín Ziegler in 1847, the most prestigious chemist in the region of Alsace, as first chemist and director of both the dyeing and printing sections. Ziegler, who was given a five-year contract and the highest salary at the firm (15,000 francs for the first three years and 18,000 francs for the following two), pledged 'to dedicate all his knowledge, experience and efforts to La España Industrial and to guard the secrets of the firm's production'. Because the dyeing and printing sections required a great deal of technical innovation and because there was a lack of skilled workers in this field, Ziegler was asked not only to direct and coordinate the operations taking place in the different workshops but also to train local workers in the new production tasks and to ensure that they complied with what was expected of them:

> The cylinder printer has begun to work today; this will allow M. Ziegler to be more able to supervise more assiduously the rest of operations and thus counter-acting the ignorance and tepidness of operatives. No doubt that the directors are conscious that at that stage we do not count on the sufficient number of skillful and intelligent workers in such a delicate and new trade.[21]

When Ziegler's contract expired, he was replaced by Jean Jacques Heil-mann, a prestigious chemist and native of Mulhouse who had acquired a great deal of experience while working in the English, German and Bohemian textile mills. He was aided by a 'second' *contremaître*, Juan Hoesly, who was a highly qualified chemist also. Like his predecessors, Heilmann was initially hired for a period of five years (1852–1856) and was offered a yearly salary of 12,000 *reales* during his first year of service, which was to increase annually by 2,000 *reales*. Like his predecessors, he pledged fidelity and confidential-ity to the firm. The first Catalan chemist to work in the firm was Josep Tay, who was hired in 1873 to work under Hoesly as second chemist in the dye kitchen. Tay had been trained in Sorèze (France) and obtained his degree in Barcelona. In 1884 he replaced Hoesly as the section director and was given his own assistant, also of Catalan origin.

The printing section also underwent a series of reorganizations and sub-divisions. In 1856 it was divided into five sections: the dye kitchen, the designer, engraving, moulding and pantography section, the mechanical-printing section, the calico-dyeing section, and the percale-dyeing section. Each of these five was run by a *contremaître* who was also a highly qualified technician. This was especially true of the *contremaîtres* for the first three sections, who continued to be brought in from other countries until the late 1880s. The only exception was Josep Capdevila, *majordomo* of the calico-dyeing section, who had finished his education in England after concluding his studies in chemistry at the Barcelona Chamber of Commerce.

The basic role of these foremen, as revealed by some of their contracts, was to improve techniques, to coordinate the different stages of production, and to train local workers in the practices generated by technological innovations. Most of the workers in the designer, engraving, moulders and pantograph sec-tion as well as in the mechanical-printing section came from Alcasia, and all were paid a monthly wage. All of these sections seem to have functioned as arti-sanal workshops composed of a master, skilled workers, apprentices and peons.

The high-quality print designs of La España Industrial were ranked among the finest of Europe, as evidenced by the firm's numerous and prestigious awards at the international exhibitions of London (1856), Portugal (1861 and 1865), Paris (1867, 1878 and 1889), Vienna (1873), Philadelphia (1876) and Barcelona (1888).[22]

The various auxiliary workshops devoted to the production, adaptation and reparation of the mill machinery (including the carpentry, locksmith, tinsmith sections, among others) were organized in a very similar way. Early in the mill's existence, they were all housed within the same section, known as the 'workshops' area; later, they were divided up according to craft. The managers of these sections, who were artisans themselves, were directly involved in coordinating the different task (and trade) activities taking place within each workshop, and in coordinating the flow of exchange between the various workshops and the sections that housed them. Here, the only element of hierarchy was the section manager, and workers organized themselves according to the traditional rules of craft workers. Thus, the locksmith workshop was made up of different groups, including designers, blacksmiths, lathe-makers and adjusters, who had their own (local) artisans and apprentices. Yet in the carpentry workshop, for example, the manager (who was a master carpenter) directly allocated and oriented the work of a small group of no more than twelve carpenters and a couple of apprentices, and also coordinated the flow of activity between the workshop and other sections. This setup could also be found in other sections, such as the locksmith, tinsmith, and shuttle workshops, in all of which the managers received a monthly wage while other operatives earned a day wage.

Foremen: Identity and Class Conflict

In the mid-nineteenth century, the directors of La España Industrial denounced the weakness of the Spanish governments' policy regarding industrial mechanics' training, and its prejudice against the development of a modern and competitive national textile industry. The restoration of an absolute monarchy in 1813, which was anti-industrialist and supporter of agrarian interests, delayed industrial training and education for several decades. As a consequence, personnel shortages forced Spanish manufacturers to hire foreign technicians. In Catalonia such technical training had come about almost entirely as the result of private initiative since the late 1700s. In 1796 the Spanish Royal Chamber of Commerce (Real Junta de Comercio) created several polytechnic training institutes, but these were closed by royal order in 1847, a period crucial for Catalan industrialization.[23]

Although the entrepreneurial association Institut Industrial de Cataluña founded new polytechnic schools in 1849 as replacements for the inoperative institutes, a year later they too were forced to shut down after another royal order demanded the suspension of the Institute's activities. The Escuela Industrial de Barcelona opened its doors just three years after La España Industrial had drafted its founding constitution.[24] In this context, it is easy to understand why the firm's managing directors criticized the shortage of highly skilled technicians, and why they actively recruited foreign technicians, especially for the printing section. Nevertheless, most of the original mechanics and spinning and weaving foremen hired by Muntadas were Catalan natives who had studied engineering, chemistry and textiles at the Real Junta de Comercio, making them part of an elite group of textile technicians.

In some cases, these early members of the managerial hierarchy came from manufacturing families, where they had received practical training that complemented their technical education. Others had been given a mostly hands-on education in the context of trade workshops or mills, in accordance with their artisan or working-class origins.[25] Muntadas's goal of making La España Industrial one of the most advanced firms of its time motivated him to send some of these technicians to prestigious French and English firms, where they completed their practical training and picked up the latest industrial trends and innovations. While Muntadas had recourse to a number of highly qualified local and foreign technicians and foremen, the company's main problem had to do with the training of local workers who were taught by senior artisans and technicians through both formal and informal apprenticeship.

Were all of the foremen at La España Industrial so highly qualified? Was this high level of education and training an exception within the Catalan textile industry as a whole? It is true that 'while illiteracy prevailed among the workers, *majordomos*, directors, *contremaîtres* and other intermediate foremen needed to be able to read the machinery instructions and to interpret mechanical plans'.[26] However, most textile manuals of the period underlined the lack of technical training among *contremaîtres* and stressed the need to set forth the basic principals of textile manufacturing in a clear, straightforward manner. As late as 1876, Manuel Brosa y Arnó dedicated his *Manual Completo de la Hilatura de Algodón útil a los contramaestres, mayordomos y fabricantes* (A Complete Guide to Cotton Spinning for Foremen, Masters and Manufacturers) to 'all cotton textile foremen and managers, in order to facilitate instruction in this field and bring you up-to-date on the most modern cotton-spinning machinery, using a very simple method that is devoid of any scientific jargon and is easily accessible even to the most limited of intellects'.[27] In 1897 the weaving master Manuel Pagés y Borí published the first manual dedicated exclusively to weaving foremen, pointing out that 'most weaving masters can barely read … making it necessary to explain the rules of the craft using clear, easily understood language'. He compared this low degree of instruction with the situation in other countries where 'the level of scientific knowledge generally possessed by the masters is truly marvellous' and argued 'against the widespread belief among foremen in the advantages of hands-on experience and the uselessness of theoretical training'.[28]

Family networks within the firm appeared to be a useful way of transmitting the skills that facilitated access to managerial posts. A few examples can serve to illustrate the importance of family ties among mill foremen. The bleaching section was run by three generations of Vendrell family members, two generations of Orriols served as foremen in the weaving section, and various Puigcorbé relatives managed the Porter's Hall. A similar evolution can be traced for the Arbós family in carpentry, the Garriga, Jover and Armengol families in yarn preparation, the Bentura family in spinning and the Marti family in print cylinders and fabric finishing. Foremen also sometimes cast their familial nets out into other sections of the mill. Such clan-like attitudes served to strengthen their status and power both inside and outside the mill. Thus, some masters and foremen held prominent local political positions. Clemente Orriols, for example, served as a town councilman between 1868 and 1869, as did Carlos Vendrell in 1872; Joan Rabada, a print designer, sat on the civic board of trustees in 1879, while the spinning master Francisco Ventura served as assistant vice-mayor in 1877; and Joaquín Oller, a weaving preparation master, and Ignacio Puigcorbé, a master in the porter's hall, were elected mayor in 1881 and 1887, respectively. Some of these foremen were also known as militant republicans and/or presidents or directors of mutual societies, while others belonged to Catholic or monarchical groups or mixed societies comprised of both manufacturers and workers. Thus, Ignacio Puigcorbé sat on the board of directors for La Fraternal, a ladies' mutual society founded in 1868, while Paula Vallés Vendrell and Maria Vendrell, members of the powerful Vendrell family and workers in the spinning section, served as president and vice-president, respectively. Likewise, Melchor Torrabela, master of printing preparation, served as president for the Monte de Piedad de Jesús Sacramentat between 1882 and 1886.[29]

Workers' associations, which perceived the foremen's professional and social mobility as a menace to class cohesion, often denounced the changes they observed in foremen who came from working-class backgrounds:

> After reaching certain spheres, the worker generally undergoes a kind of metamorphosis, which effects such a radical change in his way of being and thinking that, apart from a few noble exceptions, he becomes a stranger even to himself, forgetting who he was and his past sufferings and enjoying the advantages of his new state. In her vicissitudes, goddess of Fortune provides repeated examples of this process, and we are very conscious that it is extremely prejudicial to the proletariat.[30]

In 1887 the firm wanted to suspend employees' pay on holidays that fell during the workweek. The workers of La España Industrial went on strike, and some of the foremen protected the entry of scabs into the mill. Workers' associations later denounced the ambiguous situation of foremen, stating that 'some of the foremen, known among us as *cabos de vara* ('pole-brandishers'), defended the interests of the manufacturers without realizing that, by so doing, they were damaging their own interests'.[31]

Attempts by La España Industrial foremen to extend their power beyond the bounds of the mill were often denounced. In 1869, for example, workers association journals criticized the masters at La España Industrial for their behaviour during the first elections to be held under a system of universal male suffrage, when they not only voted for the Catholic candidate but also incited the workers in various sections to do the same.[32]

Foreman identity and the role of the 'good foreman' were also debated in reformist workers' journals. Although the members of this social group were recognized and accepted as middlemen mediating between labour and capital during times of conflict, the violence of their methods was firmly resisted:

> Except for a very few and honourable exceptions, the middlemen usually known as directors, *majordomos*, or overseers – according with the traditions of the different industries, arts, trades or occupations – constantly prove that far from looking for the harmony of the conflicting interest of owners and workers, which is the fundamental basis of security for capital, well-being of the workers, and guaranty of peace for society, enjoy stirring up the war and introducing the discord to satisfy their own will to act as tyrants upon those that once were their own peers or upon those that could be their equals some day.[33]

Over the course of the second half of the nineteenth century, craft associations gradually began to perceive these middlemen as a new threat to the traditional autonomy of qualified workers. Their main complaints had to do with the middleman's usurpation of many of their own long-standing duties and responsibilities, including the hiring of new workers, the distribution of tasks and the determining of work rhythms and rates.

Spinning and weaving foremen were most frequently targets of worker resistance, since in most factories the spinner's traditional control over internal subcontracting and his freedom to manage teams and oversee production was gradually shifted to foremen. In Barcelona, the Batlló mill introduced these changes as part of the feminization of the spinning industry. 'The masters [in the Batlló cotton mill of Barcelona] not only do not want to hire male spinners, but they have also been dismissing older female workers and young male employees in order to hire little girls who will run the machines for half the price.'[34] In La España Industrial, women ran the self-acting mules right from the start, but their wages, as we have seen, were far higher than those of female spinners in other Barcelona mills of the time. Nevertheless, we do not know whether the hiring of piecers and creel-fillers fell under the control of these female spinners.

The foremen's attempts to control the organization of labour in the weaving section at La España Industrial set them at odds with weavers as early as 1854, when Catalonia's first general strike took place. 'Some of the weavers of La España Industrial objected to their replacement on the looms by other workers, and they abandoned the factory before authority could intervene. Some fifty of them were arrested, after which all the mechanical weavers in Barcelona and the surrounding area went on strike.'[35]

Our information on workers' resistance to foremen's control of pace and discipline on the shop floor is very scant, but we do know that three of them were murdered in conflicts arising during this period. Working-class press denounced the foremen of the firm for unfairly pressuring union members:

> We reject all injustices, acts of force and the abuse of authority, no matter how often these are perpetrated by capital, which does not have the right to enslave, tyrannize and impose itself as it does. A recent occurrence in La España Industrial compels us to take up the pen and denounce an abuse, a scandal, a tyranny, an injustice. In the first wing of the mechanical looms section there was a worker who for twenty years had religiously and scrupulously done his duty towards Society; nevertheless, a week ago this worker, having caught a cold and with a pounding head, went to ask one of his co-workers for a little bit of rape tobacco, for which he was only absent from his post for a few seconds. This was enough for the *major-domo* of this workroom to issue him a reprimand, and on Saturday the director fired him for taking some snuff. Surprised, he took his case to the master, who ignored him. The despotism and injustice of this poor worker's dismissal does not surprise us, for he represents the working class.[36]

The foremen at La España Industrial were denounced not only for pressuring workers to 'stay on their toes' and for disciplining those who failed to meet their expectations, but also for deliberately targeting union members in the workshops at the mill:

> Those who work in La España Industrial are silenced and persecuted by non-union members who, supported and protected by a foreman in the spinning workshop, are insulted and provoked without taking into consideration their rights, reason and behaviour. The injustice, tyranny, and insults are carried to such an extreme that these workers are not even allowed to enter certain areas, nor are they permitted to pay the stipend and quota required by the society while they are inside the building complex. What a shame for that establishment![37]

The rise of foremen's associations towards the end of the nineteenth century, such as El Fomento de la Industria de los Telares Mecánicos (1873), El Centro Industrial de Cataluña (1877), El Fomento Industrial (1885), La Alianza Industrial (1887) and El Progreso Industrial (1892), account for the consolidation process experienced by this new and heterogeneous professional group, whose professional and class position was also a matter of debate within these associations. Some of their members defined themselves as 'technicians', some as 'mediators between [the forces of] capital and labour', and others as 'workers of the intelligence'.[38] These different views draw attention to the fact that the foreman's identity was still undefined and ambiguous. Throughout this period, workers directed their resistance against the new forms of labour organization and management – and against de-qualification of work, loss of autonomy and intensified production pace – towards the foremen.

Conclusion

During a transition period (1849–1888) different models of management and supervision co-existed at La España Industrial, a large-scale, vertically integrated textile mill. New and controversial forms of management, described in the instructive literature on textile manufacturing and implemented in some of Europe's largest manufacturing firms, were introduced to some extent.

The sections where the trades predominated functioned as artisanal workshops, governed by established rules and in which hierarchy only played a limited role. In sections characterized by new technologies and an increasing division of labour, a flexible combination of incentive wage systems, teams and a more intense supervision were introduced. This suggests that new management and wage systems were not always necessary and/or effective. While different models of management co-existed within the mill, worker supervision appears to have been stronger than in other European textile firms. Hierarchy was very well structured within each model.[39]

The highest ranks of the hierarchy were occupied by highly trained technicians and experienced workers, who were directly involved in the introduction and adaptation of new technology. The fact that local textile workers were often unfamiliar with new production techniques, meant that foremen had to play an active role in training and guiding employees. The complexity of tasks, the intense work rhythm and the need for a smooth flow of materials between sections, required intermediate foremen who transmitted knowledge and disciplined workers

On the whole, foremen constituted a heterogeneous group in terms of qualifications, roles and status both inside and outside the mill. Contrary to assumptions of Marxist and Neo-Marxist management theories, the size of the firm's hierarchy experienced no significant increase in the late nineteenth century, thanks to new, lower-maintenance technologies and automatization, which lowered the need for training and job orientation.

Evidence from the workers' press suggests that, in addition to salary issues, the foreman's authority over workers represented a key area of conflict between workers and employers. Craft societies reproached foremen for appropriating workers' traditional control over hiring, distribution of tasks, work pace and wages rates.

While the firm's directors tried to control the activities of craft societies on the shop floor by placing supervisors in positions of authority, unions tried to appeal to the foremen's loyalty to the working class. The ambiguity of the foreman's role was raised (but not resolved) in foremen's associations, created in the last third of the nineteenth century.

In the absence of similar studies, we cannot know whether La España Industrial's management policy, characterized by a combination of traditional and newer approaches, differed significantly from that of other companies in the Spanish textile industry. However, the findings in this essay might be taken as a point of departure from which to test the relationships between different models of supervision, organization of labour, technological innovations and craft traditions. At any rate, the case of La España Industrial shows that modern management methods had already come into play in the mid-nineteenth century, although their introduction was gradual and their effect on different production processes, even those taking place within the same firm, was uneven in terms of both their scope and evolution.

Notes

I would like to thank Carmen Sarasúa and Patricia Van den Eeckhout for their critiques and comments. I am indebted to Concepción Villar for her support on the designing of the database and statistical analysis. This research was supported by funds of the Minister of Education and Minister of Labour and Social Affairs (2003–2005).

1. W. M. Reddy, *The Rise of Market Culture: The Textile Trade and French Society, 1750–1790* (Cambridge, 1984); P. Lefebvre, *L'invention de la grande entreprise: Travail, hiérarchie, marché. France, fin XVIIIe–début XXe siècle* (Paris, 2003).
2. M.-G. Dezes, K. Lunn, A. McIvor and K. Tenfelde, 'Employers and Trade Unions in the Late Nineteenth Century in Britain, France and Germany', in *The Emergence of European Trade Unionism*, ed. J.-L. Robert, A. Prost and C. Wrigley (Aldershot, 2004), 204–214.
3. Regarding work organization in La España Industrial, see E. Camps, *La formación del mercado de trabajo industrial en la Cataluña del siglo XIX* (Madrid, 1995); C. Enrech, *Indústria i ofici: Conflicte social i jerarquies obreres en la Catalunya Tèxtil, 1881–1923* (Barcelona, 2005), 101–104. On foremen of La España Industrial, see A. Duarte, 'Mayordomos y contramaestres: Jerarquía fabril en la industria algodonera catalana, 1879–1890', *Historia Social*, no. 4 (1989): 3–20. On technology equipment, see M. L. Gutierrez, *La España Industrial, 1847–1853: Un model d'innovació tecnològica* (Barcelona, 1997). On the

financial analysis of the firm, see E. Ribas Mirángels, 'La España Industrial (1851–1936): Análisis económico-financiero de la compañía', in *Homenaje al Dr. Jordi Nadal*, ed. A. Carreras, P. Pascual, D. Reher and C. Sudria (Barcelona, 1999), 1125–1163. On wages, see C. Borderías, 'Salarios y subsistencia de las trabajadoras y trabajadores de La España Industrial, 1849–1868', *Barcelona Quaderns d'Història*, no. 11 (2004): 223–238.

4. I collected individual information regarding name, occupation, work organization (individual, trade, teams, brigade), work time and wages (daily, weekly, monthly, piecework, premiums) from 1849 to 1930. One week per year was selected, and all workers in this week were included in the database. Thus, this database contains individual information on about 6,000 workers.

5. The Instituto Industrial de España was founded in 1840. In 1841 it sketched out preliminary plans for what was described as a 'project for the propagation and perfection of the manufacturing industry', whose aim was to create a conglomerate dedicated to the building of wool, linen, cotton and metal mills and to industrial machinery production in various Spanish towns. The projected industrial group was to have been called La Industrial Española and was endowed with a start-up capital of some 25 million *reales* distributed in the form of 2,500 stocks of 1,000 *reales* each. However, the project was suspended after collection efforts in Barcelona resulted in only 141 million *reales*. See Gutierrez, *La España Industrial*, 75.

6. In 1865, there were 114 mules with 37,778 spindles, 22 throstles with 3,520 spindles and 7 mule-jennies with 840 spindles. See *Información sobre el derecho diferencial de bandera y sobre los de aduanas exigibles a los hierros, el carbón de piedra y los algodones presentada al Gobierno de su majestad por la comisión nombrada al efecto en Real decreto de 10 de Noviembre de 1865* (Madrid, 1867), III, 11.

7. In the mid-nineteenth century, 80 per cent of workers in Barcelona were occupied in the textile industry. The average number of workers in these textile factories was forty. The existing integrated factories at that time did not count more than 150 operatives. By 1861 there were 123 vertically integrated factories in Cataluña, which occupied around 18,335 workers. Eighty-seven per cent of them had less than two hundred workers, and only one of them – La España Industrial – had more than thousand operatives. See J. R. Rosés, 'La integración vertical en el sector algodonero catalán, 1832–1861', in *¿Qué inventen ellos? Tecnología, empresa y cambio económico en la España Contemporánea*, ed. S. López García and J. M. Valdaliso (Madrid, 1997), 249–280.

8. Manufacturas Españolas, *La España Industrial, Libro del centenario, 28 de Enero de 1947* (Barcelona, 1947), 34–59.

9. By 1856, 33 per cent of the spinners working on mule-jennies in Barcelona were female, while 79 per cent of female spinners worked on self-acting mules. In contrast, most of the spinners in the surrounding towns (Gracia, Sant Andreu, San Martí) seem to have been men, as was the case in other Catalan villages such as Cornellá, Mataró and Premiá. The mule-jennies were ruled by one spinner, but in the self-acting mules the teams consisted of a male or female spinner with one assistant, although these mules were probably quite large (with 450–500 bobbins). The women spinners working on the self-acting mules in La España Industrial represented 46 per cent of the city's total female spinners. See I. Cerdà, 'Monografia estadística de la clase obrera en Barcelona en 1856', appendix to his *Teoría general de la urbanización y aplicación de sus principios y doctrinas a la reforma y ensanche de Barcelona* (Madrid, 1867), 553–700.

10. L. C. Marshall, *The Practical Flax Spinner: Being a Description of the Growth, Manipulation and Spinning of Flax and Tow* (London, 1885), x–xi.

11. Oger, *Traité élémentaire de la filature du coton* (Mulhouse, 1845, 1855). In 1847 it was translated in Spanish and published in Barcelona by D. Francisco Arau, Profesor de Maquinaria.

12. Contract of Angel Martorell, 25 May 1847, Archive of La España Industrial.

13. Gutierrez, *La España Industrial*, 206–208.

14. Contract of Angel Martorell, 25 May 1847, Archive of La España Industrial.

15. *Traité élémentaire*, 32 (translation by Arau).

16. Ibid., 41.

17. The composition of teams in La España Industrial parallels the case of Lancashire, where spinner teams had one minder and two or three assistants. See W. Lazonick, *Competitive Advantage on the Shop Floor* (Cambridge, 1990), 79.

18. A. García Balañà, *La Fabricación de la fábrica: Treball i política a la Catalunya Cotonera (1884–1874)* (Barcelona, 2004).

19. W. Lazonick, 'Industrial Relations and Technical Change: The Case of the Self-Acting Mule', *Cambridge Journal of Economics* 3, no. 3 (1979): 231–262, here 252.

20. Reddy, *Rise of Market Culture*.

21. Archive of La España Industrial, Copiador de cartas, 2 April 1850, 208, cited in Gutierrez, *La España Industrial*, 233.

22. Manufacturas Españolas, *La España Industrial*, 113–117.

23. J. Monés i Pujol, *L'obra educativa de la Junta de Comerç 1769–1851* (Barcelona, 1987).

24. R. Solà i Montserrat, *L'Institut Industrial de Catalunya i L' Associacionisme Industrial des de 1820 a 1854* (Barcelona, 1997).

25. While many of these men had migrated from other industrial cotton districts, most came from Igualada, the Muntadas family seat and the place where they began their industrial activities. On the origins of the Barcelona cotton workers, see Camps, *La formación del mercado de trabajo industrial*; C. Enrech, *Entre Sans i Sants: Historia i política d'una població industrial a les portes de Barcelona 1839–1897* (Barcelona, 2004).

26. J. Nadal, 'El factor humà en el retard econòmic espanyol: El debat entre els historiadors', *Revista Económica de Cataluña* (1999): 9–13.

27. Manuel Brosa y Arnó, *Manual Completo de la Hilatura de Algodón util a los contramaestres, mayordomos y fabricantes* (Barcelona, 1876).

28. M. Pagés i Borí, *Completo Manual del Contramaestre Teórico – práctico en el arte de tejer toda clase de tejidos en telares mecánicos* (Barcelona, 1897).

29. See Enrech, *Indústria i ofici*, 101–104.

30. *El Obrero*, 17 December 1880, 2–3, quoted in Duarte, *Mayordomos*, 10.

31. Duarte, *Mayordomos*, 7.

32. *El Productor*, 1887, quoted in Enrech, *Industria i Ofici*, 105.

33. *El Obrero*, 3 November 1886, 2, quoted in Duarte, *Mayordomos*, 11.

34. *La Federación, Órgano de la Asociación Internacional de Trabajadores*, 26 February 1871, 3.

35. Quoted in C. Martí, *Barcelona a mitjan segle XIX: El moviment obrer durant el Bienni Progressita, 1854–1856* (Barcelona, 1979), 238.

36. *La Federación*, 1 January 1888, 2.

37. *La Federación*, 2 March 1887, 2.

38. See Duarte, *Mayordomos*, 10–19.

39. There are no specific studies on the organization of management in the textile industry of Catalonia and/or Spain as a whole during the first industrial revolution. However, indirect information on two cotton mills located on the northern coast of Spain (Guipúzcoa, 1865) indicates that the supervision in this sector was in effect very weak. This was also the case in various textile firms in the north of Spain, such as the Oria firm (located in the village of Lasarte, Guipúzcoa), which employed 73 workers in the spinning section and 85 in the weaving section, and only one *contremaître* in each section. The firm Blanc, Arbulu, Aguirre and Co. in the village of Vergara (Guipuzcoa) had 32 in the carding, 76 in the spinning and 332 in the weaving section. One foreman directed the spinning section, while two foremen ran the carding section and two the weaving section. See *Información sobre el Derecho Diferencial de Bandera*, 30.

CHAPTER 3

SALARIED AUTHORITY

The Versatile Fate of *Contremaîtres* in the
Ghent Cotton Industry (1830–1914)

Peter Scholliers

After being closed for more than ten years, the weaving section of the Ghent cotton mill Texas S.A. opened again on 22 May 1891. New buildings had been constructed and new machines installed. The reopening was a decisive moment in an operation of modernization that had started in 1876, and which brought the mill back to the top of the trade in Belgium. This necessitated a huge capital investment that was obtained by transforming the family-based mill into a *société anonyme*. The firm had a long experience with cotton spinning, weaving and printing. It started as a printer in 1790, was the first to introduce power looms on the continent in 1824, and became a vertically integrated factory in 1827 with the opening of a modern spinning division. It was one of the most important manufacturers in the city up to 1860 (with 600 workers). Then, the shortage of raw cotton and a contentious inheritance caused major difficulties, and in the early 1870s the firm barely survived. It was then that the management decided to start the modernization of the three divisions. In 1880, however, a fire destroyed the spinning section. Since the owners wished to rebuild the latter without delay, they postponed the renewal of the weaving mill. This section was closed in 1879 and its machinery was sold, while the printing division stopped activity once and for all in 1890.

The reopening of the weaving division and the recruitment of new personnel was a slow process. At the end of 1891, only fourteen workers had been taken on. With the installation of more power looms and other up-to-date weaving equipment, more workers were gradually hired, and by 1900 this division employed 120 men and women. The very first worker to appear in the wage books of the weaving section in May 1891 was a *contremaître*, Joseph Meire, born in Ghent in 1836, who had not previously worked in this mill. He remained the only foreman up to 1894, when two more were recruited. In the course of 1895 Meire left Texas S.A. During his entire stay he received a wage of 30 francs per week. The foremen's average weekly pay at the closing of the weaving mill in 1879 had been only 20 francs, and in 1895, after Meire had left the mill, the average weekly pay of the foremen in weaving again worked out at 20 francs. Clearly, Meire was highly valued during the years of the reconstitution of the weaving division.

Joseph Meire's high pay during this episode made me wonder about the tasks, position and status of foremen in factories in general. What did he do to earn considerably higher pay? Did he primarily recruit new workers and assign the work? Of no less importance is the answer to the question as to why Meire's colleagues in 1895 fell back on the *usual* wage. According to the literature, foremen had manifold tasks: they not only hired labourers and organized work, but they also controlled the product quality, applied factory rules, gave fines and premiums, mended machines, proposed (technical) advice, kept stock, and looked after safety; in short, they possessed technological know-how and authority.[1] Hence, as P. Stearns noted, they were paid 'sumptuous salaries', although some received less pay than highly specialized, skilled workers.[2]

Taking the relationship between foremen's tasks and (high) wages as a starting point, I shall explore the changes in position and status of foremen throughout the nineteenth century. To do this, I shall consider the evolution of wage differentials within one mill. In this respect, three possibilities may occur: (1) wage differentials between foremen and other workers hardly changed through time, which implies that foremen kept their position vis-à-vis other workers; (2) wages of foremen grew above other workers' wages, thus indicating a more marked hierarchy within the mill, with foremen reinforcing their position; and (3) wage gaps decreased, thus showing a weaker hierarchy, with foremen losing influence.

A debate is going on regarding the foremen's fate in the second half of the century. Some authors assert that the foremen's position in textiles was under pressure because of the introduction of ring frames, smaller power looms and faster engines. More women were employed, while complex wage systems appeared, and work (conditions) became more regulated. Also, technical changes called for more highly specialized skills and systematic organization, which the *old* foremen could not supply. Such changes entailed the decline of the foremen's position.[3] Wage gaps between foremen and other workers would therefore shrink. Other authors, however, maintain the opposite, labelling the period 1880–1914 as the 'foremen's empire'. This is linked to the decline of the spinners' and weavers' authority, which was due to new technology, and to the need to increase work effort, which entailed more control.[4] Foremen secured their role and function and, hence, wage gaps would remain stable or increase.

I shall use the results of the investigation into the wages of the above Ghent cotton mill, Voortman–Texas S.A., for which wage books are available between 1835 and 1914. I shall consider year-to-year wages of foremen in the spinning and weaving divisions, and compare these to wages of male spinners and weavers. This mill and its foremen are not representative of overseers in the Ghent textile trade or of any other industry, place or period (its history is far too particular). Yet because little is known about overseers in general and in the textile industry in particular,[5] I think my contribution may be of help in understanding somewhat better the history of foremen in textile mills.

Task Definition, Classification and (Self)image

The archives of Voortman–Texas S.A. do not contain any information about foremen's tasks and responsibilities. I shall therefore consider the way *contremaîtres* in the Ghent cotton industry were perceived and classified by contemporaries, and I shall survey the historical literature.

In 1845, the physicians J. Mareska and J. Heyman published the first, comprehensive study of the Ghent cotton industry, taking into account wages, living conditions and work organization. With regard to the foremen's task they wrote, 'The engineer is, with the clerk and the foreman, the mediator between the boss and the workers.'[6] This vague denotation reflected general difficulties with defining supervision and self-evident notions about a foreman's job. No mention is made of *savoir-faire*, which was the crucial task of foremen in French textile factories around this period.[7] Fifty years later another prominent observer of the Ghent cotton industry, L. Varlez, completely neglected the duties of *contremaîtres*, although he devoted plenty attention to the tasks of all other cotton workers.[8] Information about the foreman's job was given casually when Varlez tackled earning gaps among the weavers of one mill: he noted that weavers sometimes lost valuable time and money in waiting for a foreman to bring tools or mend a machine.[9] E. Anseele, the leader of the Ghent Social-Democrats, confirmed this when he wrote, 'The foreman does play a very important role. He may organize the job of his workers in such way that the weaver may work smoothly.'[10] Varlez and Anseele, thus, stress the organizational tasks of foremen in weaving. In an instruction manual meant for managers and foremen in spinning, published in 1914, the authors emphasized the many technical innovations of the previous twenty-five years, which required more extensive knowledge and improved schooling on the part of the foremen.[11] They stress the technical aspect of a foreman's job in spinning.

If this is too small a basis for concluding that *contremaîtres* in weaving were primarily involved with organizational matters, while their colleagues in spinning were more technically oriented, I think these testimonies at least reveal a difference between foremen in spinning and weaving.[12]

The industrial censuses of 1896 and 1910, as well as the elaborate survey of Belgium's textile workers in 1901, are helpful despite the fact that they neglected the foremen. With managers, accountants, clerks, engineers and other people who were not directly engaged in production, the *contremaîtres* were classified among the leading staff.[13] The result of such classification is that these censuses do not provide information about the overseers' wages, total numbers or age. Likewise, the *Monographies industrielles* that appeared at about the same time also neglected foremen. Next to a category 'Production workers', a category *Ouvriers des services généraux* (i.e. technical workers, engineers and the like) was created, but this did not include foremen.[14]

The original questionnaires of the industrial census of 1896 set up seven categories of people, including directors, managers, divisions' supervisors, foremen, white-collar workers, and, finally, workers. Unfortunately, when the data were published, only one partition was made: between *ouvriers* and *personnel autre que le personnel ouvrier* (*exploitants, directeurs, ingénieurs, contremaîtres, employés,* etc.), that is, between workers and all other employees. This information shows the proportion of production workers vis-à-vis other personnel. Thus, in the forty-one Ghent cotton mills there were 8,237 *ouvriers* at work for 429 other employees, that is, one 'manager' for nineteen workers.[15] Assuming that the forty-one mills had at least forty-one owners, one or two *sous-directeurs* each, a general *ingénieur*, and one or two clerks, then the group of foremen may have amounted to some 200 people, that is, about five per mill.

The historiographical literature about the Ghent textile industry shows slightly more interest in foremen. B. De Wilde's account of employers and employees in Belgian textiles tells us about their tasks.[16] He stresses the fact that overseers *represented* the entrepreneur on the work floor, that they hired and fired workers, checked whether factory rules were observed, imposed fines, and would allow advances against wages. Often, foremen were rather brutal, and their authority was limitless if they also owned a shop where workers were supposed (or compelled) to buy groceries. In the last quarter of the century factory rules became harsher in order to impose a greater work effort, and this led to more brutality by foremen.[17]

Viewed from a different angle, *contremaîtres* also emerge in G. Deneckere's history of collective actions in Belgium.[18] The so-called cotton revolt of 1839 (fierce social outbursts with demands regarding wages and work conditions) is relevant for the status, role and image of foremen in those years. In October 1839 the Ghent mayor feared serious outbursts and invited some foremen to his office, trying to persuade them to form a delegation of workers (rather than run about the streets). The foremen returned later that day, saying that the spinners had declined his offer. They then began to take an active role in the organization of an appeasing action: they met with the authorities, contributed to the writing of a petition, and became part of a workers' delegation to the king. They aimed at the leadership of the movement, wishing to calm things down.[19] Two decades later, however, very little was left of this position. Weavers and spinners decided to act on their own, and ignored foremen completely. During a strike in one of the biggest mills of the city in 1861, for example, foremen testified that they had no influence whatsoever on weavers.[20] This might suggest that in the 1850s the role of overseers in industrial relations changed. Research dealing with strikes hardly mentions overseers. Even in matters where they had their (controversial) say, such as fines, they remain absent.[21]

The investigation by K. Pittomvils into law cases before the Conseil de Prud'hommes (a labour court that was set up in Ghent in 1810) in the first half of the nineteenth century reveals that foremen were involved in only 2 per cent of cases (i.e. twenty-four).[22] Eight cases of these twenty-four involved conflicts with workers and sixteen with entrepreneurs. Overseers accused nine mill owners but only three workers, and overseers were accused by seven mill owners and by only five workers. These data by no means lead to the conclusion that overseers were in the middle of a social battlefield. Yet entrepreneurs now and then asked overseers to represent them in court.[23] Now and then collective complaints were also brought to court which involved a unpopular *contremaître*.[24] Similar research for the post-1858 period reveals only very few conflicts in the textile industry.[25]

Recent historiography about Ghent textiles therefore confirms in general the tasks of foremen, as suggested by international literature.[26] They hired and fired workers, and watched over the good functioning of machines, workers and production; they were the immediate adjutants of the owners. As for their role in Ghent industrial relations, foremen were serenely mediating between cotton workers and the authorities (a role that ended in the 1850s), but not between workers and owners. Noticeably, contemporary observers suggested a difference between foremen in spinning ('technicians') and weaving ('organizers').

Social Context of the Wage

I shall examine whether this difference between foremen in spinning and weaving is confirmed at Voortman–Texas S.A. I shall look first at geographical and social origins, length of career, and age, and then I shall consider thoroughly the wage development of both categories of foremen. Research into the Ghent population registers for one week each in 1842, 1859, 1879 and 1902 may answer questions related to the characteristics of both groups,[27] while the wage books will tell us about wage systems, levels and evolution. Using the overseers' names from the wage books, I traced back twenty-four foremen in the population registers. The total number of workers included in my four-week sample reached 761, which yields about one *contremaître* for thirty workers. Overseers are evenly divided between spinning and weaving (with twelve each).

In the population registers, six of the twelve foremen in spinning were designated by the word *contremaître*, or its Dutch equivalents *werkmeester*, *meestergast* and *meesterknecht*. The other foremen in spinning were called *fabriekwerker* (factory worker), *katoenspinder* (cotton spinner) and, mostly, *spinner*. Revealing is that foremen in the weaving division were not recorded as *contremaître* or *meestergast*, but were designated as workers (*wever*, *tisserand*, *ouvrier de fabrique*, *fabriekwerker*, *kamslager* or *katoenbewerker*). This leads to two conclusions. First, since workers themselves declared their profession to the census takers, I suggest that Voortman's overseers in spinning were more self-conscious and proud of the fact that they were foremen. They emphasized the distinction between ordinary workers and themselves. In Voortman's weaving section, on the other hand, overseers did not deem it necessary to specify their position, thus making no clear demarcation between themselves and ordinary weavers. A second conclusion would be the confirmation of a clear division between the worlds of spinning and weaving: the foremen in spinning who did not qualify themselves as *contremaître* were listed with professions linked to spinning, and the foremen in weaving were labelled with professions connected to weaving.

Foremen in spinning were slightly more local than those in weaving, although there was only a small difference, which was particularly linked to the 1902 sample. There was virtually no distinction between the place of birth of overseers in spinning and weaving prior to 1880. Thus, for the larger part of the nineteenth century, overseers in spinning and weaving originated from within the city of Ghent, and the latter hardly differed from the cotton workers of the city in general.

Foremen in both spinning and weaving lived in the immediate neighbourhood of the mill, and this was the case for the four sample weeks of the investigation. They rented houses in the working-class district of the north of Ghent, among hundreds of other textile families. Some overseers lived in *Berouw*, a small street close to the mill, where in 1837 the mill owners had built thirteen houses. These houses were roomier and had a water pump and a toilet each, and even a small yard. The wage books mention the rent that workers paid for this accommodation. Rents were directly subtracted from the weekly earnings. However, no foreman of this mill lived in these houses in 1842, 1859, 1879 or 1902.

The age of overseers in spinning and weaving differed. Although only a small number of people are involved, a pattern appears, as shown in Table 3.1. In 1842, the average age of *contremaîtres* in both sections hardly differed. In spinning their average age increased gradually, but in weaving it remained unchanged. Varlez noted the general ageing of cotton workers throughout the century,[28] which the data for overseers in spinning confirm. The fact that such did not occur for overseers in weaving may be linked to the specific employment pattern in weaving. Combining data from the wage books and data from the population registers, the lives of individual foremen of the mill can be traced. This detailed information adds to the more general picture of the overseers' milieu, but it also puts into context some of the above findings about age, origin and career.

Petrus Librecht (Ghent, 1799–1849) worked at Voortman's from 1835 to 1849.[29] He was a weaver, and was listed as such in the population registers between 1827 and 1849. From 1835 he appeared irregularly in the mill's wage books as a day labourer, but in January 1840 he was listed with the *contremaîtres* of the weaving section, earning a weekly wage of about 22 francs until 1849. He lived at one address between 1830 and 1849. He married Sophie Wyckaert, and they had seven daughters and one son. Six of the children worked as weavers at Voortman's (between 1846 and 1859). Seven died in their mid-twenties, and only Stephanie (1844–1930) lived longer, re-entering the mill in 1871 (to leave in 1879 at the closing of the weaving section). This family earned a decent living when most of its members were at work. All children started their career at Voortman's when they were twelve or thirteen years old. Very probably, their father was instrumental in taking on three of the children, and after his death this little network still operated: in 1858 six of Petrus Librecht's children worked in Voorman's weaving division.

Pierre Cedeyn (Ghent, 1805–1862) worked continuously as a foreman in the weaving division between 1835 and 1859.[30] His wage fluctuated heavily in the late 1830s (from 15.2 to 26.8 francs), but remained stable (20 francs) in the 1840s and 1850s. In the 1830s he was penalized twice (who fined

Table 3.1 *Average Age of Voortman's Foremen*

	In Spinning	In Weaving
1842	37.8	38.5
1859	41.4	40.4
1879	45.0	40.3
1902	50.0	40.5

Source: Calculated from the mill's wage registers and the city's population censuses.

the foremen?), which did not occur in the later period. He contributed 3 francs each month to the mill's sick fund from 1852 to 1859. He appeared as a *fabriekwerker* (factory worker) in the population registers, living in *Berouw* and adjacent streets. Pierre married Colette Kimpe, and the couple had ten children, five of whom died within the year. One boy, Karel (Ghent, 1841–1918), started work at Voortman's in July 1860, at age nineteen, as an overseer in weaving. His father had left the mill a few months earlier: may I assume that Pierre introduced his son to the mill? Karel seemed to have been a somewhat uncommon overseer: he did this job from July 1860 to February 1865 and, again from December 1879 to June 1880, that is, when the weaving mill had difficulties and was closed. Karel worked at the seizing machine, making more money than as an overseer. In the population registers, Karel appeared as factory worker and cotton labourer, but never as *contremaître*. He married in 1870 and had three children who did not work in textiles.

Charles Ryckaert (Ghent, 1835–1918) worked as a foreman in Voortman's spinning section from 1872 to 1898.[31] He earned a high, stable wage of about 32 francs per week during this entire period. I do not know where he had worked before starting at Voortman's. In 1860 he married Bernardine Pat, who worked in Voortman's spinning section from 1855 to 1885 (at the drawing frame, and later as a head worker at the fine frames). Charles appeared as a spinner, a factory worker, and a *meestergast in katoen-fabriek* (foreman in a cotton mill) in the population registers. The household lived in the immediate neighbourhood of the factory, moving house very frequently. Charles and Bernardine had thirteen children (two died within the year). Gustave (Ghent, 1865–?) entered the Voortman spinning mill in 1880, at age fifteen, as a maintenance worker. He earned about 10 francs per week. He did this job for twenty years, with a gradually increasing wage that reached 26 francs. In 1900 he became an overseer in the spinning mill, making 35 francs a week. He was listed as a carpenter's mate, smith's helper, and foreman in a spinning mill. This family was strongly tied to Voortman: next to Charles, Bernardine and Karel, Pauline Pat (Bernardine's sister) and Catharina Ryckaert (Karel's sister) worked in the spinning section during the 1870s and 1880s.

A last individual case is Gustave Spaliers (Ghent, 1861–1939) who worked in the mill between 1876 and 1914.[32] He started as a weaver, at age fifteen, and shifted to the seizing machines a few months before the closure of the weaving mill in 1879. In 1882 he re-entered the mill as a foreman in the spinning division. This is the one example I came across of a move from one division to another within this mill. Gustave remained a foreman until 1914, gradually increasing his weekly wage from about 20 francs in the 1890s to 30 francs in 1914. In 1882 he married Clementina Tierens, who worked as a reeler in the spinning mill from 1889 to 1891. They had a boy, Jules (Ghent, 1884–1907), who started at Voortman's weaving mill in 1897 as a warper, at age thirteen, earning about 5 francs a week. In 1900 he started to work as a weaver, and in 1903 until his death he was employed as a maintenance worker, making an average weekly wage of about 15 francs. The population registers mention Gustave as factory worker, in 1885 as foreman, and from 1900 as stock manager. Jules was mentioned as a weaver, and his mother as cotton worker. They lived in the vicinity of the mill, moving house frequently.

These examples reveal that all foremen in this mill were born in Ghent, that four out of six had a job in the mill before becoming an overseer, and that two may have been recruited from outside the mill. Two foremen were sons of mill overseers. The examples point to the fact that overseers paid fines (at least, in the 1830s), that networks through family ties existed, and that most workers were around thirty-five years old when they became foremen. Also, although wages did change over time, most overseers were paid constant high wages for long periods. And finally, the examples as well as the data of the four weeks taken from the population censuses confirm the division between foremen in spinning and weaving. Would this division also appear in their wages?

The Language of the Wage Books

As I mentioned above, account books or other documents from this mill do not provide information about the tasks of foremen. For example, it remains a question whether overseers weighed or measured output, or whether they fixed wage rates or premiums. According to Varlez, 'plain, adult helpers, somewhat better paid than ordinary workmen' measured output.[33] Voortman's wage books, however, lack a separate category of *peseurs*, but there is a category of 'general costs' (*frais généraux*) of some ten workers: could these people have measured output? In December 1895, a conflict arose at Texas S.A. Among other demands, the strike raised the question of the fair measurement of the spinners' and weavers' output. At no moment in the accounts of this strike were foremen mentioned.[34]

If wage books remain silent about some aspects, they do of course provide abundant information on other issues. Wage books are available from 1835 onward, that is, eleven and eight years after the establishment of the weaving and spinning sections, respectively. Distinct pay books existed for the spinning and weaving sections. Each ledger contained the various categories of workers, listing individual names, tariffs, output, fines, cost for oil and repairs, working time, house rent, and the actual earning. However, not all of these data were given for all categories. Working time, for example, was not mentioned for workers paid at piece rates, and the spinners' helpers did not appear in the wage books (spinners paid their helpers out of the team's pay). Wages were calculated, registered and paid each week.

In the wage books of the both divisions, the category of 'foremen, day labourers and others' (*contremaîtres, journaliers et autres*) appears from 1835 to 1914. This category was noted right below the category *frais généraux* that was present only in the ledger of the spinning mill (wage costs were neatly divided between spinning and weaving). *Contremaîtres* and *journaliers* were the only workers in the mill paid a fixed weekly wage. Their earnings were therefore not directly affected by output or working hours.[35] This mode of payment implied a particular bond between the owner and the foremen, involving an element of trust (with regard to work effort, efficiency and reliability). This made them radically different from all other workers who were paid at piece rates (spinners and weavers) or by the day or the hour (carding room, preparatory to weaving and *frais généraux*). The foremen's payment mode (weekly wage) was retained throughout the whole period. In this respect, there was no difference between foremen in spinning and weaving.

Around 1900 Varlez noticed that in some cotton mills *contremaîtres* were paid by the hour.[36] One reason was that during strikes, which seemed to be occurring more frequently in this period, foremen would no longer receive their pay (which was the case with a weekly wage). The simple fact that mill owners attempted to introduce hourly wages for overseers may indicate that their position was under pressure. According to Varlez, foremen opposed the introduction of the hourly wage: he wrote, 'Reason for this resistance: the foreman is paid as a <u>labourer</u> and no longer as a <u>member of staff</u> (dishonour).'[37] The addition of the word *déshonneur* is quite telling for both Varlez's perception and the actual shift of (some) overseers' status. And still according to Varlez, the attempt to pay hourly wages around 1900 would drive overseers towards the workers and away from the owners, 'As a consequence, foremen would get dissatisfied, which would bring them closer to the workers. They would defend bosses far less fervently, who thus force them to strike and adopt the workers' views.' Moreover, Varlez noted that more and more specialized workers (*ouvriers spéciaux*) received higher wages than the foremen, thus testifying to the loss of status of the latter.

The fact that foremen were paid by the week implies that there is no information about working hours. However, from 1887 onward the accountant did note the number of hours worked per week by foremen in spinning (and from 1891 for foremen in weaving). Could the mill owner have been considering the introduction of hourly pay for his overseers, and therefore needed the information about working time? Or did *invisible* hourly wages play a role in the calculation of the weekly wage (a premium when a certain amount of hours was reached, or less pay when this was not the case)? Why, then, start noting the hours in 1887? My suggestion is that the mill owner aimed to increase control over his foremen, by keeping a record of their actual working time. This may be linked to the sudden but continuous increase in working time in the spinning mill after 1887 (67.4 hours per week in the early 1880s, and 74.4 hours between 1888 to 1892), which contrasted greatly with the general trend of working time in the Ghent cotton mills.[38] The increase in the working time at Texas S.A. probably required more regulation by the foremen who, in turn, were controlled by having their working hours recorded

Dividing the weekly wage by the weekly working time, a theoretical hourly wage appears after 1887.[39] For foremen in spinning this fluctuated around 0.40 francs from 1887 to 1895, and then it rose to about 0.45 francs. For foremen in weaving, the hourly wage amounted to only 0.28 francs until 1905, when it oscillated around 0.30 francs until 1914.[40] The difference between spinning and weaving is of course striking: it confirms the distinct worlds of foremen in the two divisions. The weekly wage showed a more regular pattern than the theoretical hourly wage. In 1896, for example, the average working time for overseers in spinning fell significantly, but the hourly wage skyrocketed, and so their weekly earnings remained stable. And in 1904 the average working time for foremen in weaving went up to 85 hours per week, but now the hourly wage fell and, hence, the weekly earning hardly changed. If tariffs had been decisive, weekly earnings would have fluctuated much more.

Working hours of foremen in spinning show a falling trend from 1887 to 1914 (from about 70 hours per week in about 1890 to 66 in about 1910). The working time of foremen in weaving, however, rose from 74 in about 1895 to 90 in 1900, and declined in 1905 to 72 hours per week. Overall, foremen in weaving worked longer hours than their colleagues in spinning did. Moreover, *contremaîtres* in the weaving section worked more hours than the average worker in this division, whereas foremen in spinning worked fewer hours than the average worker in spinning. The presence of overseers in weaving was thus apparently more required than in spinning, which should be linked to different functions in the two divisions (see below). Observations regarding working time therefore once more confirm the divided worlds of foremen in spinning and weaving.

With only two or three overseers in each section of the mill, there is a danger that the appearance or disappearance of one foreman could influence the wage series radically. The employment of J. Meire from 1891 to 1894 illustrates this. However, this was the exception. Starting foremen earned somewhat less than their colleagues who were already working at the mill, but their pay was equal after one or two years. As noted earlier, when foremen started on their career, they were already over thirty. Consequently, a change of staff could influence the course of the wage, but only for a very brief time.

The number of foremen in both divisions hardly changed throughout the entire period (two to three in each). Yet in both divisions the number of workers and machines, and the quality of output fluctuated significantly. In spinning, for example, there were 49 workers in 1880 but 145 in 1910, and in weaving there were 148 workers around 1840, 90 in 1870 and 125 in 1910. When the number of workers rose, the almost constant number of foremen in both spinning and weaving divisions must have caused problems with regard to mending machines, supplying tools, controlling factory rules, et cetera. Surely, the *contremaîtres* then had more work. Possibly, the supervision of a larger number of workers led to rising wages for foremen. But as Varlez emphasized, spinners and weavers must have suffered from the time waiting for busy foremen to mend machines or carry out other tasks.

If foremen were put under pressure when more workers were employed, they may have feared for their jobs and wage levels if the number of workers fell. In general, however, foremen had rather regular and long careers at the mill, and they enjoyed stable earnings. Pierre Cedeyn, aged thirty, went to work as a foreman at Voortman's weaving section in 1835. He did this job for twenty-four years and left in 1859. Between 1841 and 1859 his weekly wage did not change, although the mill went through highly fluctuating employment cycles. Of course, some foremen had shorter careers in this mill, but in general they stayed for a longer period, independently of the number of workers under their supervision. This may reflect the firm's policy of retaining experienced, trustworthy and familiar overseers. Nineteen-year old Karel Cedeyn, Pierre's son, entered the weaving mill as a foreman in 1860 (note the young age), and held this position until 1865 during difficult years for the cotton trade. The mill was closed in 1862 and 1863 and all weavers were fired, but Karel stayed on. His weekly wage fell only slightly. In 1866 he started working at the seizing machine until 1880.[41]

Before considering wage hierarchies in this mill, I should mention that pay systems changed for particular categories of workers. In 1835 three systems were in use: piece rates (spinners, weavers, spoolers, etc.), day wages (scutchers, maintenance workers, etc.), and weekly wages (foremen). Two changes should be mentioned.[42] First, a clear-cut shift in the pay system occurred in October 1857, when the daily wage was replaced by the hourly wage. Second, there was a silent trend towards more piecework in spinning, but the opposite in weaving. In 1835, 45 per cent of the workers in spinning and 90 per cent in weaving were on piecework, but in 1910 the proportion of those on piecework in spinning reached 75 per cent, while in weaving it fell to 60 per cent (the remainder being on hourly wages, except weekly wages for foremen). Possibly such shifts led to less need to control the workers, which might have had consequences on the foremen's remuneration.

Pay Hierarchy

Disregarding the various wage systems, working time, and fines, the actual weekly earnings of all categories of workers at this mill may be compared in a meaningful way. Table 3.2 shows the earning hierarchy in spinning and weaving in one week of March 1902. In general, foremen were paid high wages. A clear difference, however, appeared between earnings in spinning and in weaving, with foremen's earnings in spinning some 35 per cent above those in weaving. The longer working time of foremen in weaving (in this year 75 hours as against 67 in spinning) did compensate somewhat for their much lower (theoretical) hourly wage. Yet despite their more extended effort, weekly earnings were lower. This clearly indicates different tasks for *contremaîtres* in the both divisions. The average earnings of spinners came close to those of foremen in spinning, but the average earnings of weavers were far below those of overseers in weaving.[43] Foremen at this mill were paid well, but did not receive sumptuous wages, as Stearns found for France.

There is little information by which to compare the Voortman–Texas S.A. wage level with the wages of other Ghent overseers. Varlez provided some data, which emerged from his study on Ghent wages around 1900. Foremen in the cotton mills of the city received 18.7 francs per week (no difference is made between spinning and weaving), overseers in the linen industry were paid 20 francs, and those in machine building and other metal trades were

Table 3.2 *Weekly Earnings in Spinning and Weaving at Texas S.A., March 1902*

	Category	Lowest and Highest (francs)	Average (francs)
Frais généraux		16.7 to 28.8	23.3
Spinning	Foremen (M)	32 to 35	34.0
	Day labourers (M)	22.5 to 25	23.7
	Carding room (M)	13.5 to 18.4	16.1
	Carding room (W)	6.2 to 16.5	10.0
	Spinners (M)		28.1
	Piecers A (M)		10.4
	Piecers B (M)		15.9
	Scavengers (M)		6.7
Weaving	Foremen (M)	25	25.0
	Day labourers (M)	17.8 to 19.4	18.6
	Loomers (W)	7.0 to 15.0	10.0
	Spoolers (W)	8.8 to 15.8	13.4
	Seizing machine (M)	13.3 to 18.4	16.4

Note: Whatever the wage system, all workers were paid by the week.

Source: Ghent City Archives, Fonds Voortman, nrs. 366 and 416 (wage books).

paid 34 francs.[44] Foremen at Voortman–Texas were therefore paid more than those of Varlez's account. However, fifty years earlier, Mareska and Heyman published average overseers' wages in the cotton trade, ranging from 3.66 francs per day to 5 francs.[45] Such wages were above those paid at Voortman's (approximately 2.50 francs per day).

Year-to-year series of earnings have been computed for most categories of workers of the mill between 1835 and 1913. My main interest is in the development of foremen's earnings in the two divisions. I shall compare these with each other, as well as with the evolution of earnings of male spinners and weavers (Figure 3.1).

The comparison of earnings of foremen in spinning and weaving reveals a notable reversal circa 1850 (see Figure 3.2 for a clear image of year-to-year difference in percentages). Up to this year, foremen in weaving earned over 10 per cent more than their colleagues in spinning. This changed in the early 1850s when the foremen in spinning started earning more than those in weaving, and up to 1914 the wage gap between the two grew. What happened around 1850? And why did the wage gap continue to rise, reaching a differential of 30 per cent on average (with tops of 70 per cent as in 1905)?

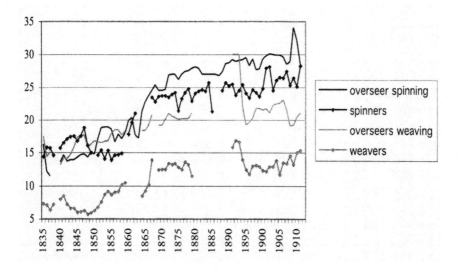

Figure 3.1 *Overseers' Weekly Earnings Compared to Spinners' and Weavers' Earnings at Voortman–Texas S.A., 1835–1912. Sources:* G. Avondts et al., *De Gentse textielarbeiders in de 19e en 20e eeuw: Lonen in de spinnerij van het bedrijf A. Voortman–N.V. Texas 1835–1914* (Brussels, 1976), 57–63, 75–78; G. Avondts et al., *De Gentse textielarbeiders in de 19e en 20e eeuw: Lonen in de weverij van het bedrijf A. Voortman–N.V. Texas 1835–1925* (Brussels, 1979), 19–23, 44–48.

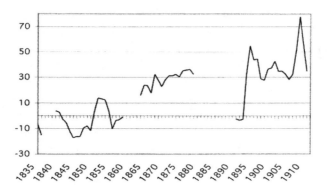

Figure 3.2 *Difference in Weekly Earnings between Foremen in Spinning and Weaving.*
Source: Based on Figure 3.1.

Voortman's weaving mill was fully operative in 1824, with 100 power looms (weavers working at one, but mostly at two looms). These were the first modern looms in Ghent, implying not only new tasks and aptitudes for the weavers but also for their supervisors. Undoubtedly, wages were high.[46] Until the late 1860s no new machines were installed. I do not know whether careers of foremen in weaving in the 1820s were as long as in later periods, but it is possible that, having been recruited in the 1820s, their experience may have led to the wage increase in the 1830s. Long careers, however, also existed in the spinning mill, so that another explanation might be called for. The general expansion of modern weaving in Ghent in the 1830s and 1840s probably played a role. The total number of power looms increased from 100 in 1824 (Voortman), to 600 in 1829, 2,100 in 1835 and 4,900 in 1846.[47] This meant the diffusion of new production modes, which included 'modern' foremen. At Voortman's, a group of foremen had been formed since the 1820s, whose experience was probably valued by competitors. Hence, foremen's wages at Voortman's increased. Pierre Cedeyn's earnings in the 1830s may illustrate this: between 1836 and 1840, his wages were 26 francs per week, which exceeded the 1902 level (shown in Table 3.2).

Moreover, the 1830s and early 1840s were a period of intense class antagonism in Ghent and particularly at Voortman's, with the closing of the mill in 1835, 1839 and again 1840 and, at the reopening, lengthening of working time, and employment of more women. Voortman's weavers went on strike on several occasions (1832, 1834 and 1839).[48] It seems highly probable that, in order to control workers and to assure a smooth employment policy (especially the hiring after each reopening and strike), Voortman paid his overseers in weaving a high wage. When peace had returned in the mill in the course of 1840, wages of foremen in weaving fluctuated much more regularly, although at a lower level. Again, the earnings of Pierre Cedeyn illustrate this: in 1838 he was paid 26.8 francs per week, but in 1841 only 20 francs. The spinning section of the mill did not show vehement class antagonism, nor was the spinning section closed. Could this be the reason why earnings of foremen in spinning evolved more smoothly up to 1850? I suggest two reasons for the rising wage gap to the advantage of foremen in weaving: the pressure on wages due to the demand for foremen in weaving, and the fact that more control was necessary to deal with rebellious weavers. This would confirm the tasks of a *contremaître* in weaving sections of cotton mills as involving primarily control over workers.

Between 1851 and 1856 the earnings of foremen in spinning leapfrogged those of overseers in weaving. Then, for a short period from 1856 to 1860, earnings moved fairly close together with a very narrow gap. The cause of the 1851 spurt is not clear. In the spinning division, there were no technical changes, work reorganization, important personnel fluctuations or tense industrial relations from 1850 to 1855, which might explain this sudden rise of the foremen's wages in spinning. It is very probable that a development occurred in spinning in the 1850s similar to that in weaving in the 1830s, in that spinning underwent rapid growth (with the total number of spindles in Ghent growing from 219,670 in 1846 to 500,000 in 1860). Hence, a sudden need for experienced foremen, and the pressure on foremen's wages in Voortman's spinning section in the early 1850s.

The earning gap between the foremen of the two sections changed radically with the cotton famine of the early 1860s. The mill was closed for a year and a half (from early 1862 to mid-1863) and all workers were laid off. The foremen and the day labourers, however, were kept on, which stresses their special position within the mill. Yet their earnings decreased by about 10 per cent. Overseers were kept on for maintaining machines, and the reduced work resulted in a lower wage. Also, I suggest that foremen were kept on as a way of keeping contact with unemployed workers.

From the weavers who were enlisted after the reopening in July 1863, 43 per cent had been working in the Voortman mill before, and for the workers in spinning this was as high as 75 per cent.[49] This latter proportion was particularly high: after all, workers had been laid off for seventeen months. Had they been bound to the mill during its closing? This was certainly not by paying workers a little 'unemployment' money, renting them a dwelling, organizing charity or by any other material link. An explanation may be found in the role of foremen who would act as go-betweens between the mill and the workers, using various kinds of invisible strings. Recruitment was indeed a task of the overseers, and by keeping them on during the closure period the mill would be more able to take on familiar, reliable and experienced workers on the mill's reopening.[50]

A major difference between overseers in spinning and weaving occurred during and immediately after the closure. When the mill reopened in 1863, the wage level of the foremen in weaving had not changed from the 1860 level, but that of the foremen in spinning had risen significantly. From this year onward, earnings of foremen in spinning were above those in weaving (except in the Meire period). Earnings of overseers in weaving did rise, but at a slower pace than foremen's wages in spinning. The result was that the difference between the two grew gradually but significantly from 20 per cent in 1865 to 35 per cent in 1879. And this difference continued to grow, with peaks of 50 per cent and more.

The growing wage gap in the late 1860s cannot be explained by a multitude of factors, in that the work organization, equipment, work rules, employment figures, industrial relations, wage systems or the workers' skills had *not* changed. One factor that seems to be of importance was the situation of the labour market, which differed between spinning and weaving. The increasing wage gap may have meant that dealing with the labour market for spinning staff required more competence than the one for weaving, which would be recompensed by paying higher wages to the *contremaîtres* in spinning. In support of this argument is the fact that this mill's owners consciously lowered their wage cost by systematically employing more women and more young workers in the weaving section.[51] The mill's owners may have assumed that not much competence was needed to organize the hiring and firing of girls and young women. Moreover, managing such a group of workers would not necessitate much trouble, since girls and young workers had the reputation of being regular and docile workers.[52] Finally, overseers in weaving would be keen to hire such workers, thus securing a more trouble-free authority.[53] A possible explanation for the growing gap between foremen's earnings may therefore be the different labour market that the different categories of foremen were dealing with.

After the cotton famine of the early 1860s, technical innovations had been introduced in spinning, particularly after the fire of 1880 when up-to-date machinery was bought. This modernization led to a larger number of workers. By 1890, this section had twenty-four up-to-date self-actors (but only two ring frames) and about 120 workers. This investment fever contrasted with what happened in weaving, where up to the closing of the weaving section in 1879, the rather antiquated, small looms were still in use. With the reopening of the weaving division in 1891, new machinery was of course installed, and, of particular interest with regard to control, work on four looms was generalized.[54] Would such major changes not influence the work, and therefore also the wages, of the foremen in the two divisions? From 1870 to 1890, a period of technical innovation, the earnings of overseers in spinning hardly changed (27 to 28 francs per week). Then a slight rise occurred, pushing earnings up to 30 francs. After the reopening of the weaving section, the earnings of overseers in weaving rose too, albeit with much more fluctuations, thus leading to very unsteady wage differentials in the 1890s and 1900s. In general, however, it would not seem that overseers in spinning had a more onerous job than before, since their earnings remained quite stable in the 1890s and 1900s. Overseers' earnings in weaving, on the other hand, rose from 1894 to 1906, after which they declined.

The suddenly gaping wage difference in 1864 may perhaps be linked to the development of wages of spinners and weavers. In Lancashire, foremen's wages were calculated on the basis of the output and earnings of the weavers.[55] Although this was not the case at Voortman's, it cannot be excluded that overseers' wages kept pace with the general output (and thus wages) of spinning and weaving or, at least, with the general wage level of both divisions.[56] Varlez's note, *Les contremaîtres: Salaires*, supports the existence of such link by mentioning, 'In these wages [of the overseers in La Lys, a big linen mill in Ghent] are included the normal premiums that foremen receive for the output of their workers.' I have not found any trace in Voortman's wage books pointing to the calculation of such premiums for foremen, or to the existence of a connection between the wages of overseers and output.

A clear comparison between earnings of foremen in spinning and spinners' wages on the one hand, and between earnings of foremen in weaving and weavers' wages on the other, is given in Figure 3.3. This graph shows that earning gaps in spinning were much smaller than they were in weaving. In the 1830s and 1840s, spinners earned more than foremen (an average difference of 18 per cent). In 1850 spinners' earnings fell, while those of foremen in spinning rose, and from then on the latter's wage was about 18 per cent above that of spinners. I do not know why this sudden alteration occurred: there were no big changes in technology nor tense social relations in 1850 (note that this was also the period when overseers' earnings in spinning overtook those of overseers in weaving). Did high demand for foremen in spinning propel wages? From this period on, the ratio of the earnings of the two categories remained fairly stable, with a closing of the gap from 1865 to 1890 (average difference of 11 per cent) and a widening after 1890 (average difference of 16 per cent). But in general and in the long run, earnings of foremen in the spinning division kept pace with the spinners' wages. Hierarchies therefore remained pretty stable in the spinning mill, particularly after 1865.

This, however, was not the case in weaving where the foremen's earnings differed greatly from those of weavers. The former never fell below the weavers' earnings. Yet in the long run there was a closing of the earning gap and, from the cotton crisis of the 1860s onward, there was a rather stable proportion up to 1910. In the 1830s, 1840s and 1850s foremen in the weaving

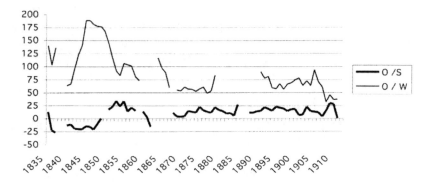

Figure 3.3 *Difference in Weekly Earnings between Foremen in Spinning and Spinners, and between Foremen in Weaving and Weavers. Source:* Based on Figure 3.1.

section could earn up to 180 per cent more than the average weaver. Such great differences were unknown after 1866. Between the late 1860s and the closing of the weaving mill in 1879, the difference between the earnings of weavers and overseers in weaving fell to about 60 per cent, a marked closing of the wage gap in comparison with the pre-1860 decades. Would this have meant a lowering of the foremen's status and authority within the weaving section? It may indicate changing tasks and responsibilities of overseers in weaving, who were dealing with a much younger and more feminine workforce than prior to 1860. Referring to this latter fact, I may suggest that the *contremaître*'s authority did not change within the weaving section, but that it probably did within the mill as a whole and, perhaps, in the textile community. After the reopening of the mill in 1891, the earning difference between the two categories reached about 80 per cent, which was due to the high wages of J. Meire. From 1894 to 1912, the difference again oscillated around 60 per cent,[57] with irregular limits between 32 and 93 per cent. In general, earnings of overseers in weaving kept pace with the weavers' earnings from 1866 to 1910.

I reached a similar conclusion with regard to the overseers' wages in spinning as compared to the spinners' earnings after 1865. May I therefore conclude that overseers' earnings in this mill were linked to general wage development in both divisions via (up till now) undetectable connections (by means, for example, of oral contracts and negotiations)? This would imply that the position and the status of overseers *in their respective divisions* would hardly have changed since the 1860s. Such a conclusion is not supported by Varlez's note of 1900, perceiving a loss of status of foremen in the Ghent textile industry (tendency to pay overseers by the hour, pushing them toward the *ouvriers*).

Authority, Labour Markets, Wages and Milieus:
Some Conclusions

An analysis of the foremen's wages at Voortman–Texas S.A. does not answer all the questions. Other than some general indications and assumptions, I do not know what foremen in this mill did precisely. But judging from the evolution of the earning gap with each other and with other adult male workers, I believe that their position in the mill, and thus their tasks and status, did change.

My investigation puts forward the existence of four different types of foremen, with 1850 as the borderline. Prior to 1850, *contremaîtres* in weaving held a particular position: they earned a very high but variable wage, which was undoubtedly due to the pressing demand for foremen in this new and expanding sector. Moreover, they played a central role in industrial relations. In the 1830s Voortman's weavers went on strike regularly and the mill was closed down on several occasions, which required from the foremen particular abilities with regard to personnel management. I link this to the high wages of foremen in weaving.

Judging from their earnings, foremen in spinning did not enjoy a special status in these years. Their pay was below that of foremen in weaving and below that of the spinners themselves. *Contremaîtres* in spinning were not confronted with tense industrial relations and a boisterous labour market: they therefore had less responsibility for personnel management. Moreover, spinning technology at this moment was not very complex. Hence, they had relatively moderate earnings.

In the 1850s all this changed, and two *new* types of foremen appeared. What had constituted the special position of foremen in weaving now contributed to their relative decline. Industrial relations in the mill calmed down, while the labour market (for both weavers and foremen in weaving) lost its restlessness. Moreover, the labour force that was taken on was assumed to be docile and cheap. Finally, when work organization changed in the 1880s (work on four looms, which caused protest in most mills), this mill was closed. As a consequence, earnings of foremen in weaving rose only moderately.

The opposite development took place in spinning. Spinning technology became more complex in the 1870s, and precisely at this moment the mill was totally renovated. This required greater experience from the workers than before 1870, which particularly affected foremen in spinning, who may have gained (technical) authority not only in the carding room but also in the spinning section. As a result, a total reversal of relations between *contremaîtres* in the spinning and weaving divisions of the mill took place.

This existence of a marked difference between foremen in spinning and weaving, particularly after 1850, is confirmed by their (self)perception (labelling in the censuses), their relative ages, and contemporaries' observations. Nonetheless, they both retained their privileges, in that they kept up their particular mode of payment (the weekly wage). On the other hand, they lost something of their privileges: their working time was recorded; something I doubt the proud foremen in weaving of the pre-1850s would have tolerated.

Notes

1. H. Gospel, 'Managerial Structure and Strategies: An Introduction', in *Managerial Strategies and Industrial Relations: An Historical and Comparative Study*, ed. H. Gospel and C. Littler (London, 1983), 1–24, here 8; S. Vandecasteele-Schweitzer, 'Comment peut-on être contremaître?' in *L'usine et le bureau: Itinéraires sociaux et professionnels dans l'entreprise XIXe et XXe siècles*, ed Y. Lequin and S. Vandecasteele (Lyon, 1990), 93–108.
2. P. Stearns, *Paths to Authority: The Middle Class and the Industrial Labor Force in France, 1820–48* (Urbana, 1978), 84.
3. S. Jacoby, *Employing Bureaucracy: Managers, Unions, and the Transformation of Work in American Industry, 1900–1945* (Mahwak, 2004), 12; Gospel, 'Managerial Structure', 8–9 (referring to 'feed and speed men'); D. Nelson, *Managers and Workers: Origins of the Twentieth-Century Factory System in the United States, 1880–1920* (Madison, 1995), 49, 52.
4. P. Lefebvre, *L'invention de la grande entreprise: Travail, hiérarchie, marché. France, fin XVIIIe–début XXe siècle* (Paris, 2003), 195, 201; Nelson, *Managers and Workers*, 39, 43.
5. It may seem relevant of the invisibility of foremen that the index of D. Farnie and D. Jeremy, *The Fibre that Changed the World: The Cotton Industry in International Perspective* (Oxford, 2004), lacks entries for 'foremen', 'supervisors' and 'overseers' (although these categories appear in the volume).
6. J. Mareska and J. Heyman, *Enquête sur le travail et la condition physique et morale des ouvriers employés dans les manufactures de coton à Gand* (Ghent, 1845), 45.
7. Lefebvre, *L'invention de la grande entreprise*, 61–63.
8. L. Varlez, *Les salaires dans l'industrie gantoise*, vol. 1: *Industrie cotonnière* (Brussels, 1901), 105–136.
9. Ibid., 131. 'Preparations were done more thoroughly, there were more foremen and helpers, workers never had to wait a long time and always had the raw material at hand.'
10. E. Anseele, 'Les sociétés anonymes socialistes en Belgique', *Les Annales de l'Economie Collective* 19 (1927): 337–352, here 341.
11. G. Pipyn and A. Vandersteen, *Handboek der katoenspinnerij, bijzonder dienstig voor fabrieksbestuurders en meestergasten* (Gent, 1914), 2.
12. Lazonick stresses the technical role of overseers in spinning ('rather than supervisory ability'): W. Lazonick, 'Production Relations, Labor Productivity, and Choice of Technique: British and U.S. Cotton Spinning', *Journal of Economic History* 41, no. 3 (1981): 491–516, here 501.
13. *Recensement général des industries et des métiers (31 octobre 1896)*, vol. 18: *Exposé général des méthodes et des résultats* (Brussels, 1902); *Recensement de l'industrie et du commerce, 31 décembre 1910* (Brussels, 1913); *Salaires et durée du travail dans les industries textiles au mois d'octobre 1901* (Brussels, 1905).
14. *Monographies industrielles. Industries textiles: Filature mécanique du coton, du lin, du chanvre et du jute* (Brussels, 1902), 16–17.

15. *Recensement général des industries et des métiers (31 octobre 1896)*, vol. 1 (Brussels, 1902), section IV, 56.
16. B. De Wilde, *Witte boorden, blauwe kielen: Patroons en arbeiders in de Belgische textielnijverheid in de 19e en 20e eeuw* (Bruges, 1997).
17. Ibid., 51, 93, 175, 178, 182, 280 (the truck system was prohibited in 1887).
18. G. Deneckere, 'Sire, het volk mort: Collectieve actie in de sociale geschiedenis van de Belgische staat, 1831–1940' (PhD diss., Universiteit Gent, 1994), 471, 474.
19. Ibid., 507–510.
20. Ibid., 597.
21. K. Tijtgat, *De geschiedenis der Gentsche socialistische katoenbewerkersvereeniging 1857–1932* (Ghent, 1932); S. H. Scholl, *Bijdragen tot de geschiedenis der Gentse arbeidersbeweging* (Brussels, 1957); W. Steenhout, 'Stakingen te Gent, 1872–1902' (MA thesis, Rijksuniversiteit Gent, 1970); L. Joos, 'Stakingen te Gent 1903–1914' (MA thesis, Rijksuniversiteit Gent, 1975).
22. K. Pittomvils, 'Alledaagse arbeidsconflicten in de Gentse textielindustrie: De praktijk van de Werkrechtersraad in de eerste helft van de negentiende eeuw', *Tijdschrift voor Sociale Geschiedenis* 21, no. 2 (1995): 181–211, here 192.
23. K. Pittomvils, 'Arbeidsverhoudingen te Gent in de eerste helft van de 19de eeuw' (MA thesis, Vrije Universiteit Brussel, 1994), 55; see also A. Green and K. Troup, *The Houses of History* (Manchester, 1999), 56, referring to the fact that 'the employer generally contented himself with sending his overlooker to answer any summons'.
24. Pittomvils, 'Arbeidsverhoudingen te Gent', 239.
25. P. Van den Eeckhout, 'Giving Notice: The Legitimate Way of Quitting and Firing (Ghent, 1877–1896)', in *Experiencing Wages: Social and Cultural Aspects of Wage Forms in Europe since 1500*, ed. P. Scholliers and L. Schwarz (Oxford, 2003), 81–109.
26. See, for example, J. Jowitt and A. McIvor, eds., *Employers and Labour in the English Textile Industries 1850–1939* (London, 1988), 93–94; R. Biernacki, *The Fabrication of Labor: Germany and Britain, 1640–1914* (Berkeley, 1995); Lefebvre, *L'invention de la grande entreprise*, 59–64; Nelson, *Managers and Workers*, 44–46.
27. City of Ghent, Bevolkingsdienst, population registers 1842, 1859, 1879 and 1902. Part of this research has been presented in P. Scholliers, *Herkomst, huisvesting, arbeids – en levensomstandigheden van de werkkrachten van het bedrijf A. Voortman–N.V. Texas* (Brussels, 1981).
28. Varlez, *Les salaires dans l'industrie gantoise*, 96–97, 180–187.
29. G. Avondts, *Levensschetsen van een aantal Gentse arbeidersfamilies* (Brussels, 1978), 121–136.
30. Ibid., 105–120.
31. Ibid., 152–166.
32. Ibid., 217–225.
33. Varlez, *Les salaires dans l'industrie gantoise*, 133.
34. In a union leaflet, for instance, the complaint was directed against the mill owner: 'Werkstaking der katoenspinnerij Voortman', January 1896, Library of Ghent University, Fonds Vliegende bladen, III, S 16. In Parliament, discussion was about whether workers were allowed to attend the measurement of their production. Who actually measured the output was not mentioned: *Annales Parlementaires de Belgique, Chambre*, 10 January 1895, 362, 364.
35. This independence of output also existed, for example, in English spinning mills: M. Huberman, 'How Did Labor Markets Work in Lancashire? More Evidence on Prices and Quantities in Cotton Spinning, 1822–1852', *Explorations in Economic History* 28 (1991): 87–120, here 91. For foremen in weaving, however, Lazonick noted that overlookers' pay was dependent on the weavers' output: W. Lazonick, *Competitive Advantage on the Shop Floor* (Cambridge, 1990), 165.

36. 'In some factories, attempts are made to introduce pay by the hour, despite the foremen's resistance'; see handwritten document: L. Varlez, 'Les contremaîtres: Salaires', undated, own collection.

37. Underlined by Varlez, 'Les contremaîtres: Salaires'. Varlez used *ouvrier* and *employé*, respectively.

38. P. Scholliers, *Wages, Manufacturers and Workers in the Nineteenth-Century Factory: The Voortman Cotton Mill in Ghent* (Oxford, 1996), 129–130, 224.

39. G. Avondts et al., *De Gentse textielarbeiders in de 19e en 20e eeuw: Lonen in de spinnerij van het bedrijf A. Voortman–N.V. Texas 1835–1914* (Brussels, 1976); G. Avondts et al., *De Gentse textielarbeiders in de 19e en 20e eeuw: Lonen in de weverij van het bedrijf A. Voortman–N.V. Texas 1835–1925* (Brussels, 1979).

40. In 1895 and 1905 there had been important strikes in this mill, which may explain the wage increases: Scholliers, *Wages, Manufacturers and Workers*, 225–226.

41. Avondts, *Levensschetsen*, 108–111, 180, 218. See also Scholliers, *Wages, Manufacturers and Workers*, 187–188, 189–190.

42. Scholliers, *Wages, Manufacturers and Workers*, 127–129.

43. Female and male weavers earned equal pay (with men working on larger looms but producing fewer pieces per week). In 1902, for example, earnings of female weavers were 13.1 francs per week, those of male weavers 12.7 francs; Avondts et al., *Lonen in de weverij*, 24, 29.

44. For more wages in the Ghent industry around 1900, see the contribution by P. Van den Eeckhout to this volume.

45. Mareska and Heyman, *Enquête sur le travail*, 99.

46. There are no wage data for the mill in this period. Varlez stressed the generally increasing wage level during the 1820s (*Les salaires dans l'industrie gantoise*, 39), and I see no reason why this increase should not have occurred at the market leader.

47. Scholliers, *Wages, Manufacturers and Workers*, 23, 219.

48. Ibid., 57–59.

49. Ibid., 68.

50. Lefebvre, *L'invention de la grande entreprise*, 125–127, stresses the 'gestion de la main-d'œuvre' by foremen in France. They had recruitment networks, knew best who to promote or dismiss, and even settled tariffs, fines and premiums. However, in doing this they were restricted by the management and local customs.

51. P. Scholliers, 'Grown-ups, Boys and Girls in the Ghent Cotton Industry: The Voortman Mills, 1835–1914', *Social History* 20 (1995): 201–218.

52. On the docility of (young) female workers, see W. O. Henderson, 'The Labour Force in the Textile Industries', *Archiv für Sozialgeschichte* 16 (1976): 283–324, here 283; C. E. Morgan, 'Women, Work and Consciousness in the Mid-nineteenth Century English Cotton Industry', *Social History* 17, no. 1 (1992): 23–41.

53. As was the case in Preston, reported by M. Savage, 'Women and Work in the Lancashire Cotton Industry, 1890–1939', in *Employers and Labour in the English Textile Industries 1850–1939*, ed. J. A. Jowitt and A. J. McIvor (London, 1988), 203–223, here 210.

54. M. Scholliers, *Bedrijfsgeschiedenis van de firma A. Voortman–N.V. Texas* (Brussels, 1976), 68–69.

55. In Lancashire weaving mills, foremen's earnings consisted of a 'commission', which was a fraction of all the pay received by workers in one section: Biernacki, *Fabrication of Labor*, 152.

56. The latter was noted by S. Pollard, *The Genesis of Modern Management: A Study of the Industrial Revolution in Great Britain* (Harmondsworth, 1968), 172.

57. In England and Germany, overseers in weaving earned between 50 and 75 per cent more than weavers did: Biernacki, *Fabrication of Labor*, 151.

CHAPTER 4

SECRETS, LIES AND CONTRACTS

Conflicts between Employers and Their Foremen
in Nineteenth-Century Ghent (1885–1913)

Patricia Van den Eeckhout

In my attempt to study the history of work and labour relations as lived experiences, I try to explore aspects of work relationships which are hardly discussed by contemporaries and historians, because they were taken for granted or remained implicit.[1] My ambition is to find out how employers and workers perceived the role and function of foremen. By studying the form, the duration and the content of their contracts, I will try to define in what respect the bond between foremen and employer differed from that between employer and ordinary worker. By looking at employers' accusations and complaints, I shall try to find out what they expected of foremen and what led to conflicts and dismissal. To a certain extent my research consists of finding out more about the content of the implicit contract between employer and employee. The implicit contract is 'the largely tacit agreement made between the two parties with regard to what will be given by each and what each will take from the relationship'.[2]

Often the answers to such questions are formulated in situations of conflict, when people become aware of the fact that what they take for granted is not necessarily shared or practised by others. The archives of the Ghent Conseil de Prud'hommes, a kind of labour court established under French rule, introduce us to the world of labour and conflict in the nineteenth century.[3] As a textile centre, Ghent was the first Belgian town to have a Conseil de Prud'hommes installed in 1810. Other cities and industrial centres followed. One of the tasks assigned to the Conseils de Prud'hommes consisted of reconciliation in minor conflicts between industrial employers and their workers individually. From the law of 7 February 1859 onwards, industrial workers were able to elect their representatives in the Conseils de Prud'hommes, as their employers already did.

Any worker or employer with complaints regarding work, wages, conditions of dismissal, etc., could bring his or her case before the Conseil de Prud'hommes. Within the latter a Bureau de Conciliation was formed, composed from 1859 on by an equal number of representatives of workers and employers. Each case had to pass before the Bureau de Conciliation, which tried to find a compromise between the two parties. When that failed, the matter was taken before the Bureau Général, also composed of an equal number of representatives of workers and employers. If that session was unsuccessful in its mediation, a judgement was pronounced.

The archives of the Conseils de Prud'hommes contain the minutes of all these sessions as well as notes and drafts produced by the clerk of the court, letters written by employers and workers, contracts, bills, etc. The language used in the documents is either French or Dutch. The most interesting files concerning foremen deal with men who had been fired before their contract ended and who contested their dismissal before the Bureau Général. This was not always the case. If a discontented foreman brought his employer before the Bureau de Conciliation and an agreement was reached then the case was hardly documented. If no agreement was reached but the foreman decided that it was not worth the fuss or if he foresaw that he would not win, then the case did not come before the Bureau Général either, and then the 'dossier' is almost non-existent.

Unfortunately not that many cases concerning foremen were presented to the Ghent Conseil de Prud'hommes: I found thirty-one between 1885 and 1913.[4] One of the problems is that the cause list does not always mention that the plaintiff or defendant was a foreman. The status of some of the workers can be discovered only while reading the proceedings. On the other hand, some of the files concerning foremen found in the Ghent archives were extensively documented, because a lot was at stake: some of the discontented foremen demanded large compensations.

One of the drawbacks of using the archives of the Conseils de Prud'hommes is the fact that they seldom contain information about the companies as such. This is no surprise since the Conseils de Prud'hommes' preoccupation was the plight of the individual plaintiff. The size and the internal organization of the company involved were seldom discussed and as a result we know far too little about the context in which the thirty-one foremen operated.

The foremen that I studied protested against allegedly unfair treatment by filing a complaint against their employer. Of course, there were also other ways to get back at him. In 1900 Gustave Vande Caspeele, who had been working as a foreman in the silk factory of De Coutere in Deinze, was brought before the Conseil de Prud'hommes. His employer accused him of what we might call small acts of sabotage. We do not learn how and why Vande Caspeele's contract ended, but it appears that before leaving the factory the foreman had damaged some goods. De Coutere accused him of maliciously destroying tools with the purpose of causing harm. As a foreman Vande Caspeele had put some indications on the dockets used in the process of silk weaving in order to facilitate the work. Before leaving the factory the foreman erased these indications. He admitted doing this, but declared there was no ill intent. The Conseil de Prud'hommes did not believe him. He received a disciplinary sanction that consisted of paying a fine of one franc. His employer, who had demanded a compensation of 1,000 francs, was allowed the sum of 5 francs.

Foreman Jules Van Bellingen, so we learn from a letter from his employer, S.A. Construction d'Appareils Industriels, took his revenge when he was dismissed due to shortage of work. The first time he had been sent away he had destroyed some models, his employer wrote, and when he was dismissed in 1911, he completely mismanaged the assembling of utensils.

Hiring a Foreman

In Ghent and in Belgium at large, the length of the contracts between industrial workers and their employers was usually not specified, and they were tacitly renewed every eight or fifteen days.[5] When a foreman was hired, however, the length of the contract was more often indicated and it appears that some employers wished to bind their foreman to their company for a longer period.

The contract that Thomas Tetlow made in 1882 with the Ghent dyer Van Damme was for six years. In 1890 Jan Baptiste Van Huffel and his employer, Gucquier Gleesener, a Ghent manufacturer of photographic plates, agreed on a contract of ten years. The contract stipulated that Van Huffel would also remain at the service of Gucquier Gleesener's children, children by marriage and his widow. In 1896 James Williams and his wife signed a contract for two years as foreman and cutter and forewoman in the Ghent shirt factory of Lousbergs. Frans De Loore had been working as a foreman barrel-maker in the wood trade Usines d'Evergem for almost twenty years when he was fired in 1906: his contract had been renewed every three years. Octaaf Haeck, who was employed as a foreman in 1909 at the toolmaker Van de Putte in Gentbrugge, signed a contract for five years. The contract agreed on in 1909 by Max Schletter, foreman in the foundry of Construction d'Appareils Industriels, was to be renewed every six months, while the contract of candy maker Henri Pauwels with candy manufacturer Van Compernolle lasted for one year. The length of the contract of cutter Camiel Roselt was not specified, but the fact that he had been hired for a yearly wage, gave the foreman the impression that he had been given a contract for a year. The contract Frans Braem and Gustaaf Van der Cruyssen made in 1912 with the piano factory of Paul & Andre Beyer was an agreement for three years. This was also the case for the contract of 1910 between foreman Frédéric Bauters and the rubber factory Colonial Rubber, and the contract of 1906 between Seraphin De Schrijver and the car manufacturer Jules Alberts.

Stipulating the length of a contract could be beneficial to foreman and employer. An employer had the certainty of being able to rely on the foreman's specialized know-how for a longer period, without the risk of losing him to the competition. But even with a contract there was no guarantee that this would not occur. Foreman Frédéric Bauters, who worked for the rubber factory Colonial Rubber, broke his contract in 1913. He left Belgium and joined a rubber firm in Portugal, so a letter from his employer's lawyer tells us. He was convicted by default and had to pay Colonial Rubber 1,000 francs compensation.

If the foreman was a disappointment, however, or if an employer wanted to get rid of a foreman for whatever reason, then a contract with a specified length was a liability. Before the law of 10 March 1900 on labour contracts, a fixed-term contract could not be broken unilaterally, even if there seemed to be legitimate reason to do so. Either the two parties agreed to end the contract or the courts gave a ruling.[6] The law of 1900 that introduced the concept of 'labour contract', made it possible (both for employer and employee) to end such a contract on the spot if there were legitimate reasons to do so. These were enumerated in the law. The employer could end the contract before its expiration if the employee had deceived him with false qualifications, in cases of gross and immoral misconduct, when material harm was caused deliberately, when trade secrets were revealed to third parties, when the employee's imprudence jeopardized the security of the workplace and generally when order, discipline and the loyal execution of the contract were undermined. But the employer had to act swiftly. In all these cases of flagrant misconduct, the end of contract had to follow before two working days expired.[7]

For a foreman, a contract with a fixed length was an asset, since he knew exactly what to expect. If the length of a contract was not specified, workers could be fired at any time. In Ghent, and in many other industrial centres in Belgium, a period of notice of eight or fifteen days was customary, unless workshop regulations stipulated otherwise. The law on the labour contract of 1900 codified this tradition: it made a period of notice of at least seven days compulsory but the latter was subordinate to particular agreements, local customs or workshop regulations that stated otherwise.[8] Workers would therefore know only about a week beforehand that they would be out of a job.

There was discussion towards the end of the nineteenth century whether workers were for or against a compulsory period of notice. According to contemporary observers, Belgian workers preferred to be able to leave their employer whenever they wanted.[9] However, it is difficult to make generalizations in this respect: workers' attitudes were probably influenced by the state of the local labour market. We lack a study of the Ghent labour market, but the fact that in the years 1877–1896 workers made complaints mostly because they were refused their customary period of notice, might be an indication that the local labour market situation was not in their favour.[10]

A foreman therefore had more chances of being employed for a fixed period than an ordinary worker. Probably not all our foremen, however, had a contract of a fixed length. In five cases (three of which were not documented at all) the foremen demanded the customary period of notice of eight days. This demand in itself is an indication that their contracts did not differ from the contracts of ordinary workers, meaning that the length of the contract was not specified and that custom ruled as regards period of notice.

Employers who wanted to entice foremen from other regions or from abroad to come and work for them possibly used a fixed-term contract to be more persuasive. Cutter James Williams, who had his own firm in Birmingham ('where he had a number of sewing machines and quite a little clientele'), was prepared to become a foreman at Lousbergs's only if he had the certainty of being employed for two years at least, so the English vice-consul Geo Hallett wrote when he came to the rescue of his compatriot. Williams and his wife sold everything in Birmingham, the vice-consul explained. They dispersed their clientele and broke up their home. Hallett suggests Williams was prepared to do that because he was 'seduced by the perspective of a position for life in Belgium, where he could raise his child in the knowledge of foreign languages'. At first Lousbergs had argued that a contract was not necessary, but the employer gave in because for Williams a two-year contract was indispensable.

Most contracts in nineteenth-century Belgian industry between workers and employers were oral, but in the case of foremen they were written down more often.[11] Of course, workshop regulations were also considered legitimate contracts, and in this respect an increasing number of workers had a written (usually printed) contract. The latter were not contracts, however, drawn up on an individual basis. Workshop regulations were unilateral conventions, imposed by the employer on a take it or leave it basis, but they were valid if they had been visibly posted in the workplace.[12] After the law of 15 June 1896, workshop regulations were compulsory for companies with at least ten workers (five workers by 1900). Foremen and other 'special' members of the personnel had their own individual contracts: workshop regulations were not applicable to them.[13] In 1887 Hippoliet Pauwels, a supervisor in a sugar factory, successfully contested the fact that workshop regulations allowing dismissal without notice had been applied to him.

Both oral and written contracts referred to the wage the foreman would receive. Sometimes working hours were also mentioned. The other terms of employment referred to dedication, loyalty, discretion and the specific know-how that the foreman was supposed to deliver. Referring to the work of the sociologist Alan Fox, Watson remarks that in the case of people with managerial positions who have a high trust relationship with their superiors, the implicit contract tends to be relatively diffuse. For people in lower positions, the implicit contract is more restricted and there is a much tighter specification of what is required of them.[14] The former is referred to as high-discretion work, the latter as low-discretion work. Our foremen can be associated with what Fox calls 'the middle range of discretion'.[15] The Conseil de Prud'hommes acknowledged that a foreman had more liberty in doing his job than an ordinary worker. In a sentence concerning the case of foreman piano maker Frans Braem, accused in 1913 of 'certain deeds', which were not specified, the Conseil remarked that the position of foreman implied 'a relatively large liberty'.

At first sight, the view on which this binary opposition is based does not seem to be applicable to the foremen I study. What the employer expected from these foremen is fairly well circumscribed: in several cases it consisted of the provision of a particular know-how that was supposed to lead to the advancement of the firm. I have never encountered such explicitness and personal accountability in ordinary workers' contracts. However, the fact that some of the foremen's duties were explicitly mentioned, either in an oral or written agreement, does not imply that the contract covered them all, and that there was no area of duty left to the discretion of the foremen. By explicitly mentioning some of the work expected, dissatisfaction with a foreman could be presented more easily as a breach of contract on his part.

According to his oral contract (1890), Jan Baptiste Van Huffel had to offer his employer, a manufacturer of photographic plates, all his knowledge and diligence so that his enterprise would become a success. He had to promise on his honour that he would not disclose any information regarding the proceedings in the factory, the secrets of manufacture and the business of his employer. In the letter that finisher Jan Baptiste Wasmijn received from his employer Eugène Bayens (warning Wasmijn that he was not satisfied with his services), a paragraph of their contract (1897) was cited. It specified that all articles had to be finished and dressed as they should be and, more particularly, as Wasmijn used to finish them in the places where he had worked before. The latter suggests Bayens had hired Wasmijn on the basis of his good reputation for the work done at his former employer's.

The written contract (1896) between cutter James Williams and his wife and the Ghent shirt manufacturer Lousbergs stipulated that the couple had to follow the instructions given to them by Lousbergs, and that they had to serve their employer with honesty and diligence. They had to devote all their time (eleven hours a day) to his service, and they were not supposed to disclose any information, plans or secrets. Lousbergs had to provide them with the necessary equipment, the contract continued, but Williams and his wife were expected to use the patterns they owned as well as those that would be approved by their employer. In this case the employer expected a combination of loyalty and obedience with specific expertise in pattern making. Again the contract suggests that the employer's choice of foreman was based on the latter's good reputation in his trade, since the employer wanted to get hold of the patterns currently used by Williams.

The written contract (1907) of candy maker Henri Pauwels with Van Compernolle stipulated that he had to produce well-finished articles and that he would not offer his services to another manufacturer. The written contract of dyer Emile Van Loo with the spinning and weaving factory of Vanderhaeghen anticipated possible bribery. It mentioned that a month's notice was required except when the foreman had received a 'commission' from one of the suppliers: in such circumstances immediate dismissal was allowed. The contract also stipulated that Van Loo had to keep a *livre de teinture* with the composition of the baths and the weight before and after dying. In this case the contract reveals an attempt to ensure that the foreman's expertise would be made available to the employer permanently.

The oral contract of Heinrich Kreitzscheck (1908) employed by the Clouterie Tréfilerie des Flandres stipulated that he was expected to tin-plate and galvanize as in the best German houses. Max Schletter who was hired as foreman for the foundry of Construction d'Appareils industriels (1909), had to take care that work was carried out as economically as possible and that machines would be used for orders of more than thirty pieces. The contract concluded with the solemn declaration that Schletter would do everything in his power to contribute to the good of the factory. It is no surprise that a machine makers' contract of 1909 contained references to the use of machines, because from the end of the nineteenth century this sector witnessed the gradual introduction of machine tools and serial production. However, the fact that the foreman's contract explicitly mentioned the obligation to use machines when a certain number of pieces had to be manufactured, suggests that it was anything but self-evident. Commenting on a strike at the Ghent machine builder Carels in 1914, the journal of the Ministry of Labour, the *Revue du Travail*, remarked that workers resented the changes introduced in the organization of work because they disturbed their old habits Apparently the foreman had to ensure that the new procedures were applied.[16]

Boilermaker Octave Haeck had to supervise other workers, his written contract (1909) with toolmaker Van de Putte stipulated, so that all the work would be done under his responsibility. In fact this was the only contract that focused on the foreman's role as a supervisor of subordinates. The other contracts emphasized the foreman's role as a provider of a specific expertise.

Trade Secrets

The content of some of the contracts reveals that employers expected their foreman to provide them with a specific know-how that would be reserved for them as long as the contract lasted. In several cases the foreman even seemed to be the only one in the firm with knowledge of the trade secrets involved, at least at the beginning of his employment. It appears that hiring a foreman could be an excellent device for entrepreneurs who had no expertise or experience in a particular trade but nonetheless wished to start up a business in a given sector. In these cases the foreman was expected to contribute all the know-how, and sometimes experience was imported from outside Belgium.[17]

The importance of the transfer of technology and know-how is often emphasized for the early phases of industrialization. S. Pollard describes how in the period 1750–1830 innovations spread by recruiting men from firms that used the most recent methods.[18] K. Bruland remarks that this continued into the later nineteenth century. In her study on technology transfer in Scandinavia it appears that the earlier immigrants were highly skilled artisans, while by the second half of the nineteenth century they were primarily supervisors and overseers. She suggests the relevant skills may have shifted from technical knowledge to organizational and managerial skills.[19] This was not necessarily the case: some of the Ghent foremen offered a combination of both.

That dependence on a foreman's expertise could be considerable is clear in the case of Thomas Tetlow, hired by dyer Van Damme. The Conseil de Prud'hommes acknowledged in its judgement that when Tetlow was first employed, Van Damme knew nothing about the trade while Tetlow was acquainted with all its secrets.

The accusations of the Ghent manufacturer of photographic plates, Gucquier Gleesener, against his foreman Jan Baptiste Van Huffel reveal that a foreman's secrets were considered a treasured possession. The employer had the impression that Van Huffel was not sharing the results of his research with him, and he accused him of acting secretively while changing or improving the fabrication process. When Van Huffel, on sick leave for five days, took home the booklet in which he had written down all the formulae, know-how and secrets, Gucquier Gleesener concluded that Van Huffel had tried to deceive him.

Foremen could play a crucial role when manufacturers started a business but lacked the know-how, as is demonstrated by the case of James Williams and his wife, hired respectively as foreman and cutter of shirts and forewoman in the shirt factory of Lousbergs. Lousbergs, an important textile manufacturer in Ghent, wanted to explore new horizons but lacked experience. 'Lousbergs wanted to add a new branch to his affairs, that of the manufacture, trade and export of shirts. He needed a man with experience to direct the cutting and manufacture', so the British vice-consul stated when he came to the defence of his fired compatriot James Williams. Vice-consul G. Hallett mentioned that Lousbergs had placed an advertisement in the Lloyd newspaper.

Heinrich Kreitzscheck, a foreman with the Clouterie Tréfilerie des Flandres, was expected to tin-plate and galvanize as in the best German houses. After some trials, he succeeded in galvanizing but failed to tin-plate, which was the reason why he did not receive the promised wage rise. Again, the employer appeared to hire a foreman for a very specific purpose: namely, to provide expertise not yet available in the company.

Urging foremen to write down the details of procedure and fabrication was a means to prevent them from monopolizing their knowledge indefinitely. But, as we learned from the Gucquier Gleesener case, these records could fuel further quarrels. Emile Van Loo, who worked as a foreman dyer at the weaving and spinning factory of Vanderhaeghen, refused to hand over the *livre de teinture* he had kept. In 1911 the two female cutters Leonie Wante and Esther Blansaer were both accused by their employer, the widow Bottelberghe, of having taken the book of patterns with them. Esther Blansaer declared she burnt it. Leonie Wante returned a small pattern book 'taken by mistake', but refused to hand over the large pattern book, declaring it was hers.

A Foreman's Wages

The wages of the Ghent foremen of my sample were mostly referred to as weekly or monthly wages, but in order to compare them I calculated wages on a yearly basis (see Table 4.1). Information from other sources on Ghent foremen's wages also mention weekly wages.[20] Vandecasteele-Schweitzer, Dewerpe and Glovka Spencer mention monthly wages in their discussion of foremen in France, Italy and the Ruhr area, respectively.[21] The fact that foremen were paid mostly by the week or by the month distinguished them from ordinary workers and had an important symbolic value. When foreman Max Schletter was degraded in 1909 from foreman to worker, he was no longer paid by the week but by the hour.

Most of our foremen received a fixed weekly or monthly wage, which suggests that there was no attempt in most cases to link their income to the output of the workers they supervised. That graded monetary sanctions were the exception can be explained by the fact that the foremen I studied were

Table 4.1 *Foremen, Wages and Compensations*

Foreman	Wage Agreement	Compensation Demanded	Compensation Received
dyer 1882;1885	1,560 fr; 2,080 fr	1000 fr	250 fr
sugar factory 1887	?	18 fr	18 fr
photo. plate 1890	1,800 fr+7% ben	18,000 fr (A)	2,000 fr
galvanizing 1896–	3,000 fr	8,250 fr (B)	nothing
brush maker 1897	?	22 fr	nothing
brewery 1897	?	20 fr	nothing
finisher 1897	?	sum not specified	45 fr
cutter + wife 1896	5,323.76 fr + travel	3,575.30 fr (C)	3,575. 30 fr
cement 1900	?	20 fr	nothing
barrel maker 1906	3,000 fr	3,000 fr	nothing
candy maker 1907–	2,184 fr	sum not specified	55 fr
car factory 1909	1,950 fr min. (D)	500 fr	nothing
foundry 1909	2,340 fr	sum not specified	work until EOY
dyer 1909	1,820 fr +0.25 ct/kg	150 fr	nothing
boilermaker 1909–	1,638 fr	740 fr	nothing
utensils 1911	?	25 fr	12.5 fr
cutter 1905–1910	4,000 fr/year	3,666 fr (E)	nothing
wood trade 1911	?	600 fr	nothing
wood trade 1912	1,980 fr/year	990 fr (F)	990 fr
machine b. 1912	3,120 fr/year	815 fr (G)	
piano maker 1912	2,080 fr/year	500 fr (J)	500 fr
pottery 1913	1,800 fr/year	1,690 fr (H)	1690 fr
wood trade 1913	?	59. 46 fr (I)	nothing
piano maker 1913	?	200 fr (J)	nothing
exhibition 1913	?	25 fr	not clear
wood trade 1913	?	300 fr (K)	300 fr
linen factory 1913	1,456 fr/year	30.50 fr	30.50 fr

Fr : franc; ct: centime

A: wages for the 9.5 remaining years of the contract + compensation for the percentage of the net benefit he did not receive; B: wage raises and bonus due since 1897; C: wages for the remaining weeks of the contract; D: employer had to provide at least fifty hours of work per week; E: wages for the remaining months of the contract; F: six months' wages; G: two months' wages + moving expenses Malines-Ghent; H: wage arrears, the foreman had free lodging; I: commission; J: sum agreed on in case of premature end of contract, K: share in profit

Note: Four cases are not included in the table because they deal with issues other than wages or compensations.

Source: Rijksarchief Beveren, Arbeidsrechtbank te Gent.

operating less as supervisors 'driving' labour, than as craftsmen with specialized knowledge. The 'driving' method of supervision consisted of 'a combination of authoritarian rule and physical compulsion' and was most apparent in highly mechanized industries, where foremen had to make sure workers did not undermine the machines' potential.[22]

Two foremen, who earned less than their colleagues, were paid partly according to results. The foreman in the photographic-plates factory and the foreman dyer, who did not earn more than some 1,800 francs per year, compensated for their lower wages with a 7 per cent share in net profit on the one hand and a bonus of 0.25 centimes per kilogram dyed material on the other hand. If the foreman dyer spoilt the articles, he did not receive his bonus. Two foremen occupied in the wood trade, but of whom we know hardly anything, also appeared to receive some incentives. Vital Baetslé who worked at the Usines d'Everghem demanded and received his share in the profits of 1911 and 1912, and Gustaaf Ramont, occupied at Remi De Jonckheere's shop, demanded the payment of his commission in 1913. However, he withdrew his complaint.

The foreman boilermaker with the lowest pay of all did not complement his wage with some form of gratuities. Is it a coincidence that it is precisely this foreman whose contract stipulated that his task consisted of supervising workers, while the other foremen were more often associated with the possession of a specific expertise?

Most of the foremen discussed in this essay earned fairly high wages. The two cutters were the most expensive employees, although in the case of Williams the pay included his wife's wages as a forewoman. A possible explanation for the cutters' high wages might be the combination of artistic creativity and technical refinement that this required. In the judgement pronounced regarding cutter Camiel Roselt, the Conseil de Prud'hommes insisted that Roselt was not an artist and that he did not produce works of art, but that he was a blue-collar worker whose labour was mostly manual. This affirmation suggests that an association with artists did come to mind.

Not all foremen were paid high wages, however. Besides the foreman boilermaker and the foreman in the linen factory who were not big earners, we have five foremen who demanded the customary eight days' notice and required 18 to 25 francs as a compensation. This sum was the equivalent of a week's wages. So besides an 'aristocracy' of foremen, we are also dealing with foremen with a far humbler position. They were occupied in factories producing brushes, sugar, cement, utensils, and one worked in a brewery.

Foremen whose work was appreciated were sometimes granted a wage rise, but promised wage increases were not paid out if there was dissatisfaction. A foreman dyer who started his career in 1882 with a wage of 1,560 francs per year, earned 2,080 francs by 1885. A foreman who was in the business of galvanizing and tin plating had the prospect of raising his wage after one year from 3,000 francs per year to 3,750. According to the oral contract, the employer was prepared to add a bonus of 750 francs extra after a year if he was pleased with the foreman's services. Apparently neither the wage raise nor the bonus was ever paid. The foreman, Heinrich Kreitzscheck, started work at the Clouterie et Tréfilerie des Flandres in 1896 and filed his complaint in 1908. The wage increases and the bonus he never received amounted to 8,250 francs. The employer argued that by not according a wage raise he showed that he was not entirely satisfied with Kreitzscheck's services. Since not once in ten years had the foreman protested, he was assumed to have agreed. The foreman had to leave the Conseil de Prud'hommes' session empty-handed and he was required to pay the cost of the case.

Expectations and Deceptions

Foremen were fired for different reasons. On the basis of the cases that I studied, I would argue that some were dismissed because they did not deliver the technical expertise and know-how that was expected of them. Others appeared to have delivered this expertise, but the transfer of their knowledge to other members of the personnel made them redundant. Their employers had to find an excuse to get rid of such expensive collaborators. Finally, some foremen were fired because their employers could not, or could no longer, trust and depend on them.

Foremen Who Did Not Deliver

The Case of Finisher Jan Baptiste Wasmijn. Jan Baptiste Wasmijn was employed as a finisher in the firm of Eugène Bayens known as Apprêts du Dock. The contract had been concluded on 31 August 1897, but on 24 December of the same year Bayens wrote Wasmijn a letter, complaining that he had not come up to expectations. Wasmijn was supposed to finish the articles as he used to do in the place where he had worked before, but it appears his employer was deeply disappointed. Bayens did not mince his words:

> Owing to incompetence or ill will on your side most of the pieces were badly finished and were ruined or damaged. Your co-workers can testify to the many reprimands and remarks you received from us, but which you ignored. You are incapable of managing the machine and mister Braun is obliged to prepare the dressing himself most of the time, because you are not able to. We cannot rely on you for one moment and in order to prevent further damage and unpleasantness, we have to tell you that we shall break our agreement if we do not obtain satisfaction. We shall be patient for four or five weeks and we shall see if there is any change in your behaviour, but rest assured that we will hold you to a strict execution of your duties.

The draft of the clerk of the court contains the following telegram-style notes: 'all the work= machine????', 'manometer', 'for 500 francs badly made pieces', 'has no order', 'lost the designs by mister Uyttendaele', 'wrote letter urging him to improve his work, if not: dismissal after five weeks of patience', 'dressing made in his fashion', 'caused disturbance', 'insulted the associate: dwazekl! (silly b—)'.

So foreman Wasmijn was not only accused of being incapable of handling the machinery and of damaging the material, but he also persisted in doing things his own way. Wasmijn could not live up to Bayens' expectations. When these technical inadequacies appeared to be combined with insubordination and a lack of order, the employer concluded that he could not trust his business in the hands of this foreman. The public humiliation suffered by Wasmijn when he was reprimanded in front of his subordinates must have undermined his authority. But this does not seem to have played a role in his dismissal, which suggests that Wasmijn's expertise was at stake, rather than his capacity to exercise authority.

Wasmijn was fired subsequently and he contested his dismissal. The parties were reconciled and Wasmijn received a compensation of 45 francs, but we do not learn why the employer agreed to this.

The Cases of Foremen Metalworkers Max Schletter and Jozef Forez. In June 1909 Max Schletter signed a contract as foreman in the Construction d'Appareils Industriels foundry. In September 1909 Schletter brought his case before the Conseil de Prud'hommes because his employer had lowered his wage to 0.60 francs an hour. He was no longer paid on a weekly basis since he was no longer employed as a foreman but as a caster in the copper and bronze foundry. In his letter to the chairman of the Conseil de Prud'hommes, the manager of the firm wrote that the foreman had accepted this decision. The employer complained that the continuous faulty production for which Schletter was responsible had already cost a lot of money. According to the manager, he was a total failure: 'His incapacity as head of the foundry is flagrant.' Schletter earned 45 francs per week (or some 70 centimes an hour), so the manager argued, but his work was hardly worth 0.30 francs an hour. Moreover he did not seem to bother: 'That man mocks everyone, he is not even doing the job of a 0.30 francs moulder and on Saturdays he is anxious to get his pay.' The parties were reconciled and Schletter finally agreed to work for 0.60 francs an hour, while he had guaranteed employment until the end of the year.

Schletter was not only accused of being technically inadequate, he also failed to fulfil the implicit contract between him and his employer. Clearly, he did not take his work to heart: he lacked the professional pride of the real craftsman and was in a hurry to pick up the foreman's wage he did not deserve.

In May 1912 machine builder Reichardt Frères offered Jozef Forez an oral contract. The latter moved from Malines to Ghent and took his family with him. In August Forez was fired. Since he did not find employment in Ghent he moved back to Malines. When Forez requested two months' wages and travel and moving expenses, his employer replied that Forez was not up to the task and that his inexperience had even caused a lot of damage. Forez did not insist.

A flagrant lack of the technical expertise expected from a foreman, could thus be a reason to fire him. However, incompetence was not always accepted as a reason for getting rid of a foreman. In 1913 the piano manufacturer Beyer broke the three-year contract of foreman Frans Braem, accusing him of incompetence, lack of punctuality and negligence. The draft of the clerk of the court mentions delays in the distribution of work, sending away the best workmen and visiting Café Belle Vue when Beyer was absent. However, the Conseil de Prud'hommes reprimanded the employer. Before signing an important and long-term contract, it was the employer's duty, so the Conseil declared, to check whether the foreman was up to the task. Since the employer was incapable of convincing the Conseil de Prud'hommes of the gravity of Frans Braem's shortcomings, the latter received the 500 francs he demanded for breach of contract.

Foremen Who Delivered Only Too Well

Down and Out in Ghent: The Case of Foreman Cutter James Williams and His Wife.

> Williams was drunk all day.... He was usually drunk when I saw him. He went out all day and came back for one hour. When he cut things wrong and we told him, he sent us away. When he came down and saw that it was his fault, he pulled the work out of our hands. He went out in the morning, drank brandy and with it, he had a lemon, so that you wouldn't smell it. He threw sink patterns at us. On the Wednesday before he left, he was very drunk. He pulled the work out of the hands of the workers and threw it at their heads.

This was what the 28-year-old seamstress Adèle Broeckhoven declared in her testimony against foreman James Williams. Williams and his wife, working respectively as foreman and cutter of shirts and forewoman in the shirt factory of Lousbergs, were fired on 19 March 1898, several months before their contract expired. Their employer argued that in the first months after his appointment Williams fulfilled his obligations, but then he neglected his duties and came to work irregularly. He took to drinking, and when he came in drunk he caused scandal among the ninety-five workers. He had been warned twice, but despite the promise to better his life, there was no improvement. Williams opposed his dismissal, while he also contested the accusations on which it was based. No less than sixteen witnesses backed up the employer's accusations. The defence produced ten witnesses who denied Williams had misbehaved.

First, relative outsiders (a cabinetmaker, a plumber, a metal worker and a driver who took Williams home after work) were questioned. The concierge of the premises declared he had seen Williams drunk four or five times a week. He brought bottles of brandy to work and asked the girls to fetch drink.

The other testimonies came from people who had been working with Williams. The seamstresses (between sixteen and thirty-four years old) reproached him with inadequate preparation of their sewing. It was his task to cut the shirts, but they had to wait for their work and sometimes he messed it up and then they had to correct his mistakes. When the work was not properly prepared, the seamstresses earned less. Williams was very rude to them, so the seamstresses complained, and he could not stand the fact that they confronted him with his sloppy work. When the women wanted to complain, he threatened to fire them. His drunkenness appears in the testimony of every seamstress: he went out during working hours, was too drunk to know what he was doing, and they all reported that Amelie Verhamme was sent out to fetch beer, gin and brandy. Ernest Mackness, a compatriot of Williams and manager of the factory, who had introduced the foreman, testified that Williams was often too drunk to know what he had measured. This gave the seamstresses a pretext, so Mackness stated, to return the shirts with the message that they could not sew them.

According to these workers, then, the foreman was responsible for the steady flow of work and indirectly for their earnings. According to the factory manager an inadequate foreman fuelled workers' imaginary complaints. In his conclusions, Lousbergs's lawyer added the element of scandal on the shop floor.

All these testimonies appear very convincing. However, most of them were from people who still worked for Lousbergs or had worked for the company in the past and possibly hoped to return. Of the sixteen witnesses testifying against Williams, nine people still worked for Lousbergs, one seamstress declared that she wanted to come back to the factory, and three artisans had worked for Lousbergs in the past.

The ten testimonies in favour of Williams came from three members of the English colony in Ghent, a former housemaid of Williams, five seamstresses who had left the factory and one woman whose relationship with Williams is unclear. Lousbergs's lawyer argued that none of these persons had been present on the shop floor in the period of Williams' dismissal: in other words, they did not know what they were talking about.

Two seamstresses who testified in favour of Williams, confirmed that they had to wait for their work, but they declared it was the result of a lack of cloth and that Williams too had had to wait. One of the seamstresses remarked that after a while Williams had a helper, and that the girls still had to wait for their work. From two other testimonies we learn that this helper was Octave

Walraet, the concierge of the factory. Walraet stated that as soon as Williams noticed that he (Walraet) could do the job, he stopped doing anything. He slept or looked through the window. After Williams had been dismissed, Walraet cut the shirts, assisted by a new helper.

On the basis of these shreds of information, we could argue that Williams's behaviour was probably not impeccable, but that this was not necessarily the main or the only reason why his employer wanted to get rid of him (and his wife). Lousbergs got hold of Williams' patterns and his know-how had been transferred to another member of the personnel, the concierge Octave Walraet. Why pay substantial wages to someone who was not entirely dependable? Hallett, the English vice-consul who tried to come to Williams' rescue by writing a letter to the chairman of the Conseil de Prud'hommes, made an allusion to the fact that the transferral of Williams' expertise had made him superfluous:

> They [Williams and his wife] are at work constantly – eleven hours a day.... They started with two helpers and now they have about 50 and Williams taught those under his supervision the specialized know-how of cutting and manufacture, all the infinite details and secrets of his trade, so that everything could function <u>on its own</u> [underlined by Hallett and written in larger characters].

The vice-consul presented Williams's dismissal as a way of lowering expenses:

> All went well until in December last, general expenses were declared too high and the factory girls had to accept a reduction on all articles, against which they protested vehemently and on 19 March ... after receiving their weekly pay as usual, Williams and his wife were told for the first time the firm did not need them any longer.

The Williams case could therefore be as much about the transfer of know-how and the subsequent redundancy of its former 'owner', as about the unruly behaviour of a foreman. The Conseil de Prud'hommes was not impressed by the employer's accusations either. The breach of contract was declared unjustified and Williams was granted a compensation of 3,575.30 francs.

Dismissed for a Quarrel: The Case of Foreman Dyer Thomas Tetlow. When Thomas Tetlow was hired for six years by dyer Van Damme in 1882, the former knew everything about the trade and Van Damme nothing, so the Conseil de Prud'hommes stated. Van Damme dismissed Tetlow in the beginning of 1885 on the basis of a quarrel. In the session of the Conseil de Prud'hommes the employer was so bold as to admit that since he now knew much more about the trade than in the beginning, he no longer needed Tetlow's costly services. He also argued that the initial contract between him and Tetlow no longer existed, since Tetlow had asked for and received a wage raise in 1884. The Conseil de Prud'hommes concluded that the employer's reaction to a simple quarrel was exaggerated and that he had made use of the event as a pretext to get rid of his foreman. Tetlow was granted compensation.

A Victim of Suspicion: The Case of Foreman Jan Baptiste Van Huffel. In July 1890 Jan Baptiste Van Huffel signed a ten-year contract with Gucquier Gleesener, a Ghent manufacturer of photographic plates. As early as January 1891 he had been fired. The employer reproached the foreman of acting secretively and of withholding knowledge and secrets regarding the fabrication process. He accused Van Huffel of avoiding the performance of experiments in his presence. Moreover Van Huffel took home the booklet in which he had written down all the production secrets and which Gucquier Gleesener considered his property. This raised suspicions whether Van Huffel did not act against the stipulation of the contract forbidding him to reveal production secrets to outsiders. Gucquier Gleesener complained that without the booklet, he was entirely dependent on Van Huffel and that this undermined trust, so that collaboration could not possibly continue.

Van Huffel contested the accusations. He admitted to withdrawing to the solitude of his laboratory, but argued that this was indispensable for the success of his experiments. At any time, he continued, his employer could enter and the latter had never made any remark in this respect. He also admitted taking home the booklet. But since all the secrets, formulas and procedures it contained were his own findings, he really had no need of the book in order to do what his employer insinuated. He had taken home the booklet because he had been on sick leave for five days and he wanted to make up for time lost. The booklet was a draft and he wanted to put it in order. Moreover, it was his responsibility to keep it and no one had ever told him he was not allowed to take it home. Van Huffel insisted that from the first until the last day, his relationship with Gucquier Gleesener had been friendly. His research had improved the fabrication process daily, and in the short period of five months that he had been working there, Gucquier Gleesener's affairs had prospered remarkably. There was no reason to doubt that he had made the utmost use of his knowledge to improve his employer's business.

The Conseil de Prud'hommes concluded that the employer's suspicions were groundless and there was no reason to evict Van Huffel from the factory in disgrace. It was not clear whether the booklet was the employer's property only, the Conseil de Prud'hommes argued, while Van Huffel's ill intent had not been proven. At his employer's request, Van Huffel returned the booklet immediately. The Conseil de Prud'hommes condemned Gucquier Gleesener to paying substantial compensation and the cost of the trial.

Again, we have a case of a foreman whose capacities and know-how were not contested and who clearly contributed to the firm's prosperity, but whose services did not come cheap: a monthly wage of 150 francs and a 7 per cent share in the net profit. The foreman had put the fabrication process on track and his know-how had been recorded in the little manual that was now in the hands of his employer.

Foremen Who Could Not Be Trusted (Any Longer)

Working on His Own Account: The Case of Foreman Brush Maker Adolf Hazebroeck. The file concerning brush maker Adolf Hazebroeck, who had been employed as a foreman at the Brosserie de l'Escaut, is very thin. His employer, Matthys-Pattyn, stated that in his absence Hazebroeck worked on his own account. He used the firm's wood and, according to Matthys-Pattyn, admitted to having sawn and made different objects, which he subsequently smuggled outside. Matthys-Pattyn had made a formal complaint for breach of trust, and the case was in the hands of a regular court. From Matthys-Pattyn's letter we learn that Hazebroeck's wife finished brushes for her husband's employer.

Workplace appropriation or the retaining of waste and surplus material from the production process, as a supplement to monetary earnings, was well known in some branches of industry, especially in the putting-out system. Sometimes manufacturers grudgingly accepted the practice.[23] At the end of the nineteenth century, brush making was still partly a domestic industry, confirmed in this case by the involvement of Hazebroeck's wife. Hazebroeck himself, however, was not a domestic worker, and he appeared to have gone further than appropriating leftovers. Not only did he take wood that was not described as 'waste', but he also stole time. His employer calculated that on one Monday Hazebroeck had worked 8 hours, but while Matthys-Pattyn had to pay his foreman 2.48 francs, Hazebroeck had in fact earned only 0.36 francs. Instead of looking after the interests of his employer, Hazebroeck had deceived him.

Dragging Workers Along to a Pub Instead of Supervising Them: The Case of Foreman Boilermaker Octaaf Haeck. Octaaf Haeck was a foreman boilermaker in the Van de Putte company. In 1909 he signed a contract for five years, but in November 1910 he was fired. Haeck contested his dismissal. A month after being fired Haeck was still unemployed. He complained that this sudden dismissal made it impossible to find another job. Being sent away like this raised suspicions regarding his honesty and craftsmanship. He suspected he would be unable to find a job for a similar wage and duration.

The Conseil de Prud'hommes invited the employer to back up his accusations by witnesses. What was Haeck accused of? Sometimes he was absent from work for a week, he had been warned several times to stop this absenteeism, but he went for a drink after his employer left the client's house, he enticed other workers to leave their work, he failed to prepare work, he did not keep order in the shop, he failed to supervise the workers and he had been found drunk during working hours. The allegations against Haeck read indeed like an inventory of what a foreman should not do. The clerk of the Conseil de Prud'hommes made notes of all the employer's allegations rephrased as questions which were put to the witnesses: do you know that Haeck was sometimes absent for a whole week? etc. The clerk's list ended with the question: do you know anything else about Haeck?

The first witness was Hippoliet Schollaert, a boilermaker employed by Van de Putte. He testified that he had missed an early train to do an urgent job outside Ghent. As he was in the neighbourhood of foreman Haeck's house, he knocked on his door and asked him what he should do. The foreman replied, 'Go tomorrow, no one will bother', after which he took the worker with him to several pubs. A publican testified that Haeck and the worker came to his pub that day, and Haeck was so drunk he had to lead him to the tram. The boilermaker reported the event to his employer. In his testimony he also told the Conseil de Prud'hommes that Haeck was often absent on Mondays.

One might well imagine that the employer found Haeck's attitude offensive. While Schollaert turned to Haeck as a figure of authority, to learn what he should do, Haeck reacted as an accomplice, 'descending' to the level of a worker taking advantage of the lack of supervision. Moreover Haeck was accused of taking off Mondays, while one would expect a foreman to impose a 'modern' work routine, not interrupted by unproductive intermissions. The fact that Haeck knew that the job to be done outside Ghent was urgent and that he made no effort to urge Schollaert to take the next train, worsened his case. Clearly, he was not looking after his employer's interests.

Two other witnesses, an apprentice boilermaker and a stoker, were linked to the event that led to Haeck's dismissal. Haeck and the apprentice boilermaker had a job to do in a place called the English Club. The stoker of the English Club had to be warned to extinguish the fire in the boiler, so that Van de Putte's men would be able to work. Haeck failed to warn the stoker, work could not start and instead of returning to the workshop, Haeck took the apprentice to a pub. In the shop a worker had to be sent home that day because Haeck had failed to prepare his work.

The testimonies of the apprentice boilermaker and the stoker tell us, however, that the employer himself had also been present in the English Club and that he too had forgotten to tell the stoker to extinguish the fire. Later that evening the employer ran into the stoker and asked him whether Haeck had warned him. Too late, the fire in the boiler would last till noon of the following day. The stoker also testified, however, that Haeck had said 'See you tomorrow', thus indicating that they would return to work on the boiler the next day. The stoker told the Conseil he did not believe Haeck, since it would not be the first time he had pulled his leg – and so the fire was kept burning.

Again, we are clearly dealing with a foreman who was not particularly zealous, but in the case of the English Club Haeck did not really mess up. His employer wanted to get rid of him and used the case of the English Club as a pretext. One could also argue that Haeck's ultimate mistake was that he failed to correct the forgetfulness of his employer. The latter was allowed to forget to warn the stoker, but that was not the foreman's privilege: he had to plan and oversee work.

The Conseil de Prud'hommes concluded that Haeck's dismissal was justified. He dragged workers along to the pub instead of supervising them, he neglected to prepare the workers' tasks, he went off to pubs during working hours, he was often absent on Mondays, he neglected his duties in a flagrant way and he gave a pernicious example to his subordinates.

We have already referred to the fact that in a judgement pronounced in 1913, the Conseil de Prud'hommes associated foremen with a 'relatively large liberty' in the performance of their duties. Since Haeck's work consisted among other things in visiting clients, he had a lot of opportunities to exercise that liberty. The latter had to be interpreted, however, as responsible autonomy: someone who looked after the employer's interests even when the latter 'was not looking'. And in that respect Haeck failed the test miserably.

Too Close to His Workers: The Case of Foreman Dyer Emiel Van Loo. In November 1908 Diomède Vanderhaeghen hired foreman dyer Emiel Van Loo. In February 1909 he was fired. A note by the clerk of the Conseil de Prud'hommes summarized what happened. Wednesday after Carnival (*mardi gras*) the workers under Van Loo's supervision were feeling a bit under the weather and so was Van Loo. At 7.45 in the morning Van Loo left the factory and all his men with him. They left without permission or without warning. On Thursday Van Loo and his crew were fined 1 franc each. On Friday, payday, workers protested that the fine was much too high and they asked Van Loo to plead for a fine of 0.50 franc. The manager refused. The workers involved left the factory, followed by Van Loo and the other workers. Van Loo accused Vanderhaeghen of breach of contract. But the latter argued that Van Loo himself had broken his contract by leaving the premises on his own initiative and taking his workers with him. Each party produced witnesses who had to back up the accusation that the other had broken the contract.

Employer Vanderhaeghen's witness declared: 'I don't know what happened in the factory. One day after the event I saw Van Loo and he told me: "It's finished here, I'm off with my crew." He told me he was going to work in the city of Ronse.' Three workers who were part of Van Loo's crew testified also. One of them, August Lippens, declared: 'Wednesday after carnival we didn't feel too well and Van Loo allowed us to leave. On Friday we learnt we had been fined. We were angry and we went to the office where mister Martiny said to us: "You Van Loo (and then he switched to French), you can leave with all your workers.'"

According to the Conseil de Prud'hommes it had been proven that Van Loo had the intention of leaving. 'He accompanied the workers who protested against their fine and left, and these workers rashly followed their leader', the Conseil stated. Reading the Conseil's judgement, it is not very clear who followed whom. However, when commenting on the testimonies of the three workers, the Conseil remarked that the latter were dependent on Van Loo, suggesting that their statements were not very credible.

The relationship between Van Loo and his workers is not clear. His contract refers to him alone, but apparently he could mobilize the whole group. At least, that is the suggestion in the testimony in favour of the employer. In the testimonies in favour of Van Loo, this is not so clear: 'you can leave with your workers' can also refer to the fact that the relationship between the foreman and his workers was much too close. Anyway, Van Loo was acting rather as a representative of 'his' workers than as the incarnation of his employer's authority. He allowed them to leave when they did not feel like working, he pleaded for a reduction of their fine and he joined them when they walked out. This attitude was not appreciated. Glovka Spencer, discussing supervisory personnel in the Ruhr area, notes that fraternization between the ranks and their supervisors was forbidden and that the latter were warned to keep their distance. Harsh supervisors had usually less to fear than foremen who were too lenient.[24]

Indecent Proposals: The Case of Foreman Cooper Frans De Loore. Frans De Loore, a foreman cooper who had been employed by the wood seller Usines d'Evergem for almost twenty years, was fired without notice in July 1906. He was accused of acts contrary to good manners with persons under his supervision. The five witnesses backing up the accusation were not eyewitnesses. Two testimonies came from the victim's colleagues, who saw her right after the event. The two remaining testimonies were from another foreman (who did not want to get involved) and the husband of the victim, who only learnt about the facts afterwards.

Maria Vossaert, twenty-eight years old, wife of Petrus Legiest and day labourer in the Usines d'Evergem, told what had happened to her:

> I heard that my brother was sick, possibly from typhus. I went to look for De Loore to ask him if I could leave at half past eleven. I found him in his office. That office has glass walls. De Loore enquired about my family and since I held my hand to my forehead, he asked me if I had a headache. I nodded and he answered he would take me to the pharmacy, to smell at a bottle. In the pharmacy they cannot see you from the outside. He told me to sit down and let me smell at the bottle.

When I wanted to leave, De Loore placed himself before me and took me in his
arms. The door was shut all the time. He asked me to kiss him and since I did not
want to, he grabbed me by the throat. I told him I was married. He replied: 'What
has that got to do with it? I am married too.' He then took me firmly in his arms,
constantly kicking his belly against me, trying to get under my skirt. I kicked him
in the chest and then he let me go. I had been absent from my work for about
an hour. When I returned to the factory, Maria Helderweerdt asked where I had
been that long. 'You have been in De Loore's claws', she said. First I denied. She
replied: 'Don't deny it, I see his claws in your neck.' After that I told her everything and to Constance De Paepe as well. I asked them not to tell anyone else,
because I was afraid of losing my job. The foremen don't mind our delays, because
we work *à l'entreprise*. There were no other workers around, nor anyone else.

The insistence on the fact that De Loore led her from a room where they
could be seen by the other workers to a room where this was not the case
suggests some premeditation. Maria Vossaert volunteered an explanation for
the fact that the other foremen did not notice her absence: since the workers were paid by the piece and not by time, foremen did not mind delays.
Constance De Paepe testified that she had had a similar experience. She felt
unwell, was taken to the pharmacy by De Loore, who wanted to unloosen her
skirt and told her that according to regulations she had to lie on her back.

Two drivers employed by the Usines d'Evergem testified that they saw the
foreman enter the pharmacy with Maria Vossaert. He let her smell a bottle,
loosened her collar and untied the ribbon of her apron. They declared the
whole scene only took a few minutes while the door was open all the time. It
is remarkable that both drivers gave the same, somewhat unusual time indication: it happened last year, 'in the fruit season', they both reported. This
might suggest that the drivers discussed their declarations beforehand, possibly to attune them. Questioned again, the victim repeated that the door of
the pharmacy had been shut. No account was taken of the fact that the drivers' declarations contradicted the victim's claim that no one had witnessed
the scene, that it had lasted quite a while and that the door had been shut. De
Loore was considered guilty. He received no compensation for the breach of
contract and he had to pay the cost of the trial.

The evidence incriminating De Loore was shaky at best. That both the
employer and the Conseil de Prud'hommes approached it as a clear-cut case
might have been the result of the fact that De Loore could in any case no
longer function as a foreman. Both the workers and his fellow foremen were
aware of the case and this undoubtedly undermined his authority. De Loore
had to go.

De Loore's employer, the Usines d'Evergem, regularly dismissed foremen.
In 1911 Seraphin Van Durme was fired on the spot for insubordination. His
employer refused to pay him the 600 francs compensation he demanded and
Van Durme did not insist.

Favouring 'His' Workers: The Case of Foreman Camiel Duprez. Another fore-man dismissed by the Usines d'Evergem was Camiel Duprez. In 1912 he was fired and accused of paying the female workers of the wood firm for work they had not done. Duprez denied the accusation and demanded six months' wages to compensate for the breach of contract. Six witnesses testified in favour of their employer: two clerks, two other foremen and two female workers. The combination of their testimonies produces the following narrative.

Women working under Duprez had always earned more than their col-leagues working under other foremen. After Duprez had been fired, several of these women left because their wages had fallen. Since wage rates did not change, the conclusion was that Duprez provided advantages for the women under his supervision. The two foremen explained the discrepancies by pointing to the fact that they measured accurately the work done, while Duprez more or less guessed. One of the foremen remarked that Duprez did not count the pieces of wood because he lacked time, since his job was more complicated. Augusta Souris, the 24-year-old worker who had accused Duprez, came forward with another explanation. Duprez always sought the company of one worker, Willemijns. He wanted to favour her and in order to avoid suspicion, he favoured all of her colleagues. Duprez, so Souris told the court, even included the hours that women spent knitting, hidden behind stacks of wood, when there was no work available.

There were also six testimonies in favour of Duprez: the former foreman Seraphin Van Durme and five former workers, among whom four women who had worked under Duprez. These women advanced another explana-tion for the higher wages earned under Duprez. Duprez's successors were less experienced, even had to seek the advice of their subordinates, did not have enough work ready or did not prepare it adequately and when work was slow, they did not distribute it equally among the workers. Moreover, since Duprez left, the women themselves had to carry the wood and that effort cost them time for which they were not paid. Under Duprez' rule another worker was given this task. Two workers asserted that Augusta Souris had sworn she would get even with Duprez if she was given the opportunity. The Conseil de Prud'hommes concluded that the accusation was unjustified and that the discrepancies in wages could have been the result of a different work organization. Duprez received the compensation demanded.

Just as in the case of cutter James Williams, the foreman's organization and preparation of work appeared to be of utmost importance for work-ers' earnings. But we also notice a tendency to rationalize the work process. Camiel Duprez who had worked for the company for at least ten years, had a rather relaxed attitude. He did not count the pieces of wood but hazarded a guess, he did not mind paying workers for some idle moments and he did not demand from them efforts for which they were not paid. His successors had a more 'rational' attitude but lacked Duprez' know-how. When Duprez left, no less than two (one testimony even speaks of three) foremen replaced him. So supervision not only became more strict and punctual, but also required more personnel.

The Foreman Who Did Not Show Up: The Case of Foreman Candy Maker Henri Pauwels. In December 1907 the candy maker Henry Pauwels signed a contract with A. Van Compernolle, the owner of Confiserie Ganda in Ghent. Pauwels lived in Evere, a place near Brussels. The contract contained the stipulation that Pauwels was supposed to work ten hours a day, unless the train between Brussels and Ghent suffered a mishap and arrived late. One day in February 1908 Pauwels did not show up at all. Van Compernolle wrote him a registered letter that same day:

> I was very surprised that you did not come to work today. As a result I could not give the other workers their tasks and since I need someone I can rely on, I have to let you know that I consider our contract as broken.... I am very sorry to have to apply this measure to you, because I was pleased with your work. The only reasons for my decision are your carelessness and negligence.

Clearly, dependability outweighed expertise as a quality required from a foreman. As in the case of Haeck, the foreman's absence prevented the good organization of work in the shop.

The foreman contested the breach of contract and requested either its continuation or compensation. The two parties were reconciled and the foreman received a compensation of 55 francs or the equivalent of almost eight days' work.

The Foreman Who Went on Strike: The Case of Foreman Piano Maker Gustaaf Vander Cruyssen. In August 1912 foreman Gustaaf Vander Cruyssen signed a three-year contract with the piano factory G. & A. Beyer. In January 1913 the foreman was fired because he had been absent in the afternoon without previous warning. Vander Cruyssen contested his dismissal and argued he had been too ill to return to work. He requested the 200 francs compensation provided in the contract in case of an unjustified termination.

Unfortunately the testimonies of the twelve witnesses heard in this case were not in the dossier, so we have only the rather laconic text of the judgement at our disposal. Compensation was granted not to the plaintiff, but to the defendant. According to the Conseil, it had been duly proven that the plaintiff had left work without reason and without giving notice. He had not been too ill to come to work, because he had been seen in town in the company of striking Beyer workers. It appears that several workers were already absent in the morning and that in the afternoon most of the other workers joined them. In the course of the afternoon and the evening, the plaintiff had been seen in the centre of the city, in the company of strikers near the house of a non-striker and at a meeting of the union.

Foreman Vander Cruyssen had thus not only deceived his employer and lied to him, he also appeared to have taken the workers' side in a strike. His presence in town in the company of strikers and at a union meeting put him down as an active participant.

Conclusion

S. Vandecasteele-Schweitzer remarks that there is no such thing as a typical foreman's job. While some men commanded five workers, others had authority over 250. Some foremen were 'drivers', *meneurs d'hommes*, with a rudimentary technical knowledge, while others were specialists in their trade.[25] Several of our foremen appeared to be representative of the foremen in the craft trades, selected on the basis of 'superior expertise and creative imagination'.[26] They were the men with fixed-term contracts, fairly high wages and relative job security, and whose expertise was supposed to contribute to the advancement of the firm. Not all the foremen with a fixed-term contract, however, belonged to this 'aristocracy' of foremen. Some were considered less as keepers of trade secrets than as supervisors of the labour force. Besides these foremen 'with a history', we have the foremen whose story is more difficult to write because their cases were not often documented. They had contracts of indeterminate duration like ordinary workers, could be fired with a week's notice and had wages that were substantially lower.

Although the turn of the century is associated with changes in shop-floor management, we can hardly find a trace of the rationalization of the work process, nor do we encounter foremen whose main preoccupation it was to 'drive' labour and impose discipline. The details of the work process revealed by these stories tell us that we are probably dealing with small companies (but big enough to need one or several foremen) who belonged to the artisanal sector.

No matter how crucial a foreman's expertise and specialized knowledge, he was unable to keep his job if his employer had the impression that he was not dependable and trustworthy. A foreman who had these qualities was able to ensure a fluid flow of work and distribution of tasks, ensuring that workers were able to earn a 'normal' wage and were not sent home or kept idle as a result of disorganization (the cases of Williams, Haeck, Pauwels and the successors of Duprez). The ideal foreman was the embodiment of a responsible autonomy, meaning that he looked after the employer's interests even if the latter was absent or distracted (the case of Haeck and Hazebroeck). The ideal foreman took his work to heart and was not only motivated by the money (the case of Schletter). He also had irreproachable moral standards: he did not take to drinking and he did not sexually harass his subordinates. Such misconduct undermined his authority and the hierarchical relations on the shop floor (the cases of De Loore, Haeck and Williams). Finally, of course, the ideal foreman never failed to remember that he was his employer's representative, rather than the companion of his subordinates (the case of Haeck, Vander Cruyssen, Van Loo and Duprez).

Notes

1. P. Van den Eeckhout, 'Giving Notice: The Legitimate Way of Quitting and Firing (Ghent, 1877–1896)', in *Experiencing Wages: Social and Cultural Aspects of Wage Forms in Europe since 1500*, ed. P. Scholliers and L. Schwarz (Oxford, 2003), 81–109; P. Van den Eeckhout, 'Van werkboekje tot arbeidscontract: De negentiende-eeuwse arbeidsrelaties revisited', *Belgisch Tijdschrift voor Nieuwste Geschiedenis* 35, no. 2–3 (2005): 153–200.
2. T. Watson, *Sociology, Work and Industry* (London, 1995), 139.
3. Van den Eeckhout, 'Giving Notice', 82–83. The Belgian and French archives of the Conseil de Prud'hommes have not been exploited that often. Apart from my own research, see K. Pittomvils, 'Alledaagse arbeidsconflicten in de Gentse textielindustrie: De praktijk van de Werkrechtersraad in de eerste helft van de negentiende eeuw', *Tijdschrift voor Sociale Geschiedenis* 21, no. 2 (1995): 181–211. See also A. Cottereau, 'Justice et injustice ordinaire sur les lieux de travail d'après les audiences prud'homales (1806–1866)', *Le Mouvement Social*, no. 141 (1987): 25–59, and the other contributions in this themed issue of *Le Mouvement Social*.
4. The archives of the Ghent Conseil de Prud'hommes are part of the archives of the Arbeidsrechtbank te Gent, kept in Rijksarchief Beveren. The thirty-one cases concerning foremen follow. Thomas Tetlow: Verslagen van de zittingen, 263, 19 January 1885. Hippoliet Pauwels: Verslagen van de zittingen, 263, 27 December 1887. Jan Baptiste Van Huffel: Verslagen van de zittingen, 264, 20 January 1891. Adolf Hazebroeck: Verslagen van de zittingen, 266, 3 February 1897; Processen-verbaal van verzoening en verzending, 167. Jan Dauwe: Verslagen van de zittingen, 266, 27 August 1897. Jan Baptiste Wasmijn: Processen-verbaal van verzoening en verzending, 168, 4 February 1898. James Williams: Dossiers van verzoening, 219, 1 July 1898; Vonnissen, 293, 19 July, 26 July 1898. Aloïs Desaffel: Verslagen van de zittingen, 266, 26 January 1900; Rol, 243. Gustave Vanden Caspeele: Vonnissen, 295, 30 January 1900. Frans De Loore: Vonnissen, 302, 3, 10, 25 January 1907. Heinrich Kreitzscheck: Vonnissen, 303, 4 February 1908. Henri Pauwels: Processen-verbaal van verzoening en verzending, 21 February 1908. Seraphin De Schrijver: Processen-verbaal van verzoening en verzending, 179, 19 February 1909. Max Schletter: Processen-verbaal van verzoening en verzending, 179, 24 September 1909. Emile Van Loo: Dossiers van verzoening, 225, 9 March 1909; Vonnissen, 304, 6, 26 April, 6 May 1909. Octaaf Haeck: Dossiers van verzoening, 226, 11 December 1909; Vonnissen, 305, 13, 20, 28 December 1910. Jules Van Bellingen: Processen-verbaal van verzoening en verzending, 181, 27 January 1911. Camiel Roselt: Vonnissen, 306, 23 May 1911. Esther Blansaer: Processen-verbaal van verzoening en verzending, 181, 2 June 1911. Leonie Wante: Processen-verbaal van verzoening en verzending, 181, 2 June 1911. Seraphin Van

Durme: Processen-verbaal van verzoening en verzending, 181, 18 August 1911. Jozef Lorez: Dossiers van verzoening, 228, 3 January 1913. Gustaaf Ramont: Verslagen van de zittingen, 267, 10 January 1913. Frans Braem: Vonnissen, 308, 14 January 1913. Frédéric Bauters: Dossiers van verzoening, 228, 26 February 1913; Vonnissen, 308, 1 April 1913. Gustaaf Van der Cruyssen: Vonnissen, 308, 4 March, 15 April 1913. Camiel Duprez: Vonnissen, 308, 20 March, 7 April, 20 May 1913. Désiré Bastin: Verslagen van de zittingen, 267, 5 June 1913; Rol, 245. Henri Dobbelaere: Vonnissen, 308, 1 July 1913. Josef Praet, Vonnissen, 308, 12 August 1913. Vital Baetslé: Verslagen van de zittingen, 267, 10 October 1913; Rol, 245.

5. Van den Eeckhout, 'Giving Notice', 88.
6. F. Laurent, *Principes de droit civil*, 33 vols. (Brussels, 1878), vol. 25, 562–565.
7. Van den Eeckhout, 'Van werkboekje tot arbeidscontract', 182–183; 'Contrat de travail', in *Pandectes belges*, vol. 113 (Brussels, 1921), 414–998, here 896–927, 934.
8. Van den Eeckhout, 'Giving Notice', 90.
9. Ibid., 89.
10. Ibid., 84–86.
11. Ibid., 88.
12. Ibid., 87; Van den Eeckhout, 'Van werkboekje tot arbeidscontract', 173–179.
13. Van den Eeckhout, 'Giving Notice', 99.
14. Watson, *Sociology, Work and Industry*, 141.
15. A. Fox, *Beyond Contract: Work, Power and Trust Relations* (London, 1974), 37.
16. E. Geerkens, *La rationalisation dans l'industrie belge de l'entre-deux-guerres* (Brussels, 2004), 53.
17. Foreman dyer Thomas Tetlow was born in Manchester in 1850. According to the population register, he lived with his parents in Ledeberg near Ghent in 1866. He married a girl from Ghent and in 1891 moved back to Manchester with his whole family (Gemeente Ledeberg, Bevolkingsregister, 1866, 1880, 1890). We already learnt that cutter James Williams and his wife were recruited in England. In the session of the Conseil de Prud'hommes, cutter Camiel Roselt declared he 'had been invited by his employer to leave the city of Rouen to come and work for him'. Roselt was not a Frenchman but a Belgian, born in Merchtem, but he moved regularly: he married in Paris and one of his children was born in Charleville, a town in the northeast of France (Stad Gent, Bevolkingsregister, 1910). Foundry foreman Max Schletter was born in Michten in Saxony (Stad Gent, Bevolkingsregister, 1900). Foreman in galvanizing Heinrich Kreitzscheck was born in Hamm in Westphalia (Gemeente Gentbrugge, Bevolkingsregister, 1890, 1900).
18. S. Pollard, *The Genesis of Modern Management: A Study of the Industrial Revolution in Great Britain* (Harmondsworth, 1968), 207–209.
19. K. Bruland, 'Skills, Learning and the International Diffusion of Technology: A Perspective on Scandinavian Industrialisation', in *Technological Revolutions in Europe: Historical Perspectives*, ed. M. Berg and K. Bruland (Cheltenham, 1998), 161–187, here 180.
20. Around 1900, four foremen in the Ghent machine building industry earned 1,560 francs, 2,168.40 francs, 1,742 francs and 1,430 francs per year, respectively: P. Scholliers, *De Gentse metaalbewerkers in de 19e eeuw: De enquête van L. Varlez* (Brussels, 1985), appendix. In 1900, the Ghent Voortman factory paid the foremen of the weaving and spinning department 1,120.60 and 1,523.08 francs per year respectively: G. Avondts et al., *De Gentse textielarbeiders in de 19e en 20e eeuw: Lonen in de spinnerij van het bedrijf A. Voortman–N.V. Texas 1835–1914* (Brussels, 1976), 78; G. Avondts et al., *De Gentse textielarbeiders in de 19e en 20e eeuw: Lonen in de weverij van het bedrijf A. Voortman–N.V. Texas 1835–1925* (Brussels, 1979), 47.
21. S. Vandecasteele-Schweitzer, 'Comment peut-on être contremaître?' in *L'usine et le bureau: Itinéraires sociaux et professionnels dans l'entreprise XIXe et XXe siècles*, ed Y. Lequin and S. Vandecasteele (Lyon, 1990), 93–108, here 95; A. Dewerpe, 'Les pouvoirs du sens

pratique: Carrières professionnelles et trajectoires des chefs d'atelier de l'Ansaldo (Gênes, 1900–1920)', in *L'usine et le bureau: Itinéraires sociaux et professionnels dans l'entreprise XIXe et XXe siècles*, ed. Y. Lequin and S. Vandecasteele (Lyon, 1990), 109–150, here 110; E. Glovka Spencer, 'Between Capital and Labor: Supervisory Personnel in Ruhr Heavy Industry before 1914', *Journal of Social History* 9, no. 2 (1975): 178–192, here 184.

22. D. Nelson, *Managers and Workers: Origins of the Twentieth-Century Factory System in the United States, 1880–1920* (Madison, 1995), 42.

23. R. Soderlun, '"Intended as a Terror to the Idle and Profligate": Embezzlement and the Origins of Policing in the Yorkshire Worsted Industry, c. 1750–1777', *Journal of Social History* 31, no. 3 (1998): 647–669.

24. Glovka Spencer, 'Between Capital and Labor', 187–188.

25. Vandecasteele-Schweitzer, 'Comment peut-on être contremaître', 95.

26. J. Melling, '"Non-Commissioned Officers": British Employers and Their Supervisory Workers, 1880–1920', *Social History* 5, no. 2 (1980): 183–221, here 191.

CHAPTER 5

'TO ORGANISE LIBERTY'

Foremen and the Effort Bargain during British Industrialization

James A. Jaffe

Among both management professionals and academics, the debate on the role of the foreman in modern industry has been both extensive and instructive. To some extent, it might even be accurate to say that the 'science' of modern management in Europe grew out of a clash of ideas over just this issue. One historian has convincingly shown that the role of the foreman was an especially key issue distinguishing Frederick W. Taylor's American system of scientific management from that of one of the leading French management experts, Henri Fayol. According to Donald Reid, 'one of the things for which Fayol is best known is differing with Taylor on the value of functional foremen. Taylor argued that specialisation was the most efficient form of management: there should be one foreman for each of eight aspects of the worker's job. Such a thought was anathema to Fayol, who believed that no employee should receive orders from more than one source'.[1]

Fayol's method of 'positive administration' published in his *Administration industrielle et générale* in 1916, has now become most widely associated with the notion that administrative authority and responsibility should be expressed in a uniform hierarchical business structure embodied in the authority of a single individual such as a chief executive officer. The irony that such an 'American' management system was expressed first by a Frenchman has not been lost upon Fayol's commentators.[2] However, as Reid's research has shown, Fayol's vision of the structure of authority within the firm was also based largely on an artisanal understanding of the labour process. Drawing upon his experience as a mining engineer, Fayol delegated extensive independent authority to small work-groups, which he celebrated for their 'ingenuity, adaptability, and

---

Notes for this chapter begin on page 127.

productivity'.[3] Management's task, correspondingly, was not to control the point of production, but, on the contrary, to facilitate as best as possible the output of these independent work-groups. As one early commentator noted, 'For Fayol ... the problem was much less to extract the extreme element of a mechanical determinism than to organise liberty.'[4]

This century-old debate on the role of management has direct relevance for the historical cases presented here. In particular, it will be suggested below that managers and foremen during the period of early industrialization often behaved in a manner that foreshadowed Fayol's theorization of 'positive administration'. That is, they delegated extensive authority to work-groups on the shop floor and perceived their role as facilitators of production – ensuring the delivery of materials, organizing transport to and from the shop floor to the point of sales, etc. – rather than as Taylorist rationalizers of labour. To be sure, Dickensian tales of abuse and exploitation were no doubt real, but many, if not most, foremen functioned within the limits of an artisanal world of work that often restrained the desire to control the point of production in favour of an even greater desire to maintain and promote output.

Unfortunately, our understanding of management during this period has not kept pace with our understanding of the economic and social history of the early industrial period. Despite the explosive growth seen in the fields of management and organizational theory during the past two decades, the study of early industrial management in Britain has arguably not yet produced a monograph to supplement or supplant Sidney Pollard's *The Genesis of Modern Management: A Study of the Industrial Revolution in Great Britain*, published in 1965.[5] Without doubt, Pollard's book was a remarkable *tour de force* and both students and historians can still gather a wealth of information from it that is not available elsewhere. However, it is also not unfair to say that the current interest in, arguments about, and understanding of Britain's industrial revolution have changed considerably since the mid-1960s, a development that Pollard himself expected to see happen.[6] Historians' understanding of both the rate and intensity of British industrialization is now substantially different than it was forty years ago. Perhaps the time has come to provisionally evaluate how such changes in the way historians now understand the industrialization of Britain may affect their assumptions about the nature and function of management during this period.

I am referring here, perhaps too obliquely, to the 'gradualist' model of British industrialization most closely associated with the work of N. F. R. Crafts and C. Knick Harley, a view, it should be noted, that has not gone unchallenged.[7] The Crafts-Harley model posits a much slower pace of industrialization for Great Britain, an 'industrial revolution' that was characterized by, among other things, the relatively limited use of steam power, low labour productivity, a limited range of exports, and the persistence of small-scale units of enterprise. While the precise speed and extent of the structural transformation of the British economy may still be a matter of some dispute, it is now generally accepted that both small and large-scale firms employing artisanal production techniques continued to constitute a substantial, and in many sectors a preponderant, position in the British economy well into the nineteenth century.[8] One prominent survey of the period up to the late nineteenth century describes this 'economy of manufacture' in the following manner:

> The production system of the period ... was an economy of manufacture. It was not an industrial economy as we came to understand the term in the twentieth century. The application of machine technology and science to production, the factory as the typical worksite of the productive process, and managerial bureaucratisation and hierarchy are the key elements to an industrial economy. Yet this manner of organising the production of goods did not emerge in Britain until the end of the nineteenth century, after which it came to dominate the economy for the next hundred years. By contrast, the economy of the period 1680 to 1880 was an economy directed by customary methods rather than one driven by 'modern' forms. The enormous and growing productive capacity of the economy was achieved through small-scale units of production – the workshop and the home preponderantly. It was an economy where technology continued to move at the speed determined by the hand rather than the reverse.[9]

Parenthetically, it should be noted that even the most prominent critics of the 'gradualist' model emphasize nevertheless the dynamism of the artisan economy during the nineteenth century as well as its expansion, which often complemented and supplemented the rise of factory production.[10]

If the 'economy of manufacture' was indeed the preponderant form of industrial organization throughout the classic period of industrialization, then our understanding of the role and function of foremen and management during this period necessarily requires substantive revision as well. The challenge before us, therefore, is to bring the theoretical and ethnographic insights of the current literature on management and the supervisory process to bear upon our understanding of the role of foremen and managers in the industrial relations process of early nineteenth-century Britain. Towards this goal, it is also especially important to keep in mind that, despite the impression that may have been left by the description quoted above, the growth and expansion of the artisanal economy during the nineteenth century did not rely solely upon small-scale units of production. Large-scale units of production based upon the 'economy of manufacture', sometimes comprised of a conglomeration or coordination of smaller-scale workshops, were also common in many sectors, including metallurgy, shipbuilding and pottery.[11] Especially in the case of mining, as Fayol clearly understood, large-scale enterprises based upon massive capital investments could be built largely upon autonomous, skilled work-groups. The quotidian process of shop-floor industrial relations entailed by the management and supervision of these work-groups during the early industrial era is the subject of this essay.

As Pollard noted long ago, there is a real 'danger of treating all industries as if they belonged to a single process called the "industrial revolution"'. This is especially so if this phenomenon is associated principally with the rise of the factory-system and the process of deskilling brought about by mechanization.[12] Berg has quite rightly stressed 'the pluralism of manufacturing structures' that characterized the early industrial period, a phrase that appropriately captures the variety of workplace experiences in the burgeoning manufacturing economy.[13]

The Effort Bargain and the Economy of Manufacture

Given the artisanal nature of the 'economy of manufacturing', all grades of supervisory personnel were continually confronted by the problem of how to elicit as much effort as possible from workers who controlled the pace and intensity of their own labour as well as the distribution and dissemination of production information. It is precisely this asymmetric distribution of control and information that is the most salient feature of what has come to be called the 'effort bargain'.

The concept of the effort bargain is associated primarily with the industrial sociologist Wilhelm Baldamus who used the term to describe the shop-floor negotiating process that sought to standardize the exchange of workers' effort for pay and output.[14] Baldamus described the effort bargain in this way: 'The formal wage contract is never precise in stipulating how much effort is expected for a given wage (and vice versa). The details of the arrangement are left to be worked out through the direct interaction between the partners of the contract. If a worker slackens his effort at one moment, the foreman's job is to remind him, as it were, that he departs from his obligations, and, in certain circumstances, it is quite possible that there may be some haggling between the two as to what is a "fair" degree of effort in relation to the wages paid.'[15] Over an extended period of time, Baldamus added elsewhere, through 'the course of the day-to-day interactions between workers in a given situation, and between workers and management, normative attitudes become standardized as a result of mutual adjustments in current conceptions of effort and earnings'.[16]

In other words, the capitalist work situation is not best described as a simple cash nexus. This is primarily because effort is not a tangible commodity that can be exchanged in the same manner as a neoclassical market transaction. As Hilde Behrend noted almost fifty years ago: 'In normal market situations, no difficulty arises in defining the commodity that is being bought, but with labour the difficulty is that the "article" that is being bought is not only difficult to define but impossible to measure. For what is being bought is a supply of effort for performing varying work assignments. Effort, however, is not a substance that can be measured. Only the effect of the application of effort – output – can be measured. Effort itself is a subjective experience, like utility.'[17] Therefore, shop-floor work presents repeated opportunities to bargain over just how much work effort is acceptable for any given amount of compensation; opportunities that may equally result in conflict or cooperation.[18] For example, any change in the quality of raw materials, the standards of production, the design or style of finished products, the speed of production, or a myriad of other changes to the production process, becomes an opportunity to re-negotiate the bargain of effort for pay.

In this shop-floor bargaining process, a worker's bargaining power is ultimately derived from his or her control of their expenditure of effort, their 'labour power' as Marx might say. Conversely, a manager's power is ultimately derived from their authority to fine, monitor or dismiss. While managers certainly possess as strong a motive to impose their authority as workers possess to resist subordination, both workers and managers nevertheless face significant costs if the shop-floor relationship is broken. Workers, of course, face the loss of income, employment, and status; managers, on the other hand, face the costs of hiring and training replacements, and, perhaps more importantly, the disruption of production and output. Both, therefore, while working within the context of a 'structured antagonism',[19] simultaneously entertain significant incentives to maintain the employment relationship; that is, to strike a bargain that satisfies both parties. If such an effort bargain can be settled and standardized, then both parties will attain a significant goal; workers may secure stability of employment and income while managers may attain a predictable level of output. Yet every bargain is necessarily a temporary one. Especially in an era of handicraft production, constant variations in inputs lead to renewed negotiations and bargaining. Thus, the effort bargain is neither a one-off deal sealed at the point of hiring nor does it necessarily result in a zero-sum solution. Both managers and workers bargain repeatedly over the course of a year and both have a stake, although certainly not necessarily a proportionate one, in the outcome.

One final point needs to be made: effort bargaining does not occur *in vacuo*, nor does it depend solely on economically rational cost-benefit analyses. Instead, the demands presented or exhibited in the effort bargain, as Baldamus observed, are ultimately circumscribed by normative values of what is fair, just and proper. That is, workers and managers bring to the effort bargain a range of social, cultural as well as economic expectations of what constitutes 'a fair day's work for a fair day's pay'. Moreover, as in any bargaining situation, the effort bargain rests upon even more subtle and complex personal exchanges of trust, honour and reputation, all of which play an important role in the success or failure of bargaining. In the end, therefore, normative cultural values are as important, or perhaps even more important, than market mechanisms in the management and employment of labour during Britain's industrial revolution.

Foremen and the Effort Bargain in the British Coal Industry

Evidence of effort bargaining is necessarily difficult to come by not only because of the shortage of sources available for such an analysis during this period, but also because of the natural 'opacity of the workplace', as Clive Behagg calls it.[20] However, sometimes one can catch a glimpse of it in the surviving correspondence or personal papers of early industrial foremen and managers. Two such groups were the 'overmen' and 'viewers' of England's northern coal industry. In Pollard's estimation, the coal viewers were 'perhaps the single most important group of professionals with managerial functions' in all of British industry. Their expertise was both scientific and managerial, and their responsibilities included the technical planning of the exploitation of collieries, including ventilation, support and excavation, as well as the conduct of industrial relations with the coal miners, especially hiring and wage negotiations.[21] Overmen, on the other hand, performed the activities more akin to that of a shift foreman and were generally responsible for monitoring production at an individual pit and assessing fines for poor workmanship. Since fines could significantly affect a miner's income, overmen were necessarily also involved in the effort bargain.

A relatively direct expression of the effort bargain is revealed in the correspondence between Lord Delaval and his coal viewer, John Bryers in 1804. In October of that year, Bryers was responsible for conducting the annual hiring of coal miners and negotiating their annual contract, the so-called bond. Under the right circumstances, the miners could demand 'binding money' or signing bonuses, if their labour was in great demand throughout the coalfield. If the viewers did not act quickly enough to engage them, their mines might be undermanned for the coming year, a situation that could severely limit their firm's production and profitability. Conversely, they might be forced to hire less skillful workers, which ultimately would have the same effect of reducing output.

In either case, viewer's investments in signing bonuses would be repaid in profits only if workers reciprocated by working harder and producing more. This simple effort bargain seems to be what Bryers reckoned on when he laid out several hundred pounds extra to sign 121 miners in 1804. 'The Pitmen's binding money', he explained to Lord Delaval, 'is an exceeding great sum and is to be paid tomorrow Evening for such as wishes to go to Newcastle the following day.' However, Bryers added this revealing note: 'I hope they will be grateful & make it up in work during the ensuing year, they promise fair, & we will not fail to remind them of their duty if they are not industrious.'[22]

Such a plain pronouncement of the way in which the effort bargain functioned as both an exchange of unpredictable levels of effort for pay as well as an exchange of honour and reputation is rare. Bryers obviously could not predict or control the miners' output for the coming year because it depended almost entirely on how much physical labour they chose to exert, or, in other words, how hard they worked. He could hope, however, that they would be trustworthy enough to uphold their promise to provide a fair day's work, a notion that had contained some sense of what was considered by both management and employees as acceptable and appropriate hours or output. This sense of what was appropriate and acceptable was culturally inscribed in the daily work practices and expectations that had developed in the northern coalfield over time. The effort bargain was thus a unique form of exchange that relied on cultural notions of trust and honour to regulate unpredictable levels of effort. In the example given here, the foreman and viewer's role was to secure adherence to these cultural codes of conduct as much as it was to monitor production.

A far more detailed and lengthy account of a complex effort bargain can be found in the diaries of Matthias Dunn, the coal viewer for Hetton Colliery in County Durham. This evidence concerns the rather obscure job of 'stowing coals', a job that required the miner to separate out the small, less valuable pieces of coal from the larger, higher priced pieces. The small coal was then stowed away in the mine and not raised to the surface.[23] In November 1831, Dunn attempted to introduce this practice. Because it required more effort, however, most firms offered higher piece rates for separation and stowing, but they also imposed stiff fines on the miners who did not adequately perform the extra labour. When Dunn first considered introducing separation, he contemplated offering the miners a bonus of approximately 7.5 per cent in return for the extra effort.[24]

Within a week, however, he had decided against this bonus system and instead offered to the miners at one of the pits in the colliery a much more sizable advance in piece rates amounting to just about 20 per cent. After conducting some trials, Dunn met with the some of the miners to discuss the implementation of this new plan. 'Had a meeting', he wrote in his diary, 'with four of the Delegates [of the miners] upon the stowing of Small Coal [;] a great deal of Discussion ensued but a meeting is necessary before any decision can be come to upon the subject.'[25] The miners' ultimate resistance to the taking up this offer and their unwillingness to expend the extra effort was noticeable, however. In the following weeks, Dunn complained repeatedly of the failure of the men to separate and stow the small coal in each of the colliery's four major pits. At the Blossom pit, Dunn noted that he had to be 'severe on [the overman] Geo. Armstrong for paying so little attention to the general orders regarding the stowing of Small Coal and other minor arrangements in his pit'.[26] At the Isabella pit, he noted that the 'stowing of Small [was] going on very tardily indeed'. In the George pit, the 'stowing of Small [was] rather doing better here, but far from complete yet' and in the Minor pit there was 'very little progress making in the stowing of Small Coals'. 'Work rather falling off generally', Dunn finally lamented.[27]

The role of the foremen, or overmen, in this effort bargain is especially interesting. Dunn was well aware of the fact that if the work was going to be executed properly he needed his overmen to enforce and supervise the change in working practices. In late November 1831, he therefore met the eight overmen employed at the colliery and 'gave the most positive injunctions to all the Overmen regarding the stowing of Small Coal'.[28] Almost immediately, however, their resistance to the plan was made known. On 7 December, both miners and overmen appeared at Dunn's office with 'serious charges given regarding Small Casting'.[29] As the month progressed, very little change appears to have occurred in the attitudes of either the men or their foremen. As late as 28 December, Dunn was complaining that there was 'still great deficiency in the article of Stowing Small Coals, as well as attention to Horses, Hay, Water, Incline Sheaves and Sundry nick nacks, entirely hinging on the management of the Overmen'.[30]

By the first week of January 1832, Dunn's frustration with his overmen was becoming even more pronounced. Surveying the Minor West pit, he expressed a 'considerable cause for fault finding in [the overman] Rob Frazers Conduct, no nicety nor pointedness [?] of arrangement whatever, the stowing of Small Coal is also dwindling away very much – Gave Rob Frazer a very severe talking to'.[31] The very next day, Dunn's survey of the Minor East pit noted a 'very great laxity of Conduct observable here also, was very severe indeed upon both [the overman] Maugham & some of his deputies'. Dunn concluded that 'if some better order cannot be obtained some virtual Change must be made amongst these Overmen – Neither as [to] the work regulated, Small [coal] Cast, nor any thing managed in a satisfactory way'.[32]

There is no surviving evidence that will fully explain the overmen's resistance. The surviving autobiography of a wagon-way wright suggests that overmen were generally quite contemptuous of the men who worked under them.[33] If that is so, then there must have been an exceptionally powerful impetus to bring the two groups together at the door of their supervisor. One possible reason is that, despite the financial incentives offered to the miners, there may have been some fear that the additional effort involved in separation and stowing may have adversely affected output. For the miners, of course, they could not be sure whether this new effort bargain would repay the additional expenditure of effort. For the overmen, any decline in output held the potential of threatening their job performance and security. The industrial relations literature cites numerous examples of foremen and workers conniving to standardize production and output on the shop floor.[34] Perhaps this is a very early example of such a connivance in the face of the imposition of new job practices that threatened to disrupt production standards and to re-open the effort bargain.

Faced with such determined resistance, Dunn eventually sought the owners' backing for a new plan to close some of the pits and transfer the redundant miners to the remaining open pits. The extra labour, he thought, might be a way to carry into effect the process of separation. However, fearing this might precipitate a strike, the owners refused to support their manager. 'The [owners'] Committee decide', Dunn noted in his diary, 'that as the men might object to have such an arrangement carried into Effect, + Stick [i.e. strike] that therefore it had better be deferred.'[35] Dunn's effort to elicit the extra effort necessary for stowing small coal did not end there. For the next several months his diary is replete with entries bemoaning the failures of his overmen to enforce stowing and the continued recalcitrance of the miners.[36] Ultimately, he admitted to being utterly baffled as to why he could not get the miners to accept this new effort bargain. 'They resist the stowing back of Small Coals', he wrote, 'under the idea that some ulterior trick is meant to be played [on] them.'[37] He could go no further than to surmise that 'the men see an object in refusing to cast', but he seemed to have very little clue as to what that object may have been.[38]

In fact, uncovering the miners' objective here may tell us a great deal about early industrial management and supervision. At one level, it would appear that the coal miners' objective was simply to withhold the expenditure of effort that was their half of the effort bargain. Their resistance, some may surmise, was a customary response by pre-capitalist, non-rational workers seeking to protect the property of their labour from the encroachment of rational, scientific management. However, as the industrial sociologist Donald Roy pointed out some time ago, contemporary notions of rational behaviour are ill-suited to the analysis of workplace behaviour. In his well-known observations, management attempts at introducing new, more efficient work practices on the shop floor had the unintended effect of disrupting production and lowering earnings. It was left to the shop floor workers themselves to bypass and undermine managerial orders to revive output and restore their earnings. As Roy concluded from his study: 'Does it not appear that operatives and their allies resisted managerial "logics of efficiency" because application of those "logics" tended to produce something less than "efficiency"? Did not worker groups connive to circumvent managerial ukase in order to "get the work out" ...? May not the common query of industrial workers, "What in the hell are they trying to do up there?" be not merely reflective of faulty communication but also based on real managerial inadequacy?'[39] It seems unlikely, therefore, that conflict between customary work practices and rationalization is necessarily the key to understanding the miners' resistance. In this case, we are especially fortunate to have surviving evidence that gives us further insight into not only how this effort bargain proceeded, but the principles and norms upon which the bargain was being informally negotiated. Over the course of the next several months, a cycle of retribution appears to have developed after Dunn sought to enforce the separation and stowing of small coal. While the miners resisted by withholding their work effort, Dunn increasingly imposed work fines and other penalties, which evoked even greater hostility and resistance. At one point, in March 1832, twelve representatives of the miners delivered a petition to the owners asking for Dunn to be discharged. The owners' committee 'received the Petition with suitable disgust', Dunn wrote in his diary, 'refusing to see the Deputation but returning a written answer in the most decisive terms'.[40]

Still, the effort bargaining did not cease altogether. By the first week of April, the owners and men appear to have made some headway toward an agreement on a plan that would have standardized the precise amount of coal to be separated and stowed.[41] Considering the fact that the amount of small coal that had to be separated and stowed varied almost daily, this proposed settlement would have had the effect of securing predictability of both earnings and output. However, at this time, the owners made a serious miscalculation. They insisted that the miners' annual contract be revised to include a clause, the ninth clause to be exact, requiring the stowing of small coals.[42] And it is here at last that we come to a full understanding of why the miners were so determined to withhold their effort. In a public handbill, the coal miners explained that it was 'this ninth clause, the alteration of which is resisted, is the grievance'.

> It says, 'that each hewer [miner] shall cast aside or stow away in the mine the small coals made in the *nicking* and *kirving*, for which he shall be paid by valuation.' On the face of it, this seems fair enough, but like many other parts of the Bond [the annual contract], it is framed only to deceive. *There is no quantity of small coals specified in the clause* [emphasis added], and when the Viewer examines the quantity cast aside, which he does once a fortnight, if he pleases to think the quantity is not sufficiently large, he orders the Overman or *Keeker* to fine the hewers 2s. 6d. for not stowing away enough, without deigning to examine whether what he considers enough could by any possibility, in fair working, be obtained.[43]

The coal miners, therefore, did not protest the rationalization of work practices through the introduction of the principle of separation of small coal nor did they resist the principle of fines, both of which were undeniably onerous. The object of their resistance was to gain a set of working rules that precisely defined how much effort they were to expend on the stowing of small coal. As Baldamus suggested, the indeterminacy of labour effort was at the root of this effort bargaining. The miners' goal was to standardize the terms of their effort bargain and to limit the unpredictability of their earnings. Therefore, they were most concerned to specify how much extra work was to be expected from them for the additional pay. That is, they needed to seal the effort bargain.

It is quite rare indeed to get such a full and lengthy account of the development of industrial relations at this shop-floor level for this period in British history. And yet it points to one further aspect of the effort bargain that was of great importance to management and other supervisory personnel. In particular, that is the role played by normative values, especially of 'fairness' in establishing the standards about which the effort bargain is determined. As has already been noted, the importance of such normative values, or what are sometimes referred to among economists as 'reputation effects', is derived from the fact that the effort bargain is a unique form of exchange, one that depends not upon the exchange of one tangible commodity for another tangible commodity, but upon the exchange of one tangible commodity, money or pay, for a range of possible work efforts.

Indeed George Akerlof, the Nobel prize-winning economist, in a justly famous article, suggested that neoclassical models of the work relationship explained very little about the behaviour of workers and managers.[44] 'The norm ... for the proper work effort', he wrote, 'is quite like the norm that determines the standards of gift giving at Christmas. Such gift giving is a trading relationship – in the sense that if one side of the exchange does not live up to expectations, the other side is likely to curtail its activities.'[45] He went on to construct an enormously influential argument that explained the work relationship as a partial gift exchange based upon norms of fairness established by outside social references rather than by market mechanisms. Simply put, Akerlof's 'fair wage hypothesis' was that average workers would work harder than stipulated by the firm's basic work rules if they could reliably expect to receive a fair, not a market, wage in return.

There were numerous ways in which 'fairness' could be expressed on the shop floors of industrializing Britain. Higher wages, seniority systems, short-time working and other management techniques appear to have been pioneered during this era in pursuit of just this effect.[46] In the example of effort bargaining between coal viewers, overmen, and coal miners, we have seen the latter struggling to clarify the circumstances under which additional pay and potential for fines could be fairly exchanged for the greater effort involved. These examples suggest that during the early industrial period, the art of management was less concerned with pushing forward the 'frontier of control' than with successfully negotiating the 'contested terrain' of the shop floor in order to establish working rules and practices that could be deemed 'fair'. In this way, both output and earnings could become more predictable and reliable in a manufacturing economy.

Foremen and the Culture of Bargaining in the London Printing Trades

Foremen therefore often found themselves acting a marginal role in mining, enforcing but not formulating the rules established by management and yet dependent upon the workers to expend the necessary effort to sustain production.[47] By way of further explication of these issues, attention will now be directed to the London printing trades, a trade whose activities took place in an environment more akin to the archetypal artisan workshop. Both the northern coal mines and the London printing shops, however, shared several features in common. In both workplaces, control of the shop floor was largely delegated to skilled, independent work-groups. Moreover, in both workplaces, foremen found themselves playing an ambiguous and marginal role in the effort bargain. In the northern coal industry and in the London printing trades, foremen could as easily find themselves at odds with their skilled employees over working prices and practices as they could find themselves in conflict with their own employer over the imposition of authority and discipline which threatened to disrupt output.

In October 1833, for example, Mr. Tugwell, an overseer at Bentley's printing house found himself in just such an ambiguous situation.[48] The quite complicated issue in this dispute concerned whether the work being done by the compositors should be cast up as 'slips', that is, as unfinished proof sheets, or as finished book pages, a process that included, among other things, extra pay for the insertion of extra spacing between lines. Commonly, slips were made up when a great many alterations were expected to be made before the finished page was set and compositors often made up these proof sheets without charge or at significantly reduced piece rates. However, Bentley, the master printer, apparently tried to circumvent this practice by having nearly finished pages of a book set as slips thereby getting portions of the book typeset for far less than they otherwise might have been.

The dispute evolved into a direct confrontation between the master printer and the compositors on the shop floor. According to the only surviving account, Bentley, the printing master, at one point in the dispute, turned to Tugwell and demanded that he cast up the 'slips' as an example for the men. Tugwell was thus put in the unenviable situation of obeying his employer and thus alienating the workmen ostensibly subordinate to him or supporting the workmen and thus angering his employer. His response perhaps illustrates the ambiguity of his position. He turned to the workers and refused to undertake the job unless the compositors approved. The papers of the London Union of Compositors record what happened next: 'Mr. Bentley was much surprised by this refusal, and told Mr. T.[ugwell] that he ought to do every thing which he ordered him to do, as a soldier obeys his general; and that if he would make the matter up, he (Mr. Bentley) would preserve him from harm. Mr. Tugwell refused, and Mr. Bentley instantly discharged him.'[49]

The confusion attendant upon the marginal role of the foremen is quite evident here. To the employer, the foreman was no more and no less than a soldier in the ranks of management whose job was first and foremost to obey orders. However, the foreman himself apparently viewed his role quite differently, acknowledging, in fact, the importance of the acquiescence of the compositors. As was the case of the miners' overman described earlier, this foreman's explanation of his actions, whether public or private, will never be known. However, some suggestions as to his motivations may be offered. It is quite possible that he acted as he did in order to safeguard his honour and reputation. For future employment, especially in the highly organized London printing trades, such attributes may have been essential to securing an effective effort bargain. Tugwell's ability to manage the shop floor, especially to negotiate working practices and prices may have been seriously compromised by what would have appeared as an abject submission to the master printer. Especially in situations in which bargaining is frequent and repeated, as on the shop floors of printing houses where bargaining might take place over each new printing job, such 'reputation effects' may have taken on even greater significance. Based upon qualities such as honour and fairness in bargaining, trust became an essential element of successful negotiations. Without such trust, the foreman's ability to ensure a reliable and predictable output from the shop may have been seriously or even irreparably eroded.

Foremen's and managers' interest in and attempts to build such reputations of honour and fairness, I would suggest, was not uncommon during this era in large part because under conditions of artisanal production management readily ceded direct control of the shop floor to skilled work-groups. Naturally, this did not prevent strikes, output restriction, or other forms of industrial conflict. Workers and employers still operated within the context of a 'structured antagonism'. However, the foreman's role was not in every case to exert direct control over the production process, especially if the attempt to do so threatened output. In the age of manufacturing, it was much more important for foremen to maintain production than seize control of the shop floor. Thus, it was not at all unusual to find foremen straddling the line between exercising authority and conspiring to maintain output.

Another such example comes from December 1831 when the overseer at Ryder's printing house in London asked the compositors' union to determine the piece rates for the printing of the *Calendar of the Persons in Clerkenwell Prison*. Here is an extraordinary case in which the shop foremen consulted with the workers' union before agreeing upon an effort bargain. According to the union records, two compositors, Messrs. Smouton and Crathern, representing the workers at Ryder's, came before the union leadership committee. 'The gentlemen then stated', the report explains

> that they sought the opinion of the Committee, not because the Work was in dispute, but in order to ascertain how the Work ought to be paid; and they were induced to act thus by the advice of the Overseer at Mr. Ryder's, who wished them to get advice upon the subject, and they considered that the overseer would think himself bound to abide by the decision of the Union Committee.[50]

The union committee, for its part, thought long and hard about this issue. They examined at least six different specimens of previous publications of the *Calendar* and voted on at least two separate motions as well as one amendment. Their eagerness to get this decision right was noticeable. In part, as I have described elsewhere, this was because the union was young and it was attempting to regulate compositors' piece rates throughout London.[51] Clearly, however, both the union and the overseer were seeking to establish reputations for cooperation and fairness apparently in an effort to more reliably predict both future pay and production.

In one final case, the overseer's desire to maintain output rather than control the shop floor is perhaps most apparent in the very lengthy dispute over 'wrappers' that plagued the printing business for several years during the mid-1830s. 'Wrappers' were the paper mailing covers used for journals, magazines, and other periodicals. As the market for weeklies and monthlies grew significantly during the second quarter of the nineteenth century, the question of whether and how much master printers should pay for composing 'wrappers' became an increasingly important and vexatious issue. In most cases, the masters refused to pay for printing up these wrappers claiming that it was customary not to do so. The compositors, on the other hand, finding that printing wrappers was an increasingly onerous task, demanded their effort bargains be renegotiated to have this task taken into account.

One of the first major disputes over wrappers occurred at the printing house of Gilbert & Rivington in June 1834.[52] At that time, three compositors had been dismissed for refusing to work on a job without being paid for casting up the wrappers. After some discussions in which the printing masters stated their opposition to paying for wrappers, the overseer intervened and approached three other compositors to undertake the job. When 'the question was put to him [the overseer] if the wrapper was to be given up with the job, and he answered in the negative', the compositors responded by claiming that they 'would not touch it under the circumstances'.

The employer's and overseer's subsequent responses are indicative of both the ambiguous position of foremen as well as the importance placed upon honour in the effort bargain. At first the overseer threatened the compositors: 'If you refuse to do this job you shall not have any more work in this house', he told them. Then the employer, Mr. Gilbert, 'requested [the compositors] to take the copy with them, and to rely on their [the employers'] honour that no advantage would be taken of them'. The compositors met to discuss this offer, but they eventually refused it. Nevertheless, they deputed a number of compositors to explain to the employer 'that the job could not be proceeded without an express promise of having the wrapper'.

Before this delegation could meet with the masters, the overseer came upon them and this time tried to mediate the dispute. As the Minute Books of the London Union of Compositors records it, the overseer 'endeavoured to persuade [the compositors] to take the copy, that no notice should be taken of any thing that had transpired, and he would do all in his power to obtain the wrappers'. Yet the compositors still refused to accept the offer. The entire shop was shut down for the remainder of the day and the compositors reassembled at 10 AM the next morning. After further discussions, the overseer met with the compositors yet again. This time he offered them a new compromise. The compositors would be paid for all the wrappers except those used in the printing of one publication, a tract that appeared very infrequently and whose wrappers used only half-sheets of paper. In response, the compositors willingly accepted this offer.

The overseer, however, had one final goal and that was to re-establish the honour and trust that facilitated and maintained output. To do so, he promised that the compositors 'might rely on his carefully abstaining from coming in collision with them on disputed points; but if any of the works now disputed were given to the journeymen [compositors] they were to go on with them without asking any questions, as the required price would be paid'. That is, in order to maintain production, both employees and management would avoid disputes, trusting in each other that when the production run was over the proper price for the job would be paid. This solution satisfied all parties and both the union and the employers ratified this course of action.

The extent to which this particular foreman was willing to go in order to secure a reliable output was perhaps unique but certainly not extraordinary. Of course, it would be unwise to therefore conclude that foremen in the printing trades always sought to facilitate production over imposing control. Overseers frequently appear, for example, in the *Proceedings of the Old Bailey* tracking down paper or books stolen from the printing houses or challenging perquisites.[53] They also appear providing testimony against illegal combinations.

However, even in this latter role, Mr. Crow, the overseer at *The Times* printing office, testified that he had tried to get the men to talk directly with their
employers: 'I could not help expressing my regret; I said, I was sorry that
they were about to go, I was loth [*sic*] to part with them; I said, the measure
was precipitate and rash; I cannot say that they made any answer, I wished
them to wait for the masters. They all went away on the 26th and the office
was left without a man.'[54]

Foremen and the Effort Bargain during the Industrial Revolution

We have come a long way from the dispute between Fayol and Taylor over
the proper role of foremen in industry. Admittedly, the way here has been
rather complicated, so let me try to synthesize the argument I have been
trying to make. As Robert Wilson, the prominent game theorist, has suggested, in many, if not all, bargaining situations, decisions are based upon
an understanding that the past behaviour of one party is indicative of their
future performance.[55] These reputation effects are extremely important for
our understanding of how work was both accomplished and supervised during the early industrial period. The exchange of reputations, I am suggesting
here, becomes an especially important and sensitive element of the general
exchange of effort for pay in situations where labour inputs are difficult
or impossible to monitor, supervise, or quantify.[56] Such a situation, where
labour effort is indeterminate and shop-floor supervision minimal, was the
central feature of the effort bargain in the economy of manufacturing that
characterized the first stages of Britain's industrial revolution.[57]

Try as they might, employers had no effective way to control a workers'
expenditure of effort and workers were rarely willing to reveal just how much
effort they could put forth. Consequently, to use Akerlof's metaphor, the
employment relationship was more akin to an exchange of gifts than to a
neoclassical market exchange. A supervisor's obligation was to recognize what
could be fairly expected from a worker and fairly reward it; the worker's reciprocal obligation was to expend an amount of effort equivalent to a fair day's
work. The repeated effort bargaining that characterized shop-floor industrial
relations therefore placed great importance upon normative values of fairness
as well as upon notions of honour and reputation. Not only did honour and
reputation affect the chances of successful negotiations on the shop floor, but
they also affected the reliability and predictability of both output and earnings.
Thus, early industrial managers and foremen found themselves enmeshed in
a complex relationship with their workers, one that did not easily distinguish
between either economics and culture or the professional and the personal.

As Steven Tolliday and Jonathan Zeitlin have argued, most accounts of the history of business enterprise, the rise of management, and the historical development of labour relations depend upon a specific set of unstated assumptions about the nature of the firm.[58] Both business and labour historians frequently take as a given the 'fact' that the labour management policies of firms are ultimately dictated by some combination of the external state of both the market and technology. However, there has long been both theoretical and empirical evidence to the contrary and the determinism inherent in such a view is rarely acknowledged. Indeed perhaps a more appropriate analytical perspective would be to view the firm as a shifting set of 'political' coalitions whose goals, in James March's words, 'are not given; they are bargained'.[59]

From this 'political' perspective, foremen and women are perhaps best viewed as one of a number of groups of actors within the firm whose shifting alignments ultimately contribute to the formulation of a firm's business policy. These coalitions, according to Tolliday and Zeitlin, may be based on any number of 'non-economic factors such as company history, power struggles, personalities and ideology'.[60] Therefore, the overmen of the northern coal industry and the overseers of the London printing trades are not best seen as 'men in the middle'. These foremen were active participants in complex, value-laden bargaining processes that ultimately produced the coalitions upon which business decisions were made.

Notes

1. D. Reid, 'Fayol: From Experience to Theory', *Journal of Management History* 1, no. 3 (1995): 21–36, here 22.
2. See D. Reid, 'Reading Fayol with 3D Glasses', *Journal of Management History* 1, no. 3 (1995): 63–71.
3. Reid, 'Fayol: From Experience to Theory', 23.
4. Ibid., 24.
5. A. Thomson, 'The Case for Management History', *Accounting, Business & Financial History* 11, no. 2 (2001): 99–115, here 104; see also D. Martin, '*The Genesis of Modern Management* Reconsidered', *Historical Studies in Industrial Relations* 20 (2005): 115–136.
6. Martin, '*Genesis of Modern Management* Reconsidered', 136.
7. C. K. Harley, 'British Industrialisation before 1841: Evidence of Slower Growth during the Industrial Revolution', *Journal of Economic History* 42, no. 2 (1982): 267–289; N. F. R. Crafts, *British Economic Growth during the Industrial Revolution* (Oxford, 1985). The most notable challenge has come from M. Berg and P. Hudson, 'Rehabilitating the Industrial Revolution', *Economic History Review* 45, no. 1 (1992): 24–50.
8. See, among others, M. Berg, *The Age of Manufactures, 1700–1820: Industry, Innovation and Work in Britain* (London, 1985, 1994); R. Price, *British Society, 1680–1880: Dynamism, Containment and Change* (Cambridge, 1999); J. Mokyr, 'The Rise and Fall of the Factory System: Technology, Firms, and Households Since the Industrial Revolution',

2001, http://faculty.econ.northwestern.edu/faculty/mokyr/pittsburgh.pdf (accessed 13 July 2006), 27.

9. Price, *British Society*, 17.
10. Berg and Hudson, 'Rehabilitating the Industrial Revolution', 30–32.
11. S. Pollard, *The Genesis of Modern Management: A Study of the Industrial Revolution in Great Britain* (Harmondsworth, 1968), chap. 3.
12. Ibid., 103.
13. See 'Factories, Workshops and Industrial Organisation', chap. 6 of R. Floud and D. McCloskey, *The Economic History of Britain Since 1700, Volume 1: 1700–1860* (Cambridge, 1994), 129.
14. For a recent evaluation of the content and influence of Baldamus's work, see J. Eldridge, 'A Benchmark in Industrial Sociology: W. G. Baldamus on *Efficiency and Effort* (1961)', *Historical Studies in Industrial Relations* 6 (1998): 133–161.
15. W. Baldamus, *Efficiency and Effort: An Analysis of Industrial Administration* (London, 1961), 35–36, 46–47.
16. W. Baldamus, 'The Relationship between Wage and Effort', *Journal of Industrial Economics* 5, no. 3 (1957): 192–201, here 200.
17. H. Behrend, 'The Effort Bargain', *Industrial and Labor Relations Review* 10, no. 4 (1957): 503–515, here 505.
18. The 'joint creation of conflict and co-operation' is a point emphasized by P. K. Edwards, 'The Politics of Conflict and Consent: How the Labor Contract Really Works', *Journal of Economic Behavior and Organization* 13 (1990): 41–61, here 42.
19. For the concept of 'structured antagonism', see P. K. Edwards, *Conflict at Work: A Materialist Analysis of Workplace Relations* (Oxford, 1986), 5–6.
20. C. Behagg, *Politics and Production in the Early Nineteenth Century* (London, 1990), 124.
21. Pollard, *Genesis of Modern Management*, 126–128. See also M. W. Flinn, *The History of the British Coal Industry*, vol. 2: *1700–1830: The Industrial Revolution* (Oxford, 1984), 57–68. Surprisingly, Flinn does not include any mention of the role or function of overmen.
22. Bryers to Delaval, 25 October 1804, Northumberland Record Office [hereafter, NRO], Delaval Papers, ZDE 4/26/68.
23. During this period, coal was an important consumer item. Like other consumer items, coal was marketed under a variety of 'brand names' that indicated their quality. Most 'brand names' reflected the name of the coal seam from which they were extracted. In addition, large, 'round' coal was most prized by consumers because it burned longer than 'small' coal. Until it was put to industrial uses in the second half of the nineteenth century, 'small' coal was almost worthless. To give but one example, between 1838 and 1840 Lord Londonderry's highest grade 'round' coal, the Wallsend brand, sold on average for 11s. 6d. per ton and earned him gross profits of nearly £80,000 each year. His 'small' coal, on the other hand, sold on average for only 5s. 6½d. per ton. With working costs varying between 5s. and 5s. 6¼d. per ton during these years, small coal was just not worth the cost of raising it to the surface: see Durham County Record Office [hereafter, DCRO], Londonderry Papers, D/Lo/E/514 (7–8). In fact, at North Hetton Colliery, also managed by Dunn, small coal was being burned as waste in November 1832. Dunn estimated that North Hetton would save £26 per day by separating and stowing the small coal underground instead of raising it to the surface. No such calculation exists for Hetton Colliery, a much larger colliery: see Matthias Dunn's Diary, 14 November 1832, Newcastle Central Library [hereafter, NCL].
24. Actually, in the terms of the day, Dunn offered the miners a bonus of 1½ corves, or baskets, of coal, for each score of baskets sent to the surface of the pit. A corf, pl. corves, was a wicker basket used to carry coal away from the seam. It was therefore a measure of volume, not weight, and its exact size varied at each colliery. Michael Flinn suggests that corves averaged between 16 and 20 pecks, but Matthias Dunn considered a 20-peck corf seriously

under measure. Flinn further notes that a 20-peck corf measured about 26 inches high and 34 inches in diameter. For Flinn's account, see *History of the British Coal Industry*, vol. 2, Appendix B, 461. For Dunn, see Dunn's Diary, 21 February, 29 March, 5 April and 23 April 1832, NCL. For Dunn's offer, see Dunn's Diary, 10 November 1831, NCL.

25. Dunn's Diary, 16 November 1831, NCL.
26. Ibid., 15 December 1831, NCL.
27. Ibid., 8 December 1831, NCL.
28. Ibid., 30 November 1831, NCL. The eight overmen were employed as follows: George Armstrong (Blossom West Pit), William Lish (Blossom East Pit), Jonathan Maugham (Minor West Pit), Robert Frazer (Minor East Pit), Morgan Frazer (Elemore Isabella Pit), Jacob Graham (George Pit, Hutton Coal Seam), William Bailey (George Pit, Main Coal Seam). See Dunn's Diary, n.d. (mid-November) 1831, NCL.
29. Ibid., 7 December 1831, NCL.
30. Ibid., 28 December 1831, NCL.
31. Ibid., 4 January 1832, NCL.
32. Ibid., 5 January 1832, NCL.
33. P. E. H. Hair, ed., *Coals on Rails, or the Reason of My Wrighting: The Autobiography of Anthony Errington, a Tyneside Colliery Waggon and Waggonway Wright, from His Birth in 1778 to Around 1825* (Liverpool, 1988), 89–90.
34. One of the most oft-cited examples is that of the experience of the sociologist Michael Burawoy related in his *Manufacturing Consent: Changes in the Capitalist Labor Process under Monopoly Capitalism* (Chicago, 1979), 60–62.
35. Dunn's Diary, 15 December 1831, NCL.
36. Ibid., 4 January, 5 January, 19 January, 25 January 1832, NCL.
37. Ibid., 8 March 1832, NCL.
38. Ibid., 15 March 1832, NCL.
39. D. Roy, 'Efficiency and "The Fix": Informal Intergroup Relations in a Piecework Machine Shop', *American Journal of Sociology* 60 (1954): 255–266, here 265–266.
40. Dunn's Diary, 19 March 1832, NCL.
41. Ibid., 5 April 1832, NCL. The precise amount varied depending upon which seam of coal that was being worked. In the Main Coal seam, the agreement stipulated 1½ corves per score and 1 corf per score in the Hutton seam.
42. Bell Collection, NRO 3410.
43. 'Address from the Hetton Pitmen to the Public', 20 April 1832, Bell Collection, NRO, 3410/ Bell/11/405. 'Nicking' and 'kirving' were techniques used to cut coal from the face.
44. G. A. Akerlof, 'Labor Contracts as Partial Gift Exchange', *Quarterly Journal of Economics* 97, no. 4 (1982): 543–569, here 548–551.
45. Ibid., 549.
46. See M. Huberman, *Escape from the Market: Negotiating Work in Lancashire* (Cambridge, 1996).
47. On the marginal role of foremen, see D. Wray, 'Marginal Men of Industry: The Foremen', *American Journal of Sociology* 54, no. 4 (1949): 298–301, although Wray minimizes the extent to which foremen were often forced by their situation to accommodate the demands of their workers.
48. National Graphical Association [hereafter, NGA], Minutes of the Union Committee, 1831–1834, 10 October 1833, Modern Records Centre [hereafter, MRC], Mss. 28/ CO/1/1/3.
49. NGA, Minutes of the Union Committee, 1831–1834, 10 October 1833, MRC, Mss. 28/ CO/1/1/3.
50. Ibid., 20 December 1831, MRC, Mss. 28/CO/1/1/3.
51. See J. Jaffe, 'Authority and Job Regulation: Rule-Making by the London Compositors during the Early Nineteenth Century', *Historical Studies in Industrial Relations* 3 (1997): 1–26.

52. For the following, see NGA, Minutes of the Trade Council of the London Union of Compositors, 1834–1836, 17 and 19 June 1834, MRC, Mss. 28/CO/1/1/5.
53. Old Bailey Proceedings Online (http://www.oldbaileyonline.org, accessed 14 November 2005), 17 April 1776, trial of Thomas Procter (t17760417–63); 3 June 1778, trial of William Blake and Mary Pearce (t17780603–53); and 28 October 1789, trial of Thomas Rumbald (t17891028–22).
54. Ibid., 31 October 1810, trial of Stephen Hurley, Robert Howlett, Edward Kidd, Guy Warwick, Roderick Pasquin, John Gee, William Clifton, Stephen Beckett, Henry Burn, Thomas Woolley, William Williams, Corbett Latham, William Coy, James Macarthy, John Macintosh, Nathaniel Collins, Malcolm Craig, John Chapman, George Westray, John Simpson (t18101031–106).
55. R. Wilson, 'Reputations in Games and Markets', in *Game-Theoretic Models of Bargaining*, ed. A. E. Roth (Cambridge, 1985), 27–62.
56. Analytically, this could be considered a condition of imperfect information, as discussed in detail in D. M. Kreps and R. Wilson, 'Reputation and Imperfect Information', *Journal of Economic Theory* 27 (1982): 253–279.
57. See also M. Huberman, 'Piece Rates Reconsidered: The Case of Cotton', *Journal of Interdisciplinary History* 26, no. 3 (1996): 393–417.
58. S. Tolliday and J. Zeitlin, 'Introduction: Employers and Industrial Relations between Theory and History', in *The Power to Manage? Employers and Industrial Relations in Comparative-Historical Perspective*, ed. S. Tolliday and J. Zeitlin (London, 1991), 1–34, here 2–12.
59. J. G. March, 'The Business Firm as a Political Coalition', *Journal of Politics* 24, no. 4 (1962): 662–678, here 672.
60. Tolliday and Zeitlin, 'Introduction', 12.

CHAPTER 6

WAGE FORMS AND HIERARCHY IN LATE NINETEENTH-CENTURY FRENCH INDUSTRY

Jérôme Bourdieu and Gilles Postel-Vinay

Two opposing views of industrialization are commonly expressed. The first emphasizes capitalism's coercion of workers into furnishing more effort than they had long been accustomed to when they themselves decided on the rhythm and timing of their work. From this standpoint, factory discipline is an essential part of capitalist development. The second point of view claims that the need for factory discipline emerged only slowly during the nineteenth century, as increasingly productive technologies rendered the closer coordination of workers essential. Both views agree that large-scale production, the division of labour, and the breakdown of tasks into individual standardized operations were essential to the industrial firm of the nineteenth century. They also agree that achieving such an organization implied reshaping labour relations within the firm and the development of a hierarchical structure of decision and control, which was implemented on the shop floor by a new figure: the foreman. However, advocates of the first view argue that foremen were a necessary condition of capitalist development, as the generalization of supervisory tasks in labour relations was a distinctive feature of the organization of new industrial plants. In the second view, foremen's importance grew over time, as a corollary of the development of large firms which raised coordination problems and required the invention of new labour relations at the expense of workers' self regulation and autonomy. To distinguish between these two views it would seem important to determine if, and at what pace, firms recruited more foremen over time. Answering these questions is fraught with difficulty, if only because foremen were not always explicitly identified, either because they may have played different roles in the firm or because their position was not defined as such.

Notes for this chapter begin on page 143.

These types of questions are usually addressed via case studies and research monographs as the best way of capturing the evolution of hierarchical organization over a protracted period of time. Here we will argue, paradoxically, that cross-sectional analysis is perhaps more suited to the systematic observation of the long-run evolution of work organization inside firms. This choice has some self-evident drawbacks. The late nineteenth-century survey we use does not do justice to the complexities of labour relations under industrial capitalism. We might say, however, that poor sources have their strength. Indeed, this survey allows reliable comparisons between a large number of firms of all sizes and all industrial sectors.

What Do Foremen Do? Two Possibilities and Two Effects

Work organization at the plant level during the nineteenth century and the monitoring of wage labour by foremen are typically viewed in two different ways: either foremen were required to coordinate workers, especially in large firms, or they helped to coerce more effort from workers than they would have freely given. Gregory Clark labelled these 'coordination theory' and 'coercion theory' respectively.[1] According to coordination theory, foremen are coordinators who became more necessary as capitalism introduced the division of labour and increasingly complex technologies. There was no need for foremen when small independent production units performed tasks (either because firms were mostly small, or because, in larger firms, work was organized by teams and crafts). Foremen became vital, however, when work organization became more complex as a result of the division of labour. At least in large firms, workers' tasks were prescribed and routinized, while foremen transmitted orders and checked whether they were carried out. According to coercion theory, foremen were supervisors hired to impose greater work effort and/or longer hours. They enforced discipline, fined or fired lazy workers, and, more generally, imposed 'factory rules' on the shop floor.

The two theories yield different results and imply different types of firm organization by affecting the wage policy, the length of the working day, and, more generally, the division of labour inside the plant. As such, the relationship we observe between the employment of foremen on the one hand, and firm characteristics and organizational choices on the other, will allow us to distinguish between coordination and coercion.

The role of foremen depends on the characteristics of the firm. In particular, it depends on size, capital intensity and industry-related characteristics (such as seasonality, for example). However, firms' policies are also affected by the presence of foremen. We can therefore reasonably assume that, depending on how many foremen they employ, firms will differ. They will have different wage policies, prefer different lengths of the working day, and while some will hire more skilled workers, others will be more likely to hire unskilled labour, possibly of rural origin.

First, firm size matters. Under coordination theory, we expect a higher percentage of foremen in the labour force in larger units, as the greater division of labour induces more complex coordination problems. Under coercion theory, we assume foremen to be always necessary in industrial firms, but we also expect economies of scale. This size variable is particularly important, as firm size grew over the nineteenth century.

Second, the firm's wage policy is also important. Wage policy may be either a complement or a substitute for other disciplinary devices: piece-rate wages, or any other form of incentive wage, induce effort with less supervision. If the coordination theory holds, the use of incentive wages may reduce the demand for foremen. However, this may be offset by increased demand resulting from coordination considerations. If the coercion theory holds, a greater use of time rate wages is likely to increase the need for foremen.

Third, the presence of foremen might be connected with the length of the working day. It depends on the nature of supervising techniques whether a longer workday results in more foremen per worker. Large plants, for example, using unqualified male workers making long hours might require a higher rate of foremen in order to enforce hard work. Foremen also have the opportunity to reduce breaks or to impose overtime. As the organization of work becomes more complex, their role in that respect may possibly be reduced.

The quality and origin of labour will have different impacts on the demand for foremen under the coercion and coordination theories. Unskilled labour and mobile workers (in the sense of often changing occupations), in particular those who are not full-time manufacturing workers, or those who have recently changed sectors, require more supervision regardless of coordination issues. On the other hand, skilled and unionized workers are heavily involved in the firm's decision-making process, through which given forms of organization and coordination emerge.

Technology also does play a role. Coordination can be achieved either by foremen or by technology. In particular, machines as such can impose a rhythm independently of foremen. To this extent, technology can be seen as a substitute for foremen as supervisors. However, as the number and thus the variety of machines grows, coordination problems are likely to increase. As such, we expect that the number of foremen depends to some extent on capital intensity.

Last, it seems likely that there was more need for coercion in certain industries. We can imagine that supervision was particularly important in the building industry, for instance (as seasonality implies high turnover), or in the iron and steel industry (due to a wide variety of separate tasks).

Data

We use a very detailed survey carried out in late nineteenth-century France by the Office du Travail.[2] Created in 1890, the Office du Travail decided to conduct a large-scale survey of wages, employment and working conditions: the *Enquête sur les salaires et durée du travail dans l'industrie française*.[3] The Office innovated in a number of ways. It produced much more detailed information than previously available on working conditions, especially by referring to precisely defined categories within the labour force. Up to that date, the industrial censuses published by the Statistique Générale de la France reported only the number of male and female workers, but the Office du Travail distinguished between foremen, skilled workers by crafts as well as unskilled workers, and also apprentices and outdoor workers.

To do so, the Office du Travail introduced a new method: instead of a general census, which was the common practice of the Statistique Générale de la France, it used a weighted sample of plants. Last, it chose to publish both its own results and the comments and reactions of employers' and employees' organizations.

This survey covered a sample of some 3,000 industrial firms, stratified by size and region. It dealt with almost all industries (even though the sampling was not carried out on this basis). Despite its potential for the question that interests us here, this data set has, of course, its limitations. First, as mentioned above, it is only a cross section. Second, information is collected at the plant level. The plant is most often one firm, but this is not always the case. As a result, it may be misleading to a certain extent to assume that organizational choices were made at the plant level (which we observe) and not at the firm level (which we do not observe).[4]

However, the data allow precise and reliable comparisons between plants. Crucially, the categories are identical for all units of observation. Moreover, the categories used in the survey were previously discussed and agreed upon. In particular, what the term 'foreman' meant seemed to be common knowledge for all those who participated in the survey. Both those who collected the information at firm level, as well as employers' and employees' unions commenting on the results, appeared to agree on the definition of 'foreman'. However, while the investigators who collected the data used the word *contremaître* as an unproblematic category with a self-evident content, the designers of the survey had a wide variety of concrete situations in mind. They wrote:

> There is a great variety in the role of foremen. The job itself can range from a supervisory role requiring no special knowledge to the chief worker who directs all the practical aspects of the jobs, sets the framework of the division of labour and substitutes for the owner in many circumstances. The definition of foreman covers a wide range of actual tasks and skills, and remunerations vary accordingly.[5]

In this context, foremen could be either surprisingly low-skilled workers assigned to supervisory tasks or high-level specialists devoted to work coordination. For the survey designers the only thing that mattered is that the foremen constituted a separate group of workers, willing to work without counting their time, entirely dedicated to the firm's interests. What matters for us is that this category embraces a large spectrum of practical undertakings covering activities of monitoring and coordination. Here we venture to distinguish between these various tasks.

For each plant we have information on the sector of activity and location. Below, we will call 'sectoral variables' the industry-specific dummy variables for each of these nineteen sectors of activity. The survey not only mentions the *département* – the main administrative unit in France – where the plant is located, but also the commune. The name of the commune is not known, but we do have information on the size of its population, which is enough to identify urban and rural firms. We consider communes with less than 2,000 inhabitants to be rural, and communes with over 2,000 inhabitants to be urban. The presence of steam engines is also reported, as well as their horsepower (hp).

The survey pays particular attention to the labour force, its size and composition. It includes the number of workers, not only by sex, category, and skill and craft, but also by type of employment (i.e. outdoor workers versus those working in the factory). Notwithstanding their potential interest, we do not use all of these variables. While the craft variable, for instance, could help address a number of questions, we here leave it for further research. We focus on the group defined as 'foremen' (*contremaîtres*) and on variables that measure divisions within the labour force and the resulting demand for coordination. These divisions may derive either from a mixed labour force (mixing skilled and unskilled workers, male and female workers, etc.) or high turnover.[6]

Finally, wages are observed in great detail. In each plant, the survey reports daily and annual wages for each category of workers, the number of hours worked per day and the number of working days per year. It also specifies the type of wage (piece wage/time wage/mixed).

Results

Simple descriptive statistics suggest some striking results. First, as Table 6.1 shows, foremen are omnipresent. In particular, far from being an idiosyncratic invention of large firms, small firms also typically employ foremen. In fact, small firms employ more foremen per worker than do large firms. While the percentage of foremen in the labour force falls noticeably with firm size, due to economies of scale, the use of foremen remains general. It is also of interest that there is no wage premium for foremen in larger plants.

Table 6.1 *Presence of Foremen and Size of Plants*

Plant Size (No. of Workers)	Percentage of Foremen	Mean Annual Wage of Foremen (FF)
<10	7.83	1,756
10–19	6.23	2,029
20–49	4.97	2,127
50–99	4.03	2,209
100–499	3.45	2,163
500+	2.93	2,182

Source: Office du Travail, *Enquête sur les salaires et durée du travail dans l'industrie française*, 5 vols. (Paris, 1893–1897).

Let us propose a benchmark that indicates how the labour force was distributed by establishment size in Western industry during the nineteenth and the early twentieth centuries. According to Kinghorn and Nye, who rely on cross-country comparisons for France and Germany in the years 1905–1913, firms with more than fifty workers employed only 38 per cent of the industrial labour force.[7] In other words, as late as the beginning of the twentieth century, establishments with less than fifty employees – those in the first three rows of Table 6.1 – employed the majority of workers and an even higher proportion of foremen. This was certainly the case – and very likely even more so – earlier in the nineteenth century.

Second, we might have expected a simple linear relation between the capital intensity of production techniques and coordination problems. However, taking the degree of steam power as a proxy for capital intensity, the relation between foremen and steam power is rather U-shaped (Table 6.2). As in Table 6.1, we do not see a wage premium for foremen in firms with more capital-intensive production technologies.

The percentage of foremen in the labour force is also affected by other variables. In particular, it varied dramatically by geographical area. Rural firms,

Table 6.2 *Presence of Foremen and Use of Steam Power*

HP of Steam Engines by Plant (Quintiles)	Percentage of Foremen	Mean Annual Wage of Foremen (FF)
Q (0–20)	5.39	2,125
Q (20–40)	3.71	2,258
Q (40–60)	4.11	2,227
Q (60–80)	4.33	2,013
Q (80–100)	5.29	2,074

Source: Office du Travail, *Enquête sur les salaires.*

for instance, usually hired more foremen than urban firms, and Parisian firms hired fewer foremen than other urban firms. This is illustrated in Table 6.3.

Table 6.3 *Presence of Foremen by Size and Location of Plant*

Plant Size	Rural Areas	Towns (Other than Paris)	Paris
<10	9.18	8.06	4.18
10–20	6.83	6.02	6.26
20–49	4.81	5.26	3.87
50–100	4.53	4.03	3.23
100–499	3.59	3.45	3.04
500+	(na)	3.03	2.06

Source: Office du Travail, *Enquête sur les salaires.*

Third, is there a direct link between the presence of foremen and the length of the working day? A comparison of the percentage of foremen in four groups of firms ranked by working time is inconclusive. The percentage is similar (4.8 per cent) for firms whose average work time is below nine and a half hours per day and those working more than eleven and a half hours. In the two intermediary groups (around ten hours per day and around eleven hours per day) the percentage is hardly higher (5.0 per cent and 5.2 per cent respectively).

Going beyond these preliminary findings requires a more systematic approach. To do so, we run a regression where the dependent variable is the percentage of foremen in the labour force, and the explanatory variables are those we presented above.[8] The results of this regression may help us to clarify the role of foremen as coordinators or as coercive supervisors.

Note that these explanatory variables omit what could be seen as a crucial part of the problem: a foreman will be in a better position to impose discipline or facilitate coordination if workers feel close to him and if he is recognized as being both able and fair. It is then possible to argue that workers were unlikely to feel close to someone whose income was so much higher than their own.[9] Leaving this argument aside, however, it is reasonable to suggest that this kind of recognition was easier to obtain for someone who had spent part of his career in the plant. Unfortunately, we do not have information on workers' careers, but we can still address the question indirectly. The fact that foremen are significantly more prevalent in the public sector or in railway companies, suggests that industries with long-term job attachment can recruit foremen more easily than other sectors can. But, clearly, other factors must also be taken into account, as Table 6.4 shows.

Table 6.4 *Explaining the Presence of Foremen*

Independent Variables	Coefficient	Std Error	t	P>|t|
Number of workers	-0.00171	0.00054	-3.19	0.001
hp/capita	0.47931	0.07386	6.49	0.000
(hp/capita)^2	-0.01193	0.00204	-5.84	0.000
Piece rate wage only	Ref			
More than one kind of wage	3.09766	0.68970	4.49	0.000
Time wage only	4.28735	0.69115	6.20	0.000
% outdoor workers	-1.22705	0.40885	-3.00	0.003
Number of hours/day	0.03311	0.12404	0.27	0.790
Average wage	0.09760	0.11614	0.84	0.401
Turnover	0.30120	0.08925	3.37	0.001
Percentage female participation	-0.91380	0.59182	-1.54	0.123
Heterogeneity 1 (1 sex/ 1 skill group)	-0.42752	0.33112	-1.29	0.197
Heterogeneity 2 (1 sex/ 2 skill groups)	-0.44295	0.30918	-1.43	0.152
Heterogeneity 3 (2sexes/1 skill group)	0.63490	0.30873	2.06	0.040
Heterogeneity 4 (2sexes/ 2 skill groups)	Ref.			
Food	Ref.			
Wood	-0.16449	0.40278	-0.41	0.683
Building and civil engineering	1.65585	0.64355	2.57	0.010
Quarries	1.56233	0.98596	1.58	0.113
Chemicals	0.57016	0.38608	1.48	0.140
Leather	0.50906	0.44927	1.13	0.257
Cabinet-maker	-0.77953	0.62795	-1.24	0.215
Cloth	0.62013	0.54015	1.15	0.251
Book industry	-0.11971	0.60088	-0.20	0.842
Machinery	0.46058	0.43774	1.05	0.293
Metallurgical industry	-0.21670	0.50026	-0.43	0.665
Iron and steel	1.28920	0.47646	2.71	0.007
Mining	0.02937	0.81301	0.04	0.971
Paper	-1.23355	0.63505	-1.94	0.052
Stones	-1.68357	0.50997	-3.30	0.001
Jewellery	-0.47222	0.80056	-0.59	0.555
Freestone	0.90214	0.99013	0.91	0.362
Textile	0.53269	0.46244	1.15	0.249
Transport	-1.18529	1.89312	-0.63	0.531
Rural	Ref.			
Urban	-0.86909	0.24505	-3.55	0.000
Paris	-1.08076	0.48429	-2.23	0.026
Public sector	4.82664	0.83387	5.79	0.000
Constant	-0.07443	1.66805	-0.04	0.964

Number of observations = 1966; R-squared = 0.1348; Adjusted R-squared = 0.1196

Dependent variable = percentage of foremen in the firm's labour force

Source: Office du Travail, *Enquête sur les salaires.*

First, the regression confirms what had already been suggested in Table 6.1: the number of workers in a plant (its size) is strongly negatively correlated with the percentage of foremen in the labour force. In other words, more workers imply fewer foremen per worker or, vice versa, the smaller the firm, the higher the percentage of foremen in the labour force. Clearly, this finding is not consistent with the coordination hypothesis. More precisely, foremen are indeed present in large firms; but they are even more so in small firms. And since firm size tended to grow during the nineteenth century, it is safe to conclude that foremen were present in both older industries as well as more recent ones. This outcome does not confirm the idea that industrial capitalism initially operated with an almost independent labour force, until large firms emerged that required foremen to solve the coordination problems induced by the new firm organization. Foremen and discipline are not latecomers.

A closer look at this size effect reinforces this conclusion. In fact, the size effect is even more important for medium and large firms. To put this into context, consider some nineteenth-century standards: the typical cotton firm, common to all of Western Europe as early as the 1830s or 1840s, employed some 200 workers.[10] It is thus reasonable to consider that above that threshold, a plant is of medium size. On this basis, we run the regression presented in Table 6.5. If we explain the percentage of foremen by the size of the plant (as measured by the number of workers) and by a dummy for plants with more than 200 workers, the coefficient on the dummy is both very significant and positive. In other words, the relation between size and supervision is still negative but shifts upwards when the size of the plant reaches a certain critical level. On this basis we can conclude that the presence of foremen in firms is subject to significant economies of scale, but is not linked to the progressive emergence of large firms during the late nineteenth century. Rather it is a common feature of any industrial nineteenth-century firm.

The Office du Travail paid only little attention to firms' technological characteristics. Nevertheless, the survey reports the presence of steam engines and their horsepower. We construct two technological variables, assuming

Table 6.5 *Size Effect*

Independent Variables	Coefficient	Std Error	t	P>|t|
Number of workers (log)	-0.717	0.0216	-33.19	0.000
Dummy: plant>=200 workers	1.114	0.0843	13.21	0.000
HP/capita	-0.004	0.0015	-2.22	0.027
No. of outdoor workers (log)	0.0386	0.0084	-4.60	0.000
Constant	4.2873	0.69115	6.20	0.000

Number of observations = 2,521; R-squared = 0.7291

Source: Office du Travail, *Enquête sur les salaires.*

that horsepower per worker is a good proxy for capital intensity. One is a simple ratio (horsepower per worker), while the second is the same variable squared to capture any possible non-linear effects (respectively (hp/capita) and (hp/capita)² in Table 6.4). Both are strongly significant. As Table 6.4 shows, more capital-intensive technologies lead to more foremen. This result suggests that factory discipline can be achieved in at least two ways: technology and/or foremen. In fact, foremen and technological constraints are substitutes up to a certain point. But only up to a certain point: squaring the same variable shows that if the technology becomes more complex, then coordination problems emerge and require more foremen. Different methods of organizing workers coexist.

If the technological variables thus lead to an ambivalent conclusion, the variables linked to the type of labour contract yield unambiguous results. All things being equal, firms hired fewer foremen when they used various forms of incentive contracts – piece rate pay (in particular in the case of outdoor workers) or any mix of time contracts and payment per piece.[11] On the contrary, firms that relied on time contracts required more foremen: without any incentive, foremen were necessary to coerce workers.

The number of working hours per day has no effect on the percentage of foremen in the labour force. After accounting for various effects of size, contract type, branch of industry etc., no direct relation between the length of the working day and the presence of foremen is captured by the regression: probably because this relation operates through complex interactions between different variables. In plants employing a large proportion of unqualified workers, for instance, the percentage of foremen increases when the workday is longer. As shown in Table 6.6, when the rate of unskilled workers increases, firms with long hours have a higher percentage of foremen, both in small and large firms. That suggests that putting to work unqualified workers for longer workdays requires more discipline. However, the linkage between working time and the role of foremen is complex. In plants employing a lower rate of unqualified workers, an increase of working time is not correlated with an increase of the percentage of foremen (for a given size of firm, the percentages in column a and b are close: 4.21 compared to 4.29 and 3.33 compared to 3.22).

This is not to deny that a part of the foreman's job consisted in coordinating groups within the labour force. But we must be precise and cautious, because if we aggregate potentially different situations, significant distinctions may be blurred. For instance, female participation is inversely but not significantly correlated with the percentage of foremen.[12] In order to identify firms where coordination problems were likely to develop, we isolate four different groups ranked by increasing heterogeneity. The first one includes firms with a homogeneous labour force – for instance, with only one level of skill (whether skilled or unskilled) and with either male or female workers. The

Table 6.6 *Percentage of Foremen by Plant Size, Rate of Unskilled Workers and Length of Workday*

| | Rate of Unskilled Workers below 65% | | Rate of Unskilled Workers above 65% | |
	a	b	c	d
Workday	11h or less	More than 11h	11h or less	More than 11h
20–99 workers	4.21	4.29	3.83	4.58
100 workers or more	3.33	3.22	3.14	3.40

Source: Office du Travail, *Enquête sur les salaires.*

second and the third group are in an intermediate position: firms with either male or female workers but with two levels of skill; and firms with both male and female workers but only one level of skill. The last group stands at the other extreme and includes firms with the most heterogeneous labour force (firms with male and female workers, both skilled and unskilled). Interestingly, the first two groups (single sex/single skill group and single sex/two skill group) need less supervision, but the coefficients are not significant. In fact, the only significant contrast is between the third and the fourth group. When male and female workers were present in both skill groups, there was only a limited competition between groups, and no special demand for coordination. On the contrary, when both sexes shared the same kind of jobs (whether skilled or unskilled), competition between men and women led to a significant increase of coordination problems and more supervision.[13]

Other variables such as the 'sectoral variables' also give some new insights into foremen's role. Surprisingly, these industry specific dummy variables are seldom significant. Actually, they have a significant effect (either positive or negative) only in four out of nineteen industries. Firms in the building industry or in the iron and steel industry hired more foremen while firms in the paper industry or in the stone industry hired less. Moreover, no straightforward reasons emerge. Firms in the building industry might have hired more foremen per worker because their highly scattered workforce needed more supervision. But this reasoning does not hold in other cases. In the iron and steel industry, one would have expected less – not more – foremen than in other sectors because in this particular industry crafts traditionally played an important role in labour organization. Firms in the stone industry hired fewer foremen than others (despite the fact that they employed a mostly unskilled labour force), and so did firms in the paper industry (who employed a mostly skilled labour force). Moreover, the dummy variable for textile (one of the largest industries) is not significant. One conclusion remains. We must indeed keep in mind that some industries were ancient and some were more recent.

Some kept the old organization and still used a lot of outdoor workers (paid by piece), others had only developed in the last few decades before the Office du Travail undertook its survey (for instance, firms in the chemical industry). In this respect, just as traditional breweries and innovative cotton mills coexisted during the English industrial revolution,[14] the various industries that coexist in our cross section can be seen as different geological layers. In both cases, we are dealing with enterprises of disparate industrial nature that originate in different periods. Thus, comparing these different industries is like comparing different historical periods. Yet it is remarkable that, in general, the degree of supervision is hardly different from one industry to another.

A last set of variables – what we call the regional variables – sheds more light on this discussion. The percentage of foremen in the labour force varied considerably across regions. Rural firms used more foremen than others in order to change customary workplace habits and to coerce workers who lacked industrial tradition and skill.[15] On the contrary, urban workers required less supervision either because they were more skilled than their rural counterparts or because they had accumulated factory experience and learned to collude to protect a standard rate or effort norm. Unionization was an urban phenomenon (a Parisian phenomenon, in particular) and, as unionized workers were more able to organize themselves, urban and especially Parisian firms employed fewer foremen.[16]

Concluding Remarks

Scholars have proposed many different and sometimes opposite views on the role of foremen within the firm. A major opposition is the coordinating versus coercive role of foremen. Foremen are sometimes considered as 'middle men' pacifying the relation between capital and labour, and able to implement a fair and accepted order in the workplace. However, as evidence presented here suggests, the main role of foremen was to secure order within the firm and elicit effort from workers by controlling the pace and quality of their work.[17]

Foremen had to be skilled craftsmen indeed. But why were foremen hired in the first place? Because of their skill or mostly in order to detect and repress attempts of resistance? In the latter case a foreman would not have to be an experienced and respected worker, but more likely a keeper and defender of the owners' interests. Overall, coercion appears as the main factor determining the demand for foremen.

This is not to deny the growing complexity of large firms and the coordination problems it induces. But, first, if the general drive to large-scale organization did raise more and thornier coordination problems during the nineteenth century, the diffusion of the factory system was far from uniform across industry, and developed within a variety of organizational forms. Second, one must take into account the fact that nineteenth-century capitalists constructed factory regimes 'not just in the immediate process of production but also through larger political and legal apparatus'.[18] While the data available allow us to catch only a glimpse of what was happening outside the firm, they demonstrate that coercion and coordination problems were not solved only within the firm. Clearly, both internal and external discipline mattered.[19]

Notes

1. G. Clark, 'Factory Discipline', *Journal of Economic History* 54, no. 1 (1994): 128–163. See also E. P. Thompson, 'Time, Work Discipline and Industrial Capitalism', *Past and Present*, no. 38 (1967): 56–97; P. Scholliers and L. Schwartz, *Experiencing Wages: Social and Cultural Aspects of Wage Forms in Europe since 1500* (Oxford, 2003).
2. See J. Luciani, ed., *Histoire de l'Office du travail (1890–1914)* (Paris, 1992); R. Salais, N. Baverez and B. Reynaud, *L'invention du chômage: Histoire et transformation d'une catégorie en France des années 1890 aux années 1980* (Paris, 1999).
3. Office du Travail, *Enquête sur les salaires et durée du travail dans l'industrie française*, 5 vols. (Paris, 1893–1897).
4. See, for instance, M. Berg, *The Age of Manufactures, 1700–1820: Industry, Innovation and Work in Britain* (London, 1985, 1994), 198–207.
5. Office du Travail, *Enquête sur les salaires*, vol. 1, 518–519.
6. Turnover is not directly observed, but the survey reports the number of workers in three ways: the maximum number of workers over the whole year, the minimum number and the average number. We thus assume that the turnover of a given firm (or plant) can be approximately measured as [(maximum number of workers – minimum number of workers)/average number of workers].
7. J. R. Kinghorn and J. V. Nye, 'The Scale of Production in Western Economic Development: A Comparison of Official Industry Statistics in the United States, Britain, France, and Germany, 1905–1913', *Journal of Economic History* 56, no. 1 (1996): 90–112.
8. Note that in the smallest plants, overlookers may not have been necessary, as workers worked directly under their employer. To avoid thresholds effects, we thus neglect here the very small plants (less than ten workers).
9. The wage gap between foremen and other workers was much larger than it is today. Admittedly, comparing a nineteenth-century wage gap and a contemporary wage gap is fraught with difficulty, if only because the categories have changed over time, see L. Boltanski, *Les cadres: La formation d'un groupe social* (Paris, 1982). In 1892, a foreman earned on average 1.67 times more than a skilled worker and 2.26 times more than an unskilled worker. In 1998, the same ratios were respectively 1.37 and 1.68. See Office du Travail, *Enquête sur les salaires*, and INSEE (Institut National de la Statistique et des Etudes Economiques), *Résultats: Les salaires dans l'industrie, le commerce et les services en 1998* (Paris, 2000), 106ff.
10. J. V. Nye, 'Firm Size and Economic Backwardness: A New Look at the French Industrialization Debate', *Journal of Economic History* 47, no. 3 (1987): 649–669; P. Sicsic, 'Labor Markets and Establishment Size in Nineteenth-Century France', *Journal of Economic History* 53, no. 2 (1993): 401–404; J.-M. Chanut, J. Heffer, J. Mairesse and G. Postel-Vinay, *L'industrie française au milieu du XIXe siècle: Les enquêtes de la statistique générale de la France* (Paris, 2000). See also Kinghorn and Nye, 'Scale of Production', 99, table 9, panel C.

11. In Table 6.4: 'Piece rate wage only' and 'More than one kind of wage'.
12. The female participation rate in the industrial labour force increased during the second part of the nineteenth century: from 30 per cent in 1860 to 37.7 per cent in 1906. See M. Guilbert, *Les fonctions des femmes dans l'industrie* (Paris, 1966).
13. M. Perrot, *Les ouvriers en grève, France 1871–1890* (Paris, 1974), 319. This result qualifies Michelle Perrot's finding: 'Bien loin de pousser à l'apathie, la mixité forme un mélange détonnant.'
14. P. Mathias, *The Brewing Industry in England 1700–1830* (Cambridge, 1959).
15. R. Trempé, *Les mineurs de Carmaux, 1848–1914* (Paris, 1971).
16. Note that various sets of rules developed by industry on a regional basis. See M. Huberman, *Escape From the Market: Negotiating Work in Lancashire* (Cambridge, 1996), chap. 8. Note also that this result is consistent with the fact that firms with only male workers needed less supervision (since unionization was mostly a male phenomenon).
17. Dewerpe describes the foremen as *les chefs immédiats* or 'direct supervisors': A. Dewerpe, 'Les pouvoirs du sens pratique: Carrières professionnelles et trajectoires des chefs d'atelier de l'Ansaldo (Gênes, 1900–1920)', in *L'usine et le bureau: Itinéraires sociaux et professionnels dans l'entreprise XIXe et XXe siècles*, ed. Y. Lequin and S. Vandecasteele (Lyon, 1990), 109–150.
18. M. W. Steinberg, 'Capitalist Development, the Labour Process, and the Law', *American Journal of Sociology* 109, no. 2 (2003): 445–495, here 445.
19. This implies that the role of foremen may differ according to the legal context. For comparisons with the English legal framework, for instance, see R. J. Steinfeld, *Coercion, Contract, and Free Labour in the Nineteenth Century* (Cambridge, 2001); Steinberg, 'Capitalist Development'.

CHAPTER 7

LEADING HANDS AT WORK

Technology, Work Organization and Supervision
in British Engineering, 1870–1914

Joseph Melling

The decline of manufacturing output within the European and North American economies during the second half of the twentieth century provides a sharp contrast with the growth of the global economy and the international division of labour a century earlier. The migration of technologies and other forms of knowledge around the world has given less industrialized countries scope for competing with those enjoying an early start. At the same time, the most affluent societies have interrogated the costs of maintaining institutional support for producers and employees in state welfare systems. Researchers who have investigated the expansion of industrial production and technology during the nineteenth century have provided detailed information on the importance of social and institutional influences, as well as the scale and pattern of market demand, on the utilization of labour power in this period. The adoption of particular technologies was usually a matter of social negotiation rather than simply being a rational choice arising from an accurate reading of current market opportunities. General narratives of capitalist innovation and management control, drawing on classic sociological and political theory, developed during the third quarter of the twentieth century have been robustly challenged in more recent research, which details the uneven pace of changes in both economy and civil society.[1] The impact of workplace conflict and wider labour resistance on management practices has been documented in more recent scholarship, as well as research tracing the influence of nation-states and inter-state regulation on the organization of distinctive groups of producers at different moments in modern business.[2] The cultural context and the symbolic importance of technological innovation has similarly been emphasized in recent research on heroic male inventors.[3]

Notes for this chapter begin on page 165.

Historical Interpretations of Workplace Management

Debates concerning the nature of capitalist development and the control of labour in the production process have received less attention in recent research than more specific discussions of authority, gender and the relationship of knowledge to the exercise of power at work.[4] In the field of labour relations, radical interpretations of scientific management and strategies of control and accommodation have been critically challenged by pluralist accounts of continuities in production and the persistence of 'craft administration' in the older manufacturing industries of the United Kingdom. Some accounts acknowledge that the benefits of skilled labour and craft autonomy appropriate in the Victorian era only became an obstacle to effective management when firms lost their freedom to alter technologies and work systems as markets changed.[5] More recent studies of productivity decline in British manufacturing have similarly stressed the long-term impediments to growth presented by a historic reliance on skilled labour and the institutional practices associated with collective bargaining, more particularly those established in the later nineteenth and early twentieth centuries.[6] The role of individual and group piecework payment systems in the management of effort within both craft and mass production industries has been widely noted by historians of bargaining in British and American industry, including the vehicle-building industry, during the twentieth century.[7] Such long-term assessments of production management and industrial performance derive from important assumptions about the organization and supervision of labour during the nineteenth century. It is remarkable, therefore, that we possess so few detailed accounts of work supervision in the major industrial societies of the years 1870–1914.

In the absence of fresh research, one of the most authoritative studies of British employment relations remains the research of Craig Littler, published twenty years ago. Littler argued that the persistence of internal contracting systems in manufacturing industry since the Victorian era, including the delegation of job control to group or gang leaders who agreed prices with employers for the completion of pieces of work in production, has been a defining feature of production management in the United Kingdom.[8] Direct and simple employment contracts were relatively uncommon during the nineteenth century, largely confined to trades where detailed planning of production was possible and among state or regulated private monopolies which developed internal bureaucracies. The power of the industrial foreman was largely restricted to such sectors, while the internal contractor was a more significant source of authority in many industries, exercising control over the employment, supervision, payment and training of labour – along with the choice of production techniques and the division of labour. The closing decades of the nineteenth century saw an increased reliance on industrial supervisors as the enforcers of work organization at the expense of internal contractors, though the growth of systematic management through new systems of incentive wages and increased use of technical staff for planning and work study also signalled the longer-term demise of the powerful foreman and forewoman. The new payment systems culminated in the elaborate system of work-study procedures and measurements designed by Bedaux, whose intricate blueprint for detailed programmes for calculating labour inputs and rationalizing effort was briefly popular in some British management circles during the 1930s. Littler charts the progress of Bedaux's ideas. Trade unionism, he suggests, exerted little direct influence on the pattern of employment relations which developed since the nineteenth century, when craft unions had arisen from confederation of petty contractors and piecework bargainers. Even in the inter-war years they could only moderate rather than sabotage schemes of scientific management.[9]

Such an interpretation of employment and wage incentives in British industry provides a valuable analysis of contractual relations but offers only a partial explanation of changes in capital-labour relations in these years. It is difficult to accept the sharp distinction between wage contracts and the range of indirect and internal contracting relations which evolved in different industries. Even where subcontracting was most prevalent, supervisors were usually employed to act as the employer's agent in overseeing production and allocating work. The craft occupations discussed by Littler usually agreed piecework prices as a supplement to hourly wages, jobs being completed by craft groups rather than piecework masters. Most forms of subcontracting declined in the later nineteenth century, partly as a result of the antagonism shown by craft and non-craft unions, who fought relentlessly to remove these intermediaries in the bargaining process as they bid up wage rates and piecework prices whenever markets permitted.[10] Littler's claim that trade unions arose from the institutional matrix of internal contracting again obscures the complex range of market institutions and bargaining practices which prevailed, with limited attention paid to the impact of new technology on changes in the division of labour in sharp contrast to Marxist accounts of comprehensive deskilling.

Closer examination of the industrial foreman during the years 1870–1914 indicates the need for a careful reappraisal of debates on development of management in British industry. In particular, it is possible to assess Littler's claim that industrial foremen enjoyed a significant but brief ascendancy in these decades, only to be undermined by the rise of work study specialists in leading firms. The evidence for this argument is, at best, uneven. For many firms who favoured progressive management placed supervisors at the centre of their reforms and also developed welfare policies to enhance the loyalty of these grades. Among those enterprises geared to domestic and imperial consumer goods were cigarette-makers such as Wills in Bristol, a noted 'paternalist' employer which combined a disciplined approach to labour with the offer of long-term employment for a significant proportion of the local population in these years. Regular meetings of foremen and forewomen were introduced at the firm in 1906, and its members were involved in designing systems to strengthen supervisory control of factory life as well as monitor the administration of the generous pension benefits funded by the enterprise.[11]

It is true that labour markets and working conditions were very different in such craft-intensive and export-oriented industries as shipbuilding and engineering, from which many of our impressions of 'traditional' foremanship are drawn. Before considering the experience of these industries in more depth, it is worth outlining a general interpretation of workplace supervision in this period. In contrast to scholars who have stressed the dominance of both internal contracting and craft administration in British industry at this time, it is suggested here that the male foreman was already established as a significant figure in many, possibly most, manufacturing and building trades by the mid-nineteenth century. His influence was greatest where the employer depended on the supervisor's technical knowledge and practical aptitude in regard to arranging and completing work. The key to the supervisor's practical value lay in the individual's possession of social as well as technical knowledge in particular labour markets and production systems. Technical standards and specifications became more demanding in metalworking firms undertaking inventive and innovation orders, including those related to armaments production, in the period 1870–1914. There were significant advances in machine tool and other forms of technology at this period, though their impact was uneven across the metalworking industries. There is some evidence that the drawing office staff became increasingly important in regard to the preparation and planning of such orders, as well as becoming a more significant training ground for management staff. At the same time, some older forms of apprenticeship contracts changed as employers made some formal provision for technical training. The growth of collective association among employers as well as labour in response to the growth of collective bargaining was mirrored by the spread of technical, professional and vocational bodies among industrial managers and senior technical staff.

It was in this setting of growing association that there emerged the first conscious management culture among most industries in the United Kingdom. Faced with evidence of trade union attempts to preserve and expand their influence over labour markets, wage bargaining and working conditions, including industrial technology, employers frequently highlighted the vital responsibility of the foreman to represent their interests in the workplace. British industrialists rarely contemplated and more rarely attempted a radical reorganization of production to lessen their dependence on skilled labour. Nor did they make systematic provision for the training of supervisors, technicians or managers beyond practical instructions mainly learned at work. Their rationale for limited, practical and piecemeal changes can be explained not only in terms of prevailing market conditions but in the light of their relatively good performance in domestic and overseas markets as well as their collective success in containing if not suppressing the challenge from the craft and non-craft trade unions. There was no crisis of foremanship before 1914 because their employers were relatively successful in meeting their competitors and asserting their control over production while containing the craft unions.

The next section considers the responsibilities of male supervisors in mid-Victorian industry and the impact of some technical changes in metalworking after 1870. This is followed by a survey of reforms in payment methods and the pattern of industrial bargaining in engineering workshops before 1914.

Overlooking Technology: Supervising Labour in Metalworking, 1870–1914

Historians of work differ in their interpretation of the impact of technical change on the capacity of employers to monitor labour effort during the nineteenth century, though most scholars agree that employees even in highly mechanized sectors such as cotton textiles retained considerable discretionary control over the arrangement of their work.[12] Firms recognized the benefits of assimilating and adapting handicraft techniques and operative skills from earlier occupations rather than sweeping aside earlier production methods and their attendant relationships.[13] Such ties were underpinned in handicraft trades by institutions designed to give their members easier access to the labour market, as well as defending their acknowledged fair wage rates.[14] Some historians have presented these institutional supports in terms of a discussion on the 'social construction' versus technical content of skills, though it is self-evident that technology has a necessary social context.[15] Nor were these technical aptitudes insignificant. The contribution of the workforce to the process of incremental invention, innovation and adaptation is acknowledged by many historians of technology, including the empirical discovery of new techniques in iron-making works.[16]

Samuel Smiles recognized the presence of numerous foremen among the early generations of engineering entrepreneurs.[17] William Fairbairn, a pioneering engineer, emphasized the importance of effective supervision of machine makers by trained millwrights.[18] Whether the employer had personal understanding of technical requirements or little practical vision of production, an experienced foreman often played a vital role in the initial success of the firm.[19] E. J. Harland was apprenticed at Stephenson's works in Newcastle (spending one year in the drawing office), before joining J. & G. Thomson's on Clydeside and returning to Tyneside in the 1850s. After joining an engineering firm in Belfast during a labour dispute, he immediately demonstrated his value by importing strike-breakers from west Scotland and later a chief foreman from a former Newcastle employer.[20] His achievements were secured after fifteen years in Belfast, where he trained a full staff of foremen 'promoted from the ranks', as well a works manager and the outstanding draughtsman, W. J. Pirrie, later head of Harland and Wolff.[21]

The engineering industry which emerged from the third quarter of the nineteenth century retained a significant degree of regional and local specialization as well as sectoral distinctions between the manifold trades which comprised this key area of metalworking. These differences in part reflected both supply and demand, which continued to be regionally concentrated even as the international export economy expanded in the nineteenth century. Many engineering enterprises remained family concerns possessing at most three or four main departments devoted to heavy, light, foundry and brass or copper work. The diverse sectors of engineering retained their distinctive identity as well as differences in their use of skilled labour within production during the years 1870–1914. Economic historians have long debated the extent of technological change and the diffusion of 'American' machine tools and methods of work organization in this period. There is little need to rehearse the arguments and evidence, though it is worth distinguishing three related technical changes after 1870 and more particularly from the 1880s. Firstly, the introduction of new, lighter machine tools increased the precision, power and speed available to engineering workers. This new generation of lighter and faster machine tools, including the cheaper lathes manufactured in the United States, laid the foundations for the subsequent introduction of high-speed carbon-steel tools which permitted much higher revolutions at the lathe.[22] In addition, the increased use of jigs, fixtures and other means of setting work gave greater scope for a division between setting of machines and the simpler, repetitive tasks associated with machine labour. Thirdly, many larger and better-organized firms sought to extend the use of detailed plans prepared by their drawing office staff, as well as collating production data associated with the costing of jobs completed.

As important as the introduction of new technologies in the late nineteenth century was, their impact on production and the working life of engineering labour was diverse and uneven. In lighter trades such as bicycle and sewing machine manufacturers, these machines were widely hailed during the 1890s and later as the first wave of automation which reduced labour and removed much of the discretion over jobs which had been previously exercised by skilled workers, though even here there was a recognition that firms found it profitable to ensure that the setting of machine tools was undertaken by 'only skilled men'.[23] Employers such as Alfred Herbert welcomed the new technology as an instrument which allowed the rise of a new elite tool and jig makers, rate fixers and process setters within the workforce, though they also created a body of less skilled 'machine men' or 'machine labourers', as well as provoking resentments within the workforce.[24] Herbert made a familiar point in contrasting the reasonable standards of finish gained in the mid-Victorian years by craftsmen carefully 'playing' their machines 'at an appalling cost in time', compared to the tighter and more consistent standards gained from the new lathes.[25] Herbert's point needs to be corrected to the extent that in both periods it was also the responsibility of the shop managers and foremen rather than the craftsmen alone for securing accuracy in finished work by devising jigs and other fittings for more intricate jobs.[26] The new technology did permit a more elaborate division of labour in the engineering shops. By 1914 Barbara Drake detected at least four distinct groups within the ranks of engineering workers ranging from the highly trained to the machine minder.[27]

Working conditions in the heavier, more specialized and technically more complex sections of the engineering industry were different from those linked to the lighter repetition work possible on standard items, including new consumer goods. Machines to sheer, punch and bend the frames or parts of engines were steadily introduced to locomotive and marine engine works during the 1870s. Such equipment was designed to meet many different purposes and required the employment of experienced manipulators to achieve results.[28] In the heavy-engine shops there appears to have been a growing trend of restricting roughing work to the blacksmiths in the foundry rather than setting up the biggest cutting and boring machines in the workshops, for the limited use which could be made of such machines meant that any 'gain in this direction would not justify the additional capital outlay', as well as taking up valuable space.[29] The reluctance of engineering employers to abandon older machines even when superior technology became available is also well attested in contemporary and later sources. The impression of workshop production and limited mechanization is confirmed in Watson's vivid picture of employers who are extremely reluctant to abandon older redundant machines, and of even advanced enterprises which attempt to combine the modern with the antique in such places as the Bleak House Engineering Company. These firms could often serve as the refuge of the traditional craftsman in flight from the pressures of the larger works, particularly when the smaller plants continued to supply major employers with limited batches of specialized parts. Firms such as David Napiers retained the use of an antiquated table engine (salvaged from a paddle steamer), prime mover to drive workshop lathes at the end of the nineteenth century.[30] As Watson pointed out from the longer perspective of the 1930s, modern plant operated alongside geriatric machines. Mass production could only justify the heavy investment in equipment where specific machinists could expect to be employed on very large runs of standardized work.[31]

As governments and private customers demanded increasing sophistication in marine engines and vessels, including more interchangeability of engine parts, precision in design and finish rose to new standards. Among the most advanced and complex products demanded of the engineering industry in this period were those manufactured by private and government armaments enterprises. The large Elswick works of Armstrong-Whitworth specialized in field artillery and heavy ordnance. Leading technical specialists Noble and Rendel led the firm's drive to supply British governments in competition with the state's own arsenal at Woolwich as well as rivals such as Maxim-Nordenfeld and Vickers.[32] Engineers pointed out in the 1920s that the drive to achieve more interchangeability required a level of craft competence which was 'rarely entirely dependent on, but is very often entirely independent of the accuracy of the machine [tool]'.[33] Large machine parts in particular, which could not be fixed or secured as with smaller jobs, required well-trained workers to complete.[34] One manufacturer of marine gear and engine parts, G. & J. Weirs of Cathcart, near Glasgow, exploited the new machine tools during the 1890s, deploying lighter and faster equipment such as Potter and Johnson automatic lathes, which allowed the employment of less skilled 'handymen'. Both machines and labour could be readily replaced as demand altered.[35] The introduction of such technology permitted more precise gearing ratios and acceleration as well as the detailed observation and measurement of output from individual operators, though expert observers again stressed the role of the skilled craftsmen in setting jigs and fixtures even when production was carefully designed.[36] As one employer had told a gathering of London foremen in the 1880s, 'the more tools we introduce, the more demand there is for intelligent manual labour'.[37]

The need for firms to rely on both traditional and fresh standards of manual competence among their engineering workers was more apparent where specialized goods were required and where fine tolerances in experimental and finished work were demanded. The experienced foreman was expected to perform the role of leading hand in the engineering workshops of the mid-nineteenth century. Joseph Newton, a vociferous advocate of foremen's interests and keen journalist, declared in 1876 that the supervisor must acquire his credentials in the workshop itself and 'have for his teachers Practice and Experience'. The foreman engineer who lacked this basic qualification would never 'be of real value to his employer, or avoid the contempt of those he is supposed to govern'. This theme of government in the workshop was developed in Newton's analysis of the foreman's domain.[38] Such men were invariably recruited from the most able of the skilled workers, and it was not until the arrival of increasing numbers of machinists and workshop labourers at the end of the nineteenth century that the appointment of non-craft supervisors became a realistic prospect. The strategic value of the skilled foreman is apparent in the case of Armstrongs, which rose rapidly in the last quarter of the century to become a leading supplier of armaments to the British government. During the important strike of 1870 in support of a trade union demand for a nine hour day in the engineering industry, hard-pressed foremen were responsible for managing blackleg labour imported from Germany and Scandinavia as well as overlooking the work of apprentices.[39] As the firm struggled to meet the unprecedented standards required by Woolwich Arsenal, the foremen at this north-east firm were directly responsible to Noble and Rendel for the completion of prototypes and consequently bore the strain of disappointment when completed work was rejected.[40] The perils of investment in new technology without effective control of costs were apparent at another supplier to the Woolwich Arsenal. David Napiers manufactured specialized machinery for the Woolwich plant along with machine tools and cranes, before narrowing its catalogue of specialist manufacturers to light armoury and printing machinery as the workforce fell to a handful in the 1880s and the foreman was evacuated from his glass office at the firm's Lambeth works to make way for an experimental project.[41]

The evidence suggests that technical change in the British engineering trades during the years 1870–1914 was a diverse and complex process rather than a decisive transformation of production which entailed a comprehensive deskilling of the workforce during the period 1870–1914. There were significant advances in power generation, transport and tooling which led to the growth in precision work and a greater divide between the skilled setting of work and the less demanding tasks of completing routine machined jobs. The pace of innovation and growing sophistication of products also led to a reallocation of responsibilities as designers and drawing office staff were engaged to meet higher specifications while the practical tasks of completing fine work continued to rest on the shoulders of experienced management and journeymen. There is little evidence that the majority of firms in the leading districts perceived new technology as a means to radically reconstitute workplace labour or supervision. Employers consistently emphasized that in the expanding markets of these decades the need for skilled workers remained as great as it had been in the mid-Victorian years, though there was considerably more scope for the employment of less-skilled machinists.

The appointment of engineering foremen reflected these wider contours of production in the metalworking trades. In the mid-Victorian years they were senior craftsmen invariably selected to overlook the more skilled operations of the industry. They were also men capable of commanding sufficient respect to lead the workforce. During the 1880s some industrialists argued that the most able supervisor were not necessarily drawn from the ranks of the most gifted journeymen, since organizing abilities were more important in modern production.[42] Even these commentators recognized that an effective foreman required the respect of the craftsmen and could not be effectively employed where he faced active resistance from experienced tradesmen. Elevation to supervisory responsibility was frequently depicted in terms of the survival of the fittest, as leaders arose by natural selection within the shop itself. The improvement of supervision could be achieved only by raising general standards and by promoting the most able candidate, rather than the deferential charge hand.[43]

By the end of the 1890s, employers and unions were engaged in the most serious dispute since 1852. During this struggle the position of the industrial supervisor came under close scrutiny. These formed part of wider discussions about the various qualities which foremen should possess and the emphasis which could be given to their technical skills. The two responsibilities which continued to be most commonly cited by employers as the criteria of effective supervision were the improvement of 'the craft as a whole', and the representation of management authority to the shop floor.[44] This frank acknowledgement of craft vitality as well as individual competence remained even after the Great War, when senior marine engineers insisted that the all-round talents of the respected supervisor continued to be an essential asset in general engineering as compared with mass production sectors.[45] The aggressively managerial journal *Cassier's Magazine* acknowledged in 1901 that technical ability and personal capacity remained the primary recommendation for foremanship, noting that the supervisor must stand out as 'a master among his men, in skill as well as in knowledge'. The same journal stressed the need for cooperation between supervisors and workers to achieve maximum output.[46] The question which increasingly became an issue of managerial authority in the pre-1914 period was whether the foreman derived greater legitimacy from his craft credentials than from his position within the enterprise. It was not solely in regard to the firm's control and disposition of its capital equipment that the question of managerial prerogatives and supervisory authority arose in the British engineering industry. The question of workplace organization, the surveillance of the workforce and specifically the design and operation of payment systems all drew attention to the strategic value of the supervisor in battles for control over effort in the workplace.

Managing Organization: Workplace Reforms and Payment Systems in Engineering

Historians of industrial management in Britain, including Littler, have often emphasized the importance of a transition from internal contracting to new methods of systematic piecework and the spread of scientific management practices as a fresh strategy for controlling labour output before the First World War.[47] In recent years scholars such as Rose have argued that we should

understand the place of such reforms not only within the larger programme
of scientific management but also a rhetoric of personal surveillance which
featured in many areas of human and social sciences in the early twentieth century.[48] From the 1880s there emerged a distinctive literature on the management of production and a concept of 'management' itself as a discrete set of
activities subject to fundamental principles. Earlier initiatives by philosophers
such as Charles Babbage, Jeremy and Samuel Bentham, made little impact
outside state enterprises, though the railway companies and other concerns
which required substantial coordination developed organizational practices in
Britain as well as the United States in the later nineteenth century before the
appearance of management theories associated with Frederick Taylor.[49]

Surveys conducted by the advocates of Taylor's model of comprehensive
management reform and workshop control indicated that the full-blown
schemes outlined by Taylor were restricted to little more than a hundred
plants even in the contemporary United States.[50] The pioneering theorist
was surprised that his work on the art of cutting metals and tool steel became
a much more popular text than his broader theories of workshop planning
and control, including his programme for eight distinct functional foremen,
under the Shop Disciplinarian or superintendent. British industrialists and
their trade journals evidently received his general claims with scepticism.[51]
While Taylor had insisted that his schema could not be introduced piecemeal, this is how pragmatic British admirers approached his opus – including
apologists who omitted to discuss functional supervision in their exposition
of his radical agenda.[52] It is not difficult to demonstrate the limited support
for wide-ranging blueprints of Taylorism in British manufacturing before
1914, though it is also important to register the extent to which management
reforms were introduced or attempted and the impression which Taylor's
ideas (or changes what were assumed to be inspired by his writings), made
upon workers as well as younger managers during these years.[53] One Glasgow
manager was clearly influenced by Taylor's ideas in identifying five basic principles of scientific management in 1917: the effective organization of work by
management rather than by men; the provision of the best-quality machinery
and tools; the selection, grading and training of workers by management for
specific jobs; the provision of healthy working conditions; and a pre-calculated
system of payments by results designed to reward individual performance.[54]
The pattern of technological change has already been considered and will be
touched on only briefly here, but some consideration of progress after 1870
in the major areas of management identified in 1917, offers some impression
of the transition from older forms of work organization and internal contracting to the systematic management of production.

The principle that production should be the sole responsibility of management gradually pervaded the growing vocational literature for managers

and commercial staff at this time, including practical manuals on the introduction of measured payment systems.[55] Such texts stress the advantages of
cost accounting, stock control and accurate file systems, as well as increasing
the commercial and marketing capacities of the enterprise.[56] Some writers
argued that problems associated with the growing scale of many enterprises
and loss of personal contact between masters and men could be resolved by
the introduction of a management system which restored to the principal the
unitary power to command and direct.[57] Many organizational improvements
to distinguish line and staff responsibilities in business were canvassed before
1914, though it is apparent that employers remained unsympathetic if not
hostile to the creation of elaborate bureaucratic systems in their firms. The
card-filing system proposed by the Taylorists withered in the face of criticisms
from Glasgow industrialists that the collation of production data had been
found unwieldy and expensive to implement.[58]

Engineering employers were more ready to appreciate the advantages
of faster lathe speeds than accessible filing information. More imaginative
and ambitious industrialists and managers were exploring the possibilities of
improving product design to achieve output improvements, including greater
standardization of jobs and parts. William Thomson confirmed the views of
many management commentators in claiming at an international engineering
congress at Glasgow in 1901 that accurate and powerful tools must be used in
conjunction with an effective payment system and good working conditions
to secure maximum productivity. Machine tools at his own works had been
given higher gearing ratios for increased power, and trusted older relics were
abandoned if their measured performance was found lacking. He also advocated the standardization of parts to increase labour output and reduce wage
costs, particularly where high levels of specification and machining were envisaged.[59] Most firms could not hope to match the elaborate organization of
plant and investment in specialist machinery undertaken at the great Elswick
works of Armstrongs, with its tens of thousands of employees.[60] Other kinds
of armaments work such as the Admiralty demand for naval vessels from the
Clyde shipbuilding yards and marine engineering shops before 1914, emphasized the need for highly specialized fittings to vessels and engines rather than
offering scope for standard designs, machining of similar parts or replicated
working methods.[61] On the other hand, some of the enterprises supplying
marine parts and machine tools in west Scotland were in the forefront of
efforts to standardize parts and introduce rigorous management controls over
production in the first two decades of the twentieth century.[62]

In arguing for central control over production as a means of securing
greater output from the workforce, management theorists in the United
States and Europe emphasized the vital importance of a deliberate policy for
the selection, grading and training of workers before their employment in

the workshop. Advocates of personnel recruitment favoured the introduction of 'labour departments' which would accumulate detailed information on individuals and advise senior management on their eligibility for promotion, rather than relying on the personal recommendation of individual foremen. One experienced commentator recommended that the works manager should personally approve all engagements, promotions and changes in pay and conditions drawing on these confidential files of character references, complemented by information provided by the timekeeping office and production records.[63] The benefits of such a policy was strengthened for many writers who witnessed production reorganization during the Great War.[64] Most engineering firms remained sceptical about the benefits of labour departments, particularly as long-established practice of craft apprenticeships continued to be universally recognized as the primary source for the supply of skilled workers.[65] Employers became convinced of the need to develop a system of enquiry references and discharge certificates as one means of excluding trade union activists from engineering trades in west Scotland and other districts before 1914, though the controversial and much-resented system was far from the systematic grading of employees envisaged by the Taylorists.[66]

Few scholars have noted the extent to which Taylor and his followers advocated healthy working conditions and a congenial working environment as a foundation for achieving greater efficiency in output. Employers such as William Thomson recognized orderly working conditions as one facet of the effective arrangement of men and materials which ensured a flow line in shops where all tools and supplies could be brought to the stationary and well-supervised workforce.[67] Leading British engineering firms acknowledged the value of careful works design and lay-out from the 1880s onwards, particularly where heavy lifting and carrying equipment could be installed to improve the movement of hardware and reduce the reliance upon muscle power in the works.[68] Whitworths introduced important personal benefits and collective profit-sharing schemes for its supervisors, though there was a considerable reluctance among employers and trade unionists in the heavy metalworking to support substantial programmes of welfare investment that was associated with consumers industries employing large numbers of females. There are also numerous testimonies of working engineers to the primitive and even brutal working conditions encountered in British manufacturing shops in these years. Boy labourers as well as 'machinemen' were deployed on lathes and other equipment for long periods while the prevalence of systematic overtime suggests the continued reliance on labour as a flexible factor of production to be hired and fired according to demand. Such policies provoked bitter resentment among tradesmen against these lesser workers as well as their employers.[69] It was the outbreak of war in 1914 which increased interest in what was identified as 'industrial fatigue' in the 'human factor', coinciding with the influx of substantial numbers of fresh male and female recruits to the strategic munitions industries.[70]

Contemporary evidence suggests that the pattern of innovation in British engineering firms after 1870 was extremely varied and ranged from radical technological innovations in the larger armaments and marine engine manufacturers to piecemeal and fragmentary alterations in the host of plants and workshops which populated late Victorian industry. Capital-labour relations in the workplace and the larger world of institutional bargaining were also governed by a number of structural, cyclical and technical influences, which contributed to significant conflicts over management's right to control production in the two decades before 1914. Littler's analysis captures a part of this shifting narrative of innovation and resistance, though it is in the area of payment systems that his argument for the transition in internal contracting must stand or fall. His claim for the ubiquity of autonomous contracting in British industry during the Victorian decades provides the foundation for his subsequent discussion of the belated arrival of Taylorism in the form of management systems derived from Bedaux's ideas.

One survey of the engineering industry in the 1860s revealed important variations in piece working across and within different manufacturing regions. Textile machinery manufacturers in Lancashire and locomotive builders in South Yorkshire and Swindon in southern England used such payments extensively while marine engineering centres such as west Scotland made little use of piecework.[71] Group or gang employment under a piece master or subcontractor was reported in central Lancashire but not elsewhere and a strong campaign against piece working generally had contained its use until a resurgence under pressure from the employers in the mid-1880s.[72] Taylor was only one of a number of management reformers in the United States and Britain who recognized the fundamental value of controlling workers' efforts by a calculated system of premiums or rewards for improved individual or group productivity. It was partly in response to the deficiencies of crude piece working, including the ability of workers to restrict effort and avoid rate cuts, that Scottish engineers devised such methods as the Rowan bonus system, which offered a scale of (diminishing) rewards for progressive increases in output.[73] Its spread to general and marine engineering districts, where quality finishing had deterred the practice earlier may be partly explained as the consequence of the erosion of differential rates between regions. as a low-wage area such as Clydeside emerged as a high-wage district by 1914 and employers sought to improve productivity.[74] A number of practical experts in such regions found that the careful measurement of individual jobs and comparison of tools as well as employees pointed to the need for greater standardization and division of work between setters and machinists as well as more advanced technology in their firms to achieve a smoother flow of work through the shops.[75] Although most firms seemed little concerned with the scope for radical overhaul of production advertised by the designers of premium systems, the spread of calculated bonus arrangements sensitized employers to labour costs in places such as the moulding shop where trade unionists fought the introduction of measured output payments in one Scottish firm in 1903.[76]

Management experts usually claimed that such resistance could be overcome by a demonstration of the scope for increased earnings under the new system, though British reformers recognized the deeper roots of craft hostility before 1914. Richardson acknowledged during the war that the success of the new system depended on the conditions prevailing in particular workshops and the way in which it was introduced.[77] Managers with practical experience of such schemes urged the need to cultivate employee support for reform which would build confidence and enable estimates for new work to be integrated in the existing model rather than re-timing fresh jobs.[78] It is also arguable that the introduction of premium payments strengthened the growth of union representation and informal shop bargaining in engineering, as well as employer support for shop committees to deal with grievances at leading firms in regions such as west Scotland. At the same time, the persistence of older forms of piecework in many shipbuilding and related engineering trades as well as the spread of measured incentive payments, encouraged the craft trades to fight for advances in standard wage rate after 1900, as their employers argued that earnings should be increased by the adoption of payments by results systems and overtime working.[79]

Early discussions of premium wage schemes gave occasion for disparaging remarks about the limitations of supervisors' intelligence, including claims that 'as for the more complicated bonus systems they do not understand them at all'.[80] Such criticism of the male supervisor as an epitome of rule-of-thumb, outdated practice and imprecise methods were more likely to arise when ambitious management reformers presented the 'traditional' foreman as the most unlikely instrument of progressive policies. Architects of incentive-pay systems almost invariably opposed suggestions that trade foremen be given power to set job rates or given direct authority over a specially trained rate fixer, citing examples of supervisors encouraging resistance to the programmes of production engineers.[81] In this respect the undoubted popularity of the new premium schemes with British manufacturers appeared to mark the passing of the firm's reliance on their foreman's power of persuasion in the workshop and a decided decline in the supervisor's own influence.[82] Some larger firms did appoint more specialized rate fixers to set times and check targets, assisted by 'investigators' who carried out original timed operations and ensured that workers did not slow or sabotage times. The timed speed method of feeding individual machines was another specialized task, while output inspectors were appointed to monitor the quality of finished parts.[83]

Such appointments were mostly confined to substantial enterprises where specialist staff members could be justified, though in some cases the firm embarked on a radical review of labour when difficult trading conditions forced the owners to scrutinize costs. The hydraulic engineers Glenfield and Kennedy only became a company in 1899, building a new foundry in 1902. The difficult competitive conditions of 1907–1911 enabled the ambitious David Strathie to persuade his board to establish departmental organization with detailed cost accounts reported to board committees on a monthly basis. Within four years of becoming a director in 1908, Strathie replaced his more cautious predecessor as chairman.[84] Such comprehensive reorganization of the enterprise around a dynamic management reformer was unusual. Much more commonplace was the increasing employment of timekeepers issuing brass disks inside a clocking office at the works entrance. This innovation reflected a growing view that the supervisor should concentrate his attention on the workshop rather than the administration of the workforce.[85] More serious for the craft foreman was the prospect that the new 'production engineers', such as those employed at Armstrongs after 1900, would be promoted from the ranks of non-apprenticed and unskilled workmen, thereby heralding the demise of time-served foremanship and the diminution of his historical responsibilities as senior workman, job organizer and output inspector.[86]

Another form of organizational change in the engineering and shipbuilding industries which held some dangers for the Victorian foreman's empire was the rise of the drawing office. As standards increased and engineering tolerances diminished with the growth of interchangeability in parts, there was a discernible advance from the blue-cloth working sketches carried by the foreman in the 1870s to the more detailed specifications prepared by an enlarged complement of draughtsmen and male or female tracers in the pre-1914 era.[87] Management in plants manufacturing sophisticated, expensive items were increasingly supported by a technical staff responsible for calculating stresses as well as designing the fine detail of production. One employer observed in 1919 that the age when the firm relied on supervisors and principal workmen to read and implement drawing office plans had given way to one where drawing office staff formed a 'thinking department' of the enterprise while the workplace provided merely the hands to complete the physical task of production.[88] As firms became more conscious of the need to distinguish 'line' and 'staff' duties (administrative and commercial employees outside the command structure of the enterprise), production and administrative departments prepared estimates and monitored contracts, while the works foreman was more clearly confined to production duties.[89]

The discussions recorded in contemporary technical and professional journals of the engineering and shipbuilding industries indicate the advanced thinking of more progressive enterprises which embarked on organizational as well as technical innovations. A recurring theme in these projects was the rearrangement of machines to allow 'overlooking by the minimum number of foremen', while the supervisor was himself framed in a glass office above the shop.[90] Such accounts frequently give a misleading impression of the scale or organizational changes and their culmination in a diminishing role for the industrial foreman in British manufacturing before 1914. In some instances employers welcomed premium bonus as an effective alternative to close supervision in craft-based trades, workers being given the burden of chasing supplies and reducing job time.[91] This move to use output bonuses as a substitute for tight supervision on day wages became a significant feature of British assembly engineering and among some leading vehicle manufacturers during the interwar years.[92] Other commentators pointed out that premium bonus systems increased the responsibilities of the works foreman and instead of 'running after the men, the men run after him, and he becomes a very harassed individual'.[93] For the production supervisor was required to monitor finished work when continuous inspection was not practicable. Where job inspectors were employed, the foreman usually directed the checking on quality.[94] Across the engineering and shipbuilding trades more generally, payment systems do not appear to have dislodged the industrial supervisor from his key role in the directing workplace production before 1914. Barr and Stroud reported in the 1920s on the key role of the supervisor in dealing with ruptures and breakdowns in production, issuing 'emergency cards' to cover the contingency and protect bonuses.[95] Where group payments were common, the foreman was needed to arrange or approve the gangs, organize the less efficient and place or oversee apprentice workers.[96] Experienced foremen were in a position to arbitrate in disputes over the achievement of bonus rates as well as the timing of unusual jobs and where machinery was inadequate or inappropriate.

The reluctance of most British manufacturers to assemble a large cadre of ancillary production personnel left them dependent upon the competence and loyalty of production managers and supervisors at a time when radical reformers advocated the destruction of craft autonomy and subdivision of foremanship. Clerical and technical staff responsibilities were restricted to supporting roles while the majority of employees in the drawing office were themselves subject to an increased division of labour before 1914, rather than being given extensive production design and planning duties. Increased use of timekeepers had limited impact of the foreman's position in the workplace, where he remained responsible for the 'distribution and technical supervision of the work' itself.[97] The foundations for the continued power of the works supervisor can be found in his knowledge of the quality of the labour market and his direct command over the hands who worked beneath him. Observers agreed that the works supervisor in most works hired and also discharged the shop hands for indiscipline or when trade slackened.[98]

Taylorists and labour activists joined together in demanding the removal of the powerful foreman who had been promoted 'because of their driving power and energy', arguing that authoritarian supervisor damaged labour relations 'which the management, with best intentions, has no power to soften or control'.[99] Other authors argued that the management should not be directly exposed to the antagonisms and grievances which arose over employment, and that by hiring hands personally the foreman provided a protective shield against this outcome.[100] Engineering employers' understanding of the balance of power within the enterprise was probably closer to Alfred Marshall's military analogy of line and staff duties in the firm, where he suggested that staff departments could prepare for the campaign, but the 'exigencies of an army in the field require that complete authority be given to every officer, commissioned or non-commissioned, in regard to all doubtful matters'.[101] The practical understanding of management authority suggested to contemporary firms the need to hold on to a strong line of command reaching from the employer to the shop floor.

The rising tension in capital-labour relations also helps to explain the continued dependence of British metalworking firms on the industrial supervisor in the period 1870–1914. By the end of the century, leading manufacturers were arguing that the growing scale of plants and enterprises as well as deepening labour conflict with engineering unions point to the need for renewed contact with their foremen. As Summers Hunter told North East engineering masters in 1899:[102]

> The friendly feeling which should exist between employers and the workmen really commenced with the foremen, and that made it so important that they should be so particular in the selection of a foreman ... [who] might have under him a hundred men or more, so that there was really a lot of money in his hands, and [he] ... could make or lose money for the works.

One consequence of alienating such a key grade of employees was the sabotaging of management reform. British Westinghouse, one of the most vociferous advocates of Taylorist reorganization and training, expanded one Manchester department under a production superintendent. At least one foreman actively opposed the scheme covertly, demonstrating to the manager that 'passive resistance was the worst kind of resistance'. The foreman was dismissed.[103]

Determined employers were able to press ahead with their reorganization plans but there remained the danger that disaffected supervisors would aid and abet the workers if not their trade unions in thwarting reformers. Bitter industrial conflict culminated in the famous battle of 1896–1897 over the 'machine question' and other issues. Thereafter the leadership of the engineering employers as well as the main skilled union followed a course of conciliation when aggressive firms such as Weirs of West Scotland dismissed hundreds of workers while introducing automatic machines. Other firms in the same region successfully sought the cooperation of the workforce in developing more systematic management policies at this time.[104] In either situation the works foreman remained the instrument by which firms introduced their policies on the shop floor and his loyalty remained a key consideration.

Conclusions

During the late nineteenth and early twentieth centuries the British engineering industry became an important battleground. The contest involved not only questions of employers' right to manage production but also for the terms in which labour should be organized under the systematic control of management. Contemporary literature includes dramatized accounts of innovation as well as conflict at work as the protagonists sought to emphasize the significance of their struggle. Historians and sociologists have followed contemporaries in viewing engineering as a classical example of technical change and labour relations during these decades, as firms sought to modernize the industry against entrenched craft unions. In his influential account of capitalist production in Britain, Littler argued that internal contracting characterized industrial production and shaped labour relations before the late nineteenth century, giving way to a brief golden age of foremanship before the rise of scientific management. This essay has argued that such a model of capitalist relations is misconceived and that the evidence from metalworking industries, among others, shows that the supervisor was well established as the key figure in workshop organization by 1870 and remained as the front line of management authority throughout these decades.

The pace of technological change was different in the distinctive sectors of the engineering industry. Engineering firms did not fail to innovate more quickly or radically because of effective opposition from craft regulation any more than they were obstructed by the immovability of internal contracting. More recent research has revealed a complex relationship between industrial structure, market demand, technical change and the division of engineering labour rather than the portrait of deskilling and systematic management found in studies of the 1970s and 1980s. In contrast to what some contemporary apologists claimed, new technology and work design did not suggest its own unproblematic pattern of development. The increased division of labour between more demanding preparatory or job-planning skills and the less demanding tasks of standard machine work attracted comment, though there is limited evidence of deskilling across the engineering workforce as a whole. Contemporary evidence suggests that supervisory discretion and the capacity to make flexible use of tools and labour may have become a more significant element in the productive efficiency of the workshop during these years.

There is little sign of a decisive shift towards Taylorized shop organization among British firms in this period, though discussions in technical and professional societies indicate the steady advance of a more systematic approach to management and the emergence of a distinctive group of progressive innovators in regions such as west Scotland. The number of drawing office staff, rate-fixers, production engineers and timekeepers all increased during this period, though most employers appeared reluctant to extend line and staff grades unless there was a strong output rationale. While many 'common sense' assumptions were being challenged by data provided in premium bonus charts, most firms were guided by their expectation of profits and losses rather than an elaborate audit of production costs. The continuing commitment of British industrialists to fairly simple hierarchies of command and control in the workplace can be traced to at least the middle decades of the nineteenth century rather than following the chronology indicated by Littler and other writers.

The expectations which British firms had of their labour force were informed and recast by the growth of a discernible management culture in the collective trade associations of industries such as engineering. Within the rhetoric of 'scientific' approaches to management expressed at such gatherings were traces of Taylor's tightly engineered model of workplace control and individual reward. Such ideas were entwined with more generalized expressions of economic and social Darwinism which presented competitive struggle as essential to industrial survival. Common to many different commentaries on industrial efficiency was a pervasive concern with discipline and a persistent analogy with military command and an appeal to the masculine 'sense of honour' which would bind the non-commissioned officers to their superior officers as well as the men. Foremen rather than clerical or administrative staff were perceived as this vital link in the chain of command.[105] Apologists for scientific management argued for the benefits of enlightened despotism where employers established absolute control, guided by a rational and transparent system of incentives and rewards. British industrialists and most of their works managers perceived their opportunities for innovation within an evolving practical masculine culture of experienced men commanding sufficient respect to direct the workforce rather than relying on a corps of trained production technicians.

This commitment to a direct, personal line of command and a continued reliance on the individual qualities of foremen promoted from the ranks was strengthened rather than diluted by the widespread awareness of increasing conflict between capital and labour in these decades. Employers as well as labour activists believed that increasing scale of enterprises and the loss of personal contact between masters and men was contributing to the growth of class politics in the workplace. The tangible counterpart to the rise of vocational association among managers was the spread of trade defence and bargaining organizations among employers. National federations of industrialists provided a central leadership which defended the autonomy of regional associations and the prerogatives of individual concerns, while in practice seeking to maintain a 'reasonable' understanding with responsible trade unionism. The appearance of the foreman as a key figure in discussions about the right to manage during the 1890s and again before 1914 underlined his strategic as well as functional importance to the governance of the British workplace.

Notes

The research for this chapter was completed with the assistance of an ESRC project award and a grant from the Arts and Humanities Research Board.

1. K. Marx, *Capital I* (London, 1912), 423–424; H. Braverman, *Labor and Monopoly Capital: The Degradation of Work in the Twentieth Century* (New York, 1974); cf. B. Jones, 'Destruction or Redistribution of Engineering Skills? The Case of Numerical Control', in *The Degradation of Work? Skill, Deskilling and the Labour Process*, ed. S. Wood (London, 1982), 179–200, here 190 and passim, an important case in modern engineering.
2. W. Lazonick, 'Industrial Relations and Technical Change: The Case of the Self-Acting Mule', *Cambridge Journal of Economics* 3, no. 3 (1979): 231–262, here 231–232, 245–248; P. Joyce, *Work, Society and Politics: The Culture of the Factory in Later Victorian England* (Brighton, 1980), 100–103, 183–184, 231–232; W. Lazonick, 'Production Relations, Labor Productivity, and Choice of Technique: British and U.S. Cotton Spinning', *Journal of Economic History* 41, no. 3 (1981): 491–516, here 491–499, 510–513; C. K. Harley, 'Skilled Labour and the Choice of Technique in Edwardian Industry', *Explorations in Economic History* 11, no. 4 (1974): 391–414.
3. For example, C. Macleod, 'James Watt, Heroic Invention and the Idea of the Industrial Revolution', in *Technological Revolutions in Europe*, ed. M. Berg and K. Bruland (Cheltenham, 1998), 96–116.
4. S. O. Rose, *Limited Livelihoods: Gender and Class in Nineteenth-Century England* (London, 1992); N. Rose, *Governing the Soul: The Shaping of the Private Self* (London, 1999).
5. J. Zeitlin, 'The Labour Strategies of British Engineering Employers, 1890–1922', in *Managerial Strategies and Industrial Relations*, ed. H. F. Gospel and C. R. Littler (London, 1983), 25–54; R. Harrison and J. Zeitlin, eds., *Divisions of Labour* (Brighton, 1984).
6. Recent literature on productivity is reviewed in A. Booth and J. Melling, 'Workplace Cultures and Business Performance: British Labour Relations and Industrial Output in Comparative Perspective', in *Making of Modern Management: Output Performance and Politics of Production in Postwar Britain in Comparative Perspective*, ed. J. Melling and A. Booth (Aldershot, 2008), 1–26.
7. S. Tolliday and J. Zeitlin, 'Shop Floor Bargaining, Contract Unionism and Job Control: An Anglo-American Comparison', in *On the Line: Essays in the History of Auto Work*, ed. N. Lichtenstein and S. Meyer (Urbana, 1989), 219–244, here 232–233; cf. W. Lewchuk, 'Men and Monotony: Fraternalism as a Managerial Strategy at the Ford Motor Company', *Journal of Economic History* 53, no. 4 (1993): 824–856, here 846–847, 850–851; S. Babson, 'Restructuring the Workplace: Post-Fordism or Return of the Foreman?' in *Autowork*, ed. R. Asher and R. Edsforth (New York, 1996), 227–256, here 227–230, 241–242.

8. C. Littler, 'Deskilling and Changing Structures of Control', in *The Degradation of Work? Skill, Deskilling and the Labour Process*, ed. S. Wood (London, 1982), 122–145, here 124–125: 'It seems difficult to exaggerate the extent of some forms of contracting.'

9. Ibid., 124, 128–131, 133–135, 138–139; see also C. Littler, *The Development of the Labour Process in Capitalist Societies* (London, 1982).

10. Cf. ibid., 126.

11. 'Minutes of Meetings of Foremen and Forewomen, 1906–1919', Bristol Record Office, Papers of W. H. Wills, 38169/E/7/1, 25 April 1907: 'Secretary said he had ascertained what each individual Foreman and Forewoman was actually doing with regard to Stairs & Corridors, had it all written out on different sheets of paper for Committee to look into.'; ibid., 1 May 1907: 'Chairman submitted plan for keeping order in Stairs & Corridors ... which made every Foreman & Forewoman responsible for some part of the Factory, as workpeople are either entering or leaving, also at Meal Times, going to & from Dining Rooms'; ibid., 13 February 1908: The firm contributed £100,000 to supervisors' pensions in some years before 1914.

12. Lazonick, 'Industrial Relations and Technical Change', 245–248 and passim.

13. K. Burgess, 'Technological Change and the 1852 Lock-Out in the British Engineering Industry', *International Review of Social History* 14 (1969): 215–236, here 217, 229–230.

14. C. R. Dobson, *Masters and Journeymen: A Prehistory of Industrial Relations 1717–1800* (London, 1980), 39, 60.

15. J. V. Pickstone, *Ways of Knowing* (Manchester, 2000), 17–20; cf. C. More, *Skill and the English Working Class, 1870–1914* (London, 1980), 57, 154, for an earlier emphasis on social construction.

16. J. R. Harris, 'Skills, Coal and British Industry in the Eighteenth Century', *History* 61 (1976): 167–182, explores technology transmission and the reliance on non-literary communication of technical knowledge in early English iron making compared with France.

17. S. Smiles, *Industrial Biography: Iron Workers and Tool Makers* (London, 1886), 241–243, 293–294; C. H. Wilson and W. J. Reader, *Men and Machines: A History of David Napier and Sons, 1808–1958* (London, 1958), 3–4, for William Murdoch, Scottish foreman at Watt and Boulton and reputed inventor of gas lighting at their works.

18. W. Pole, ed., *The Life of Sir William Fairbairn, Bart, Partly Written by Himself* (Newton Abbot, 1970) (orig. ed. 1877), 47: 'The improvements in tools changed to mode of doing mechanical work, by rendering necessary large and carefully laid out manufactories.... This led also to a division of labour; men of general knowledge were only exceptionally required as foremen or out-door superintendents; and the artificers became, in process of time, little more than attendants on the machine.'

19. W. M. Neilson, founder of the Neilson locomotive building enterprise at Springburn, Glasgow, noted the importance of securing William Tait, an experienced foreman, as his lieutenant in founding a plant: W. M. Neilson, 'Autobiographical Notes', University of Glasgow Deposit, 10 5/1, 17, for entries relating to 1844; J. Thomas, *The Springburn Story: The History of the Scottish Railway Metropolis* (London, 1964), 65–66, 69; J. A. Morris, *A Romance of Industrial Engineering: The Story of the Growth of Glenfield and Kennedy* (Kilmarnock, 1939), 36, 47–48, 58–59, 69, for resignation of a foreman in 1871.

20. J. G. Pierson, *Great Ship Builders or the Rise of Harland and Wolff* (London, 1935), 5–8.

21. Ibid., 15–16. W. J. Pirrie (1847–1924) entered Harland and Wolff in 1862 and displayed such talents as to become a partner by 1874.

22. A. Herbert, 'Machine Tools', *Transactions of the North East Coast Institute of Shipbuilders and Engineers*, no. 35 (1918–1919): 179–226, here 191.

23. Anonymous, 'Speeding Machine Tools', *Engineering Times*, 14 February 1907, 197; Editorial, 'Settlement Terms', *Engineering Times*, 7 February 1907, 173; Joseph Chilton at Herbert, 'Machine Tools', for example; T. Bell, *Pioneering Days* (London, 1941), provides a politicized account of technical change and syndicalist organization at the Clydebank works of Singers.

24. Herbert, 'Machine Tools', 185–186, 188.
25. Ibid., 199, while noting 'this class of labour has been recruited from the more intelligent, and the more thoughtful among the rank and file'; F. Watson, *Machines and Men: An Autobiography of an Itinerant Mechanic* (London, 1935), 12–13.
26. K. Burgess, *The Origins of British Industrial Relations* (London, 1975), 25–26, 32–34.
27. B. Drake, *Women in the Engineering Trades* (London, 1917), 10–11. Drake distinguished between workers who could 'mind the machines' but not 'work the tools'.
28. J. Hume, 'Shipbuilding Machine Tools', in *Scottish Themes*, ed. J. Butt and S. G. Lythe (Glasgow, 1970), 158–180, here 167, for heavy marine engineering and shipbuilding.
29. H. I. Brackenbury and W. J. Guthrie, 'Workshop Methods in Heavy Engineering', *Transactions of the North East Coast Institute of Shipbuilders and Engineers* 43 (1926–1927): 99–112, here 103.
30. Wilson and Reader, *Men and Machines,* 26–27, 56–57.
31. Watson, *Machines and Men,* 27–28, 119, 179, 183: 'Mass-production pays only when there is a continuous demand for a standard article, and if a firm is equipped for mass-production, the cost of adapting the plant for a few hundreds or even thousands is too great; it is cheaper to send the job out.'
32. B. Weekes, 'Craft Unionism, Primitive Democracy and the Right to Manage: Engineering, 1880–1914' (Mimeo, University of Warwick, 1979), chap. 2 for a discussion of leading enterprises and armaments.
33. Watson, *Machines and Men*, 186.
34. Ibid., 105.
35. North West Engineering Trades Employers' Association (hereafter, NWETEA), Minutes, 15 January 1914, Glasgow City Archives (hereafter, GCA); W. J. Reader, *The Weir Group: A Centenary History* (London, 1971), 6–7, 13–15, 74.
36. W. R. Thomson, 'The Manufacture of Machine Engines: Some Factors Affecting the Economical Manufacture', *Engineering*, 13 September 1901, 379–380.
37. Speech of C. M. Palmer reported in *Foreman, Engineer and Draughtsman*, 1 May 1884.
38. J. Newton, 'What a Foreman Engineer Should Be', *Foreman, Engineer and Draughtsman*, 3 August 1876, 129–131: 'Chosen for his personal skill, he is called upon to be a ruler really of a little kingdom. His rule is personal and for assistance he has to depend really upon himself.' Newton was the leading light in the Foreman's Association formed in the 1870s and editor of its journal.
39. Ibid., for important insight into the strains upon foremen as foreign and blackleg labour introduced to a works during the 1870 strike movement.
40. T. Emerson, 'Works and Private Diary [1871]', Tyne Record Office MF 941, entries 23 March 1871 to 24 February 1872. Also 28 January 1871 to 17 February 1871. My thanks to Norman McCord for tracing this source.
41. Wilson and Reader, *Men and Machines,* 26–27, 30–31, 42–43, 49–50, 54–56.
42. 'Second Report: Minutes of Evidence', 1884, Royal Commission on Technical Instruction, C3981-II. Evidence of William Anderson of the Erith Iron Works, ibid., Q1791: '[M]y view is that you do not want a first-rate workman in a foreman at all; it does not follow because a man is a good workman that he is a good foreman; it is quite often the reverse.'
43. Ibid., cf. Q1786, where Anderson insists that supervisors must be drawn from the most cultured and accomplished of workmen, encouraged by education to improve themselves.
44. M. P. Higgins, 'The Foreman Machinist', *Cassier's Magazine* 20 (1901): 238–242, here 239.
45. K. M. Sloan, 'Remedies for Some Engineering Workshop Inefficiencies', *Transactions of the Institute of Engineers and Shipbuilders in Scotland* 73 (1929–1930): 498–528, here 521, for comments of C. H. Wright.
46. Higgins, 'Foreman Machinist', 239–240: '[T]he foreman and the men must work together to determine the maximum feed and speed.'
47. Littler, *Development of the Labour Process*, 48–79, outlines the arguments.

48. Rose, *Governing the Soul*; M. Thomson, *Psychological Subjects: Identity, Culture and Health in Twentieth-Century Britain* (Oxford, 2006); S. Clegg, 'Foucault, Power and Organizations', in *Foucault, Management and Organization Theory*, ed. A. McKinlay and K. Starkey (London, 1998), 48–51, 53.

49. See A. D. Chandler, *Strategy and Structure* (Boston, 1962), for pioneering text on railways; L. Urwick and E. Brech, *The Making of Scientific Management* (London, 1949), for an earlier classic account.

50. C. B. Thompson, 'Scientific Management in Practice', *Quarterly Journal of Economics* 29, no. 2 (1915): 262–307, here 264–265, which estimated that 140 plants or less were directly approved by the Taylorists; also C. B. Thompson, 'The Case for Scientific Management', *Sociological Review* 12, no. 4 (1914): 315–327, where Thompson's Taylorist criticisms of Cadbury were made.

51. Anonymous, 'Cutting Tools', *Engineering Times*, 17 January 1907, 69; F. W. Taylor, 'The Art of Cutting Metals', *Engineering Times*, 18 April 1907, 452; Editorial, 'The Utilisation of Labour', *Engineering Times*, 20 June 1907, for comments upon Taylor's arguments; F. G. Burton, *The Commercial Management of Engineering Works* (Manchester, 1905), 217–219.

52. J. Richardson, 'The Question of Scientific Management', *Transactions of the Institute of Engineers and Shipbuilders in Scotland* 61 (1917–1918): 154–205, here 159–161, for his own definitions.

53. Watson, *Machines and Men*, 90; A. Williams, *Life in a Railway Factory* (Newton Abbot, 1969) (orig. ed. 1915), 302–304. Williams was openly hostile to such changes as well as being aggrieved at his failure to gain recognition and promotion at the Swindon railway works.

54. Richardson, 'Question of Scientific Management', 159–161 and passim.

55. NWETEA, *Practical Problems in the Operation of Systems of Payment by Results* (Glasgow, 1925), 19. This publication comprised a series of essays from managers and others in various engineering and shipbuilding firms of Clydeside.

56. E. L. Orde, 'The Financial Organisation of Factories', *Transactions of the North East Coast Institute of Shipbuilders and Engineers* 33 (1916–1917): 50–62, here 51. Orde's paper was presented along with those of A. D. C. Parsons and G. H. Tweedell under the general rubric of studies in 'Works Organisation' convened by the Institute in 1916; W. E. Cowans, 'Shop and General Establishment Charges in Engineering Works and Their Relation to Costs and Estimates', *Transactions of the North East Coast Institute of Shipbuilders and Engineers* 15 (1898–1899): 221–256, here 221; D. Cowan, 'Administration of Workshops, with Special Reference to Oncost', *Transactions of the Institute of Engineers and Shipbuilders in Scotland* 44 (1900–1901): 263–293, here 264–266 (Cowans delivered his paper in the North East in 1899, whereas Cowan presented his in Scotland during 1901 – one year after another paper by him on the same subject in Scotland); Morris, *Romance of Industrial Engineering*, 92–93, 105, photographs indicate a significant increase in counting house and secretarial staff during the 1890s, especially when compared with 1879–1880.

57. D. Cowan, 'Workshop Administration', *Transactions of the Institute of Engineers and Shipbuilders in Scotland* 43 (1899–1900): 227–265, here 229, 243.

58. Ibid., 257.

59. Thomson, 'Manufacture of Machine Engines', 379–380.

60. Originally prepared as a lecture to the Elswick supervisors, A. Cochrane, *The Early History of Elswick* (Newcastle, 1909), 44–45, 75–88: 'The difficult operation of rifling this [1855] gun was done by Mr Bradley, during the night, watched by Mr Armstrong ... Bradley was more than fifty years in the Company's service, and was one of our leading foremen'; R. J. Irving, 'New Industries for Old? Some Investment Decisions of Sir W. G. Armstrong, Whitworth & Co. Ltd., 1900–1914', *Business History* 17 (1975): 150–175, here 151, 162.

61. W. R. Scott and R. Cunnison, *The Industries of the Clyde Valley during the War* (Oxford, 1924), 74–75, for capacity of the Glasgow region and some leading firms.

62. Morris, *Romance of Industrial Engineering*, 123–124, for development of mass-produced sluice valves and new jet dispersers after the war.

63. Burton, *Commercial Management*, 217–221, 243,

64. A. W. Kirkcaldy, 'The Need for Improved Organisation in Industry', *Transactions of the Institute of Engineers and Shipbuilders in Scotland* 60 (1916–1917): 73–93, here 85: 'By means of the grading of labour you may use any type of man from the most skilled to the least skilled, from the most efficient to the least efficient, because under a really good grading system, the man simply earns what he is worth.'

65. D. Kirkwood, *My Life of Revolt* (London, 1935), 72–73, for craftsmen and the connections with foremen in settling of conflict.

66. NWETEA, Minutes, 3 August 1909, GCA, when the Association argued that the system of Enquiry Notes 'as an ordinary act of administration not calling for discussion with the Unions. [It] had been in operation in Shipyards for almost three years, and it had recently been decided by Engineering Employers to extend it to Engine Shops.... The Employers pointed out that the signing of the Notes by the firm would act as a protection to the workmen against vindictive Foremen'.

67. Thomson, 'Manufacture of Machine Engines', 380.

68. T. Mudd, 'Plan and Construction of Marine Engine Works', *Transactions of the North East Coast Institute of Shipbuilders and Engineers* 3 (1886–1887): 55–71, here 59; Hall at discussion on Mudd, ibid., 67; T. Westgarth, 'On Works' Organisation', *Transactions of the North East Coast Institute of Shipbuilders and Engineers* 15 (1898–1899): 87–92, 189–190, here 88.

69. NWETEA, Minutes, 24 December 1903, GCA, for example, of Amalgamated Society of Engineers members allegedly intimidating a machinist.

70. J. Melling, 'British Employers and the "Human Factor" in Industry: The Ideology of Welfare Management in Britain, 1880–1930', *Social History Society Newsletter* 6 (1981): 9–10, for some comments; J. Melling, 'Employers, Industrial Welfare, and the Struggle for Work-Place Control in British Industry, 1880–1920', in *Managerial Strategies and Industrial Relations: An Historical and Comparative Study*, ed. H. Gospel and C. Littler (London, 1983), 55–81.

71. M. Jefferys and J. B. Jefferys, 'The Wages, Hours and Trade Customs of the Skilled Engineer in 1861', *Economic History Review* 17, no. 1 (1947): 27–44, here 29–32, 38–39.

72. Ibid., 38–39, 41, 43–44; N. B. Dearle, *Industrial Training* (London, 1914), 243–244, for comments on boy labour in engineering.

73. W. R. Thomson, 'Some Aspects of the Labour Remuneration Problem in the Future', *Shipbuilder* 20 (1918): 91–94, here 92; W. H. Riddlesworth, 'Premium Bonus Systems', *Transactions of the Institute of Engineers and Shipbuilders in Scotland* 61 (1917–1918): 43–77, here 43–44; James Andrews at Riddlesworth, ibid., 69.

74. W. W. Knox, *Industrial Nation: Work, Culture and Society in Scotland, 1800–Present* (Edinburgh, 1999), 112–113.

75. W. R. Thomson, *The Premium Bonus System* (London, 1919), 379; NWETEA, *Practical Problems*, 12, 18–19, for the comments by Ian Garvie of Barr and Stroud.

76. Morris, *Romance of Industrial Engineering*, 105–106, for Glenfield and Kennedy.

77. Richardson at Riddlesworth, 'Question of Scientific Management', 73.

78. NWETEA, *Practical Problems*, 16.

79. R. Johnston, *Clydeside Capital, 1870–1920: A Social History of Employers* (East Linton, 2000), 169–199.

80. J. M. Scott Maxwell at Richardson, 'Question of Scientific Management', 193.

81. Ibid., 23, 47, for criticisms of the 'traditional' foreman by James Macfarlane of Barclay Curle and George Ross of Beardmores.

82. Thomson, 'Some Aspects', 91.

83. NWETEA, *Practical Problems*, 17, for Garvie.

84. Morris, *Romance of Industrial Engineering*, 110–113. Dr Munro welcomed the project after 1908.
85. David Keachie at Sloan, 'Remedies', 521, for a later comment.
86. Anonymous, 'Speeding Machine Tools', 197. The author remarked, somewhat ingenuously, that he was surprised to find that 'this innovation is very much resented by the workmen, but that is probably because of the dislike to change which we all of us possess': D. F. Schloss, *Methods of Industrial Remuneration* (London, 1907), 3–7.
87. Herbert, 'Machine Tools', 182.
88. Ibid., 181–182; cf. Westgarth, 'On Works' Organisation', 89, who noted that employers provided the best tools but the 'majority consider that a large staff is a waste of money'.
89. Cowans, 'Shop and General Establishment Charges', 264–266, for one of the earliest discussions; David Keachie at Sloan, 'Remedies', 521; A. D. C. Parsons, 'Manufacturing Organisation', *Transactions of the North East Coast Institute of Shipbuilders and Engineers* 33 (1916–1917): 34–49, here 35, 41, where it was argued that no part of the works 'can be expected to work to the best advantage if the foreman is continually elsewhere'.
90. Mudd, 'Plan and Construction', 56.
91. Ibid., 45.
92. W. Lewchuk, 'Fordism and British Motor Car Employers, 1896–1932', in *Managerial Strategies and Industrial Relations,* ed. H. F. Gospel and C. R. Littler (London, 1983), 82–110, here 84–86, 105–106, for the uneven impact of 'direct control' strategies amongst motor manufacturers and the significance of incentive payments during the inter-war years.
93. NWETEA, *Practical Problems*, 32.
94. Ibid., 50.
95. Ibid., 15–16.
96. Ibid., 72–73, for Macfarlane of North British Diesel.
97. Orde, 'Financial Organisation of Factories', 52.
98. A. M. Henderson at Westgarth, 'On Works' Organisation', 108; 'With special regard to foremen, they also had to be picked men; who required special training to select and handle the men under them. They went up to the gate and had almost to pick them by head-mark. They had to use an infinite amount of tact': Watson, *Machines and Men*, 16, for foremen hiring at gates.
99. Watson, *Machines and Men*, 124; cf. 125, 130–131, for varying accounts of foremen laying off workers; Anonymous, 'Industrial Reconstruction: An Employer's View', *Athenaeum*, March 1917, 135 and passim. This article became a celebrated reference point for such managerialist and administrative theorists as S. Webb, *The Works Manager of To-day* (London, 1917).
100. Burton, *Commercial Management*, 217.
101. A. Marshall, *Industry and Trade* (London, 1927) (orig. ed. 1919), 371.
102. Summers Hunter at Westgarth, 'On Works' Organisation', 94–95.
103. G. H. Nelson at Parsons, 'On Works' Organisation', 114.
104. NWETEA, Minutes, 15 January 1914, GCA. In characteristically aggressive style, Weirs had introduced eight Potter & Johnson automatics and were preparing to install a further seven amidst serious redundancies.
105. Burton, *Commercial Management*, 242: 'The class of men from whom gatekeepers are usually selected is not one to be trusted with any semblance of authority over technical officers or competent clerks'; cf. ibid., 217: 'The foremen over the different departments are in their separate spheres miniature works managers, and will frequently be consulted by him, and by the general manager.... They should therefore, like their superiors, be activated by the truest *esprit de corps*, and a desire to render to every man the recompense which his conduct deserves.'

CHAPTER 8

'STEALING THE SOULS OF MEN'

Employers, Supervisors and Work Organization
(ca. 1890–1939)

Richard Coopey and Alan McKinlay

The supervisor has long been understood as the 'man in the middle', caught between the conflicting pulls of capital and management, on the one hand, and labour and the work-group, on the other. Here we shall argue that this construction was caused by major shifts in the terrain of labour relations, employer strategies, and work organization in the two decades before 1914. That is not to say that there were not tensions inherent in the foreman's workplace role but rather to argue that institutional and technical changes opened up a new discursive space in which the nature of supervision had to be rethought. We begin by charting the creation of the Foremen's Mutual Benefit Society (FMBS) in 1899 as a direct response to the awkward position of craft foremen, poised between their memberships in craft societies and their roles in clearly articulated managerial structures. The two decades before 1914 were crucial in the construction of the foreman as the 'man in the middle', a term with several distinct meanings. We then turn to the inter-war years, a period dominated by profound and prolonged manufacturing depression. Our focus is on the fate of the foreman in British heavy manufacturing and in the car industry. Here, our main objective is to offer a corrective to the depiction of the foreman's role as exclusively coercive. Rather, we point to the persistence of ties between the foreman and the craft community, on the one hand, and the complex negotiation of authority relations in car factories where Taylorist management had greater purchase.

The Foremen's Mutual Benefit Society: 'The Bastard Organization Which Has Been Stealing the Souls of Men'

Two years after the 1897 engineering lockout, the employers launched the Foremen's Mutual Benefit Society.[1] For the employers, supervisory membership of the craft societies was a critical weakness in the workplace and in collective bargaining. For the employers, supervisory expertise was held hostage by the craft community. The Engineering Employers' Federation's (EEF) reflection on the engineering dispute had confirmed the 'startling' range and 'extraordinary interference' of unions with foremen 'which show the necessity for foremen being placed in a position of independence, and not left under the influence of their union'.[2] One exasperated employer 'urged' his 'fellow Masters' that no union foremen should be employed 'as they were worse than useless and strengthened the engineering union's [Amalgamated Society of Engineers, or ASE] men's position to an enormous extent'.[3] The initial take-up of FMBS membership by individual foremen and their employers was hesitant. Even those firms which did take out corporate membership did not – or were unable to – enrol any of their foremen, drawing the ire of employers' association strategists.[4] Even where local employers' associations voted to make it compulsory for their member firms to become contributory members of the FMBS, this was only partly successful.[5] Increasingly, however, firms were insistent that any newly hired foremen were not members of a trade union and were prepared to discharge those whom they later discovered had retained a covert membership.[6]

For the engineering employers, union incursions into managerial authority had become intolerable: from union bargaining over machine manning to increasingly assertive shop-floor delegates trying to negotiate over wages and earnings and managerial personnel. The time was ripe, argued Thomas Biggart, secretary of the powerful Clydeside employers' association, to 'strike back', not just to rebuff union claims on an ad hoc basis but 'to assert itself … to have a voice that the future will hear'.[7] For the employers, 1897 was a watershed, the moment that consolidated their national organization and forced the powerful craft unions to accept 'managerial prerogative' and the prospect of labour relations being defined by the employers. 1897 was, in short, an investment in permanently reshaping industrial relations. In the wake of the engineering lockout, management drove forward a strategy to consolidate their national victory inside Britain's factories and shipyards. But this had paradoxical effects upon the power, authority and status of their supervisors. Management's search for lower costs, the drive to introduce new technologies, and the insistence upon managerial prerogatives all contributed to the intensifying pressure on craft foremen. Modernizing management spliced together new production technologies and managerial systems, notably management accounting, with inherited forms of craft administration.[8] Each of these managerial innovations, however hesitant, represented an incursion into the autonomy and tactical discretion enjoyed by supervisors.[9] Such innovations in managerial systems were far from universal and often fell far short of scientific management. Nevertheless, there was a significant increase in the deployment of payment by results that invariably had an impact upon the relations between the supervisor and the shop floor. Conventional practices based on craft notions of an equitable spread of work and of fair work pace were now subject to supervisory challenge mediated by individualized – and individualizing – payment systems. Supervisors were themselves now subject to managerial scrutiny as to how effective they were in accelerating the work process and reducing labour costs. The result was an increase in the demands made upon the foreman to intervene in the work process. In 1913 the workers of Brooks and Doxie, Manchester textile machinery manufacturers, complained that 'the labourers in previous years used to divide the work out in equal shares for the men to do. Not so with [this foreman]. He will divide it in lots, the same as if he were playing banker. He will give a man a lot with an ace if he wants him to have it ... these men can do the work three or four times quicker in a day than what the others can do, and then he is constantly saying, "So and so has done before you. He is waiting for you."'[10] Changes in the form of payment systems did not necessarily signify the rise of impersonal control but, rather, deepened the personal role of the foreman.

The foreman was the critical figure in authority struggles in the workplace. On finalizing the draft constitution of the FMBS, the scheme's architect confided to his fellow employers that 'no scheme would lay hold of the [fore]men in the complete manner which I am almost certain this would'.[11] Initially, FMBS membership was restricted to federated firms. The firm joined the FMBS for five guineas and paid weekly contributions of five shillings, divided equally between the firm and the foreman. Individual membership was broadly defined and open to skilled, 'superior' workmen 'in a position of trust': the defining feature, then, was the personal control of labour. Members were eligible to the same range of welfare benefits as those available through the craft societies.

By far the most important condition of entry was that the supervisor had to forsake trade union membership. Covert union membership was not tolerated and resulted in expulsion from the FMBS.[12] For the individual this was virtually a point of no return. To join the FMBS, the supervisor had not only to write off all prior contributions to his craft society but also to accept that he was unlikely ever to be readmitted. As the individual and his employer's contribution fund increased, so, the EEF anticipated, any lingering ties to the craft society would evaporate. Equally, union hostility to FMBS members was consistent. John Hill, General Secretary of the Boilermakers' Society, warned supervisors that 'the employers are providing a trade union for you, just in the same way as our present government are providing and paying for a trade union for the police of this country ... you have burnt your boats ... and you are their tool for the rest of your lives'.[13] This was more than a stern warning. Hill was pointing out that foremen who left their craft unions were permanently surrendering the independence that was the hallmark of the craft community. To surrender this independence was not just to lose membership of the craft union but also to risk emasculation. The hallmark of the craftsman was autonomy and self-reliance at work and in the labour market. To be bound to an employer was to jeopardize this freedom and the right to associate with other craftsmen.[14] More than this, to ally oneself with the employer was to turn skills acquired and validated through membership of the craft fraternity against their interests. FMBS membership entailed far more than economic calculation as it involved an irreversible rejection of any allegiance to the craft community. This made it imperative that the employers' Federation maximize the number of firms that both assumed a corporate membership and actively enrolled their foremen. For, if a significant proportion of federated firms remained outside the FMBS, it made membership for the individual foreman singularly unattractive because it restricted his future possible employers.[15]

The contested loyalties of supervisory workers were subjected to unprecedented pressures in the three decades before 1914. The ambiguous pressures experienced by supervisors were perfectly captured by the chief foreman boilermaker of the shipbuilding firm, Barclay Curle, in 1911. Responding to an oath of loyalty to the firm offered by a director at a company dinner, the boilermaker lamented that foremen were 'a body of men who had capital in the form of marked energy and ability, and who labour in the exercise of these qualities; who are sometimes regarded by Capital as being allied to Labour and who are, unfortunately, often regarded by Labour as being in league with Capital to oppress them'.[16] Independence, then, did not necessarily imply neutrality, save in placing foremen in a hostile no man's land, suspected by, and assailed from, both sides. Addressing some four hundred foremen engineers in 1915, one shipyard owner remarked that 'without any attempt at flattery, no class required more tact, for the working man had been the spoiled child of the nation for some years.... It lay with foremen to prove that they were the true friends of the workers and, as the intermediary between Capital and Labour, to convince them that if one fell both would fall'.[17]

The FMBS was the cornerstone of engineering employers' strategy to institutionally insulate foremen from trade unionism. In response, the craft societies intensified the pressure on foremen and charge hands to retain their union cards. In 1912, coppersmiths in Fairfields engine works threatened to strike unless the status of one of their foremen – Donaldson – was clarified. Nor was this a recent development or one that centred on a particular flashpoint. As the coppersmiths' union delegate put it, '[T]he discontent of the workmen had existed for some years and ... it was now coming to a crisis.'[18] The coppersmiths insisted that Donaldson abstain from using tools, should be given staff status, and not paid overtime. In terms of his employment contract and his day-to-day work, Donaldson – as all foremen – should be quite distinct from the men he supervised. Unless these contractual and working adjustments were made, the coppersmiths would refuse to obey or even 'recognize' him as 'their' foreman. The craft societies *and* management refused to accept any redefinition of the foreman that left him as a neutral 'man in the middle'. The craft societies no longer tolerated the foreman as a tradesman invested with some degree of managerial authority. The implication was that if the foreman was to exercise managerial authority he now had to do so from outside the craft community.

For the employers, the coppersmiths' demands amounted to the power to define their supervisors' contract and status, a gross incursion into the principle of managerial prerogative established by their victory in the national lockout of 1897–1898.[19] Little more than a decade after the 1897 lockout, the coppersmiths' 'grotesque' demands constituted an assault upon the principle of managerial prerogative, the employers' very claim to legitimate authority inside their factories.[20] One foreman boilermaker who wished to rescind his union card to join the FMBS found that 'the Union had declined to allow him to leave' by waiving his weekly dues and insisting that as a union member he remained bound by the conventions of the trade.[21] Such actions denuded managerial power of all authority. Craftsmen were claiming the right to veto supervisory appointments, a right that implicitly demanded that foremen not only respect craft protocols, but actively guard them against undue management pressure. Equally, the craft societies were placing an obligation upon management to clarify and delineate the contractual and hierarchical status of their supervisors. The craft societies' drive for clarification of the supervisor's role, contract, and status was a key part of their guerrilla campaign against the FMBS. For a supervisor to be defined as outside to the craft community diminished, perhaps eliminated, his reserves of authority derived from his acknowledged skill and experience. Conversely, the cost to the craft societies was that they relinquished the concept of the foreman as a fellow craft worker. This cost was not insignificant given the supervisors' considerable powers over employer and work organization.

Failure to make this clarification resulted in the craft societies' retention of the supervisors' loyalty, an attribute that the supervisor could not relinquish unilaterally nor management simply appropriate. Faced with such direct challenges to managerial authority, employers were torn between, on the one hand, a desire for a decisive and irreversible victory over the craft societies, and, on the other, a bitter pragmatism that yielded to the unions.[22] In short, grassroots struggle by skilled workers was unpicking the employers' formal victory of 1897.

For the foreman, membership of the FMBS did not necessarily signify allegiance with the employers, far less hostility towards the craft community or society. Rather, the FMBS members struggled to articulate a robust definition of their neutrality. Before 1914, the FMBS membership remained divided between discourses that stressed the supervisor's neutrality and those that avowed the importance of remaining part of the craft community. There were no voices that spoke of undivided loyalty to their employer. The EEF's pursuit of supervisory loyalty had limited purchase on the supervisors' languages of craft and class. The president of the Clyde FMBS reminded his audience, employers and foremen alike, that, above all, foremen were representatives of the craft community and should not just acknowledge but celebrate this allegiance.[23] 'It would be well for the best interests of the country, if throughout the whole industrial army, from the Captains through the Lieutenants down to the Common Workman, loyalty to craft, and ambition for craft, were ever the dominant note.' Similarly, any attack on trade unions was liable to draw criticism from the foremen, even those who had relinquished their union membership and were active inside the FMBS.[24]

Before 1914 employers remained divided over the value of the FMBS. For firms that estimated that less than 50 per cent of their supervisors were union members, the Federation's strategy was secondary to their immediate interests.[25] In 1909 the FMBS secretary, the lawyer who also served as the secretary of the powerful Clyde employers' associations, estimated that only around 22 per cent of federated firms were 'active supporters of the Foremen's Society'.[26] At the local level, the FMBS also attempted to provide a regular series of events that drew employers and supervisors closer together, factory visits, and dinners hosted by employers that provided 'abundant refreshment, complete with fine wine, whisky and cigars'.[27] The rule restricting corporate membership of the FMBS to federated firms gradually became eroded, despite the EEF's insistence that its member firms must retain their exclusive rights. This process reflected the rapid drift of the FMBS away from its EEF parent. In 1906, just seven years after its inauguration, the FMBS gently proposed that it enlist members from firms organized in employer associations 'kindred to the EEF'. By 1914, despite the formal position that only federated engineering firms were eligible for corporate membership, there were contributor firms from the iron and steel and chemical industries. On the surface, the foremen's dissatisfaction was about their contracts and the employers' half-hearted support of the FMBS, not least the EEF's failure to ensure that all federated firms were full members. But beneath contractual and actuarial concerns lay a deeper, unstated anxiety that far from being strengthened, the foreman's independence was compromised by the employers' failure to involve them in decision-making processes inside the firm and continued union incursions into their authority.[28] An implicit part of the employers' pursuit of supervisory loyalty was that they would support any foreman faced with trade union challenge, no matter what the allegation or how compelling the evidence. 'Employers', an exasperated ASE official noted in 1912, 'make a harder fight on a job of that kind than anything else. They will fight harder for their own officials even though they know he is a bad man.'[29] Indeed, the employers freely acknowledged that they simply would not countenance discharging a foreman: '[I]t is a demand which no one in this Federation has considered in any way whatever, that a foreman should be discharged.... No matter what the cost we are going to keep the foreman.'[30]

The battle to secure supervisory loyalty remained finely balanced in 1914 on the eve of the First World War. The FMBS had increased its corporate and individual memberships but was far from a universal presence in engineering or shipbuilding. Not all firms shared the strategic vision of the employers' federations. Foremen and employers articulated alternative versions of the nature of supervision, supervisory authority and the source of his legitimacy. Some employers, but very few foremen, pursued the ideal of the foreman as part of a managerial chain of command. Other employers, perhaps the majority, as well as most foremen, defined the supervisor as a neutral broker between capital and labour. A third group of employers and foremen continued to regard supervisory authority as largely, if not exclusively, derived from the respect they were accorded by the craft community. These institutional and linguistic questions were raised in novel ways in the two decades before 1914 but remained unresolved.

Supervisory Power and Authority in the Workplace, 1919–1939

Despite being established and financed by the EEF, the FMBS was an independent organization, at least nominally. Based in Glasgow, FMBS affairs were administered and managed by Thomas Biggart, a prominent figure in local and national employers' organizations. There was an inherent tension in the relationship between employers and their supervisors' society. The FMBS constantly strained at the tight control exerted by the EEF. Indeed, during the pre-1914 labour unrest the FMBS was urged to move its headquarters from Glasgow to London, the more closely to be under the eye of the federation.[31] The FMBS resisted these overtures. This strained relationship remained largely unchanged until 1919 when the emergence of the rival supervisory trade union, the National Foremen's Association (NFA), falling pay levels, and an ever more assertive shop stewards' movement, the Coventry FMBS founded the Foremen's Mutual Welfare Society (FMWS). The significance of the FMWS lay not so much in its language of independence from both capital and labour, but in its search for collective bargaining rights. This was a complex institutional and linguistic turn. The FMWS's first rule was that membership was only open to individual FMBS members. By

1920 the FMWS had progressed from conferences with particular employers
to proposing a general wage claim that all foremen receive at least £1 more
than their supervisees. The Coventry Society argued that it was 'keeping the
foremen out of the National Union of Foremen [NFA] to which the Society
is strongly opposed'. The FMWS also stressed its allegiance to capital and
its rejection of sympathetic overtures from the craft unions, particularly the
ASE: 'Up till now ... the men have looked upon the foreman as part of the
management, but now the trade union movement is coming along in their
views are changing, and they want to take the foreman over to the part of the
men.... It is us few fellows who are trying to combat it.'[32] There was a latent
threat to the FMWS position. That is, according to the FMWS, an organization determined to remain loyal to the employers, if granted limited bargaining rights would blunt the appeal of both independent supervisory unionism
and the craft societies. For the EEF, even this veiled threat was insufficient to
warrant acceptance of the 'undesirable attributes' of the FMWS – specifically,
bargaining rights. However, the local employers' association did hire a recruitment agent to bolster the FMBS's falling local membership.[33] The employers
moved quickly to head off the movement inside the FMBS to become a quasi-
union: preferential hiring of foremen or redundant foremen, paying their society subscriptions during spells when they returned to 'the tools', and moral
and practical support is confronted by 'Trade Union oppression'.[34] Despite
the employers' federation's strategic awareness of the precariousness of their
hold on the FMBS and of foremen inside the workshop, there was little sus-
tained commitment from employers to support local society initiatives. Only
closer employer involvement at the grassroots level could provide the 'safety
valve' necessary if foremen were to be deterred from developing some form of
independent trade union or being re-absorbed back into the craft societies.[35]
This attempt to construct a durable bargaining role for foremen, acceptable
both to management and the craft unions, was checked by the onset of reces-
sion in 1921 and the 1922 engineering lockout.

The 1922 engineering lockout was a watershed in engineering industrial
relations. As a result of its defeat the premier craft society, the Amalgamated
Engineering Union (AEU) was virtually bankrupted, procedurally emascu-
lated and thoroughly demoralized. Shop steward networks were devastated
by a systematic comb-out of shop-floor activists synchronized through local
employers' associations. After the 1897 lockout engineering workers rebuilt
their organizational strength and workplace controls through local struggles:
the situation after 1922 was unfavourable to any similar revitalizing process of
grassroots resistance. Against the bleak backdrop of mass unemployment the
dissolution of workplace union organization continued unabated until the
beginning of rearmament in the mid-1930s. Few in number and restricted in
their power to represent their fellow workers, shop stewards largely reverted

to their primary pre-1914 role of covert union recruitment officers rather than front-line negotiators.[36] The collapse of workplace union organization and the exposure of engineers to unchecked managerial initiative was a vital element in the individualization of shop-floor bargaining, a process in which foremen played a crucial, and highly personalized role.

The foremen's sense of their role, with affinities to both capital and labour and yet distinct from both, was a consistent theme in the inter-war years. The foremen's associations struggled to conceptualize their role as brokers between capital and labour inside the factory. 'We must be regarded as expressing the views of Management as distinct from Capital and Labour.' In their daily activities the foremen struggled to reconcile 'two seemingly opposing principles, discipline and freedom', a conflict that only management could hope to contain if not defuse. Similarly, the prevalence of piecework had made the foremen the cutting edge of the employers' drive to reduce costs, a process that had made their role as intermediaries more difficult as the employment relationship was reduced to a brutal 'cash nexus'.[37] The historic basis of the supervisor's authority derived from his craft mastery and the respect of the shop floor was losing legitimacy in the employers' eyes. The question of supervisory authority was mediated through debates about technical training for foremen and their relative standing against emerging forms of technical labour.

Post-war debates about the modernization of manufacturing management systems raised questions about supervision. Again, we hear the foremen insisting upon their unique role as intermediaries, a role that was challenged by the rise of new technical staff. Addressing 107 Clydeside foremen at their association's 1923 general meeting, a consultant delivered a lecture on 'the new foremanship'. The 'old' foremanship was bound to archaic, inexact methods and had to give way to 'scientific methods', a process which, the speaker insisted, would enhance rather than diminish the status of the foreman. While there was broad agreement about the need for the further education of foremen, there was dissent from the floor. One voice argued that education 'should start at the top management amongst those who are in authority over the foremen', an intervention that implied that managerial ignorance of production methods was profound and deep-seated. This is an implicit statement of the autonomy of the foreman. A second voice 'stated very cordially that in spite of all the American methods of education for foremen, that the Clyde type were still suspicious of them all'.[38] More trenchantly still, another foreman volunteered his 'wholehearted opposition to office-bound clerks dictating how quickly a bolt should be tightened or how long it takes to rivet six inch plates'.[39] Similar debates surrounded eligibility for membership of the FMBS. The flourishing Glasgow Association of Foremen routinely admitted around a dozen new members every month without quibble. In November 1923, however, one nominee stimulated 'considerable discussion'. The nominee, a chief progress chaser, was eventually accepted for two reasons. First, the foremen pragmatically acknowledged that this was an example of 'the many new positions which had arisen owing to the new systems of Shop Management', technical roles that they had to reach an accommodation with, if not an alliance. Second, only those applicants who had completed a recognized apprenticeship and exercised some authority over staff – *chief* progress chaser – were acceptable.[40] The foremen's ruling on eligibility paralleled that of the employers' federation. For the EEF, FMBS membership was not determined by the performance of coordinative, administrative or technical tasks which made it essential that management secure loyalty but their control function: their position in the factory's authority hierarchy.[41] During the inter-war years FMBS membership, both corporate and individual, rose steadily. Corporate membership rose sharply after the engineering employers' victory in 1922: 423 firms were contributory members in 1914, jumping to 1,186 in 1922, and remaining at over 1,200 for the next decade. Individual membership displayed a similar pattern, rising from 3,166 in 1914 to 12,317 in 1922, and rising steadily to around 16,000 until 1933.[42] No doubt the weakness of the trade unions and the employers' willingness to use the FMBS as a source for new supervisors increased the society's attractiveness, although employers preferred to promote from within even if a prospective supervisor came highly recommended by another firm.[43] Indeed, foremen displaced by the inter-war depression faced both bitter hostility from men they had previously supervised and pressure to return to their craft union.[44] In 1926 Wigan manufacturers privately reported to the EEF that their unemployed foremen were unable to collect their benefits from the comparative dignity of a union lodge but were 'obliged to herd with the more or less casual labour' at the town's public labour exchange:

> The men who formerly worked under them have taken this opportunity of joining up in the queue alongside these foremen and making themselves objectionable, and informing the bystanders of their social downfall, to what they describe in Wiganese as 'the sanguinary bosses men'. As you can imagine this is rather tending to undo the work we have tried to carry out in encouraging the FMBS as they are made to feel very forcibly that by being members of the FMBS they are outcasts.[45]

After 1933 the FMBS was opened up to clerical and design office members, a departure that makes it impossible to assess the number of foremen members.

Inside the workplace, foremen generally worked in isolation, secretive about their department's costs and indifferent to the impact their decisions had on other sections. A 1939 review of the internal administration and costing regime of a shipyard engine works concluded that 'the various shops are semi-independent and are almost entirely in the hands of the foremen who seem to be capable, but have little interest in what goes on outside of their shops'.[46] Even elaborate production control systems did not necessarily centralize or guarantee control of the movement of parts or cost reduction. Clerical control did not necessarily equate to physical control on the shop floor. Illicit hoarding of finished bonus tasks by machine operators negated any drive to establish costs precisely and left foremen unable to control and plan detailed production flows.[47] Such criticism was misplaced. Craft foremen were not ignorant of such abuses of production control and bonus systems but rather complicit in them. For the astute foreman, coercion was likely to prove counter-productive, especially when dealing with a stable workforce. Turning a blind eye to workers' manipulation of the piecework system was an important part of the foreman's way of establishing and maintaining the reciprocal ties that bound him and the work-group together.[48] Conversely, insisting on the strict adherence to a piecework system was a powerful super-visory sanction against a recalcitrant individual or group. Just as respect differs from fear so power is not synonymous with authority. The foreman's authority hinged on his awareness of his constrained power; an acceptance that he was open to examination and sanctions from below as well as his responsibilities to management. Such subtle diplomatic skills had to be honed still further when the foreman confronted union shop stewards. For the general secretary of the independent foremen's union, the NFA, while technical expertise contributed to supervisory authority, dealing with unionized workplaces required the fore-man 'to be as wily as the serpent and as harmless as the dove'.[49]

Even in avowedly Taylorist regimes, the foreman's power remained formi-dable: he hired and fired, allocated short-time and overtime, was responsible for apprentice training, and distributed tasks with different bonus earnings potential. His nominal power ranged over every aspect of the technical and social division of labour. As one progressive manager put it, irrespective of organizational innovations, the foreman remained 'the vital link between Management and workmen, between design and execution; carries through into production according to plan, arranges the routine of the jobs, selects the right men for jobs and the right jobs for men; he is responsible for quality as well as quantity of production'.[50] Again, we can hear an implicit acknowl-edgement, perhaps even a note of frustration, that the foreman's brokerage role remained stubbornly fixed in place, little changed despite the employ-ers' victories in 1897 and 1922, despite the introduction of more systematic forms of management. The foreman necessarily had to rise from the shop floor or, better still, from a specific workplace. The foreman could not be formed *ab initio* but had to retain a certain affiliation to the craft commu-nity if his knowledge base was to be legitimized and accepted by those he supervised. The prime source of the foreman's authority was his knowledge of production techniques and of the abilities of individual workers. This was a powerful current in managerial, not just worker, opinion. Suggestions that supervisory training in planning and coordination would gradually supersede the traditional craft foremanship drew sharp responses from the manufacturing director of instrument makers, Barr and Stroud:[51]

> The leadership of the foreman we are told must rest today upon the fact that he is a good organizer, with suitable personality, tact, power to handle men, of methodical habits, courage, initiative.... Now these are all very well so far as they go but though a man possesses them all, without proficiency he is nothing.... The true respect of shop workers will only be won when they are convinced that the foreman knows his job.... The real training ground for foremen today, in our opinion, is the works themselves.

Typically, craft foremen kept personal records of the competences of current and previous workers.[52] It was this knowledge and his reputation for fair dealing that legitimized his authority among his shop-floor peers and was the basis of his autonomous power. But supervisory authority was more complex than just a matter of knowledge of production systems. Authority on the shop floor could derive from a dense web of family and friendship ties. We can see this in the case of Mavor & Coulson, a leading Glasgow manufacturer of coal-cutting machinery.[53] 'The foundation of the family spirit in M&C was', wrote Sam Mavor, 'that so many of us have grown up together from boyhood, and have spent all or most of our working lives here as co-workers and friends, we are in fact both an industrial and social unit. Our relations with each other do not begin and end at the starting and stopping hours.'[54] Durable family networks were the basis of consensual labour relations. In 1930, management estimated that 134 members of the 'M&C family' worked directly alongside 'at least one other member of their immediate family circle': there were 'thirty instances of two generations represented by father and son, father and daughter, mother and son, and of a father, two sons and a daughter. Other family relations represented are twenty-three brothers and two brothers with a sister and four pairs of sisters'.[55] At least 25 per cent of the factory's employees worked beside one of their immediate family. Not only was labour recruitment through kin networks of the labour force a cheap and efficient screening mechanism it also underwrote a powerful paternalist ideology. The mutual obligations of family and friendship networks enforced the high standards necessary to maintain their collective, often inter-generational, reputation independently of factory discipline.[56] For a new or sponsored recruit to infringe factory discipline was to endanger the reputation of their sponsor and others in their kin network.[57] Crucially, over time, reputation became attached to the kin network as a whole rather than to the initial or current sponsor. For supervisors, cultivating the density of family employment networks through preferential recruitment was a powerful method of reinforcing their power and authority.

Management well understood the importance of patrimonial sponsorship both as a traditional prerogative of the craft community and as an endorsement of the firm's employment practices: '[A] man who brings his son to us for training can pay us no greater compliment, for it is evidence that he finds congenial the atmosphere in which he himself works.'[58] The 'quiet, efficient and industrious' Jamie Moffat ensured that three of his four sons followed in his footsteps as a skilled engineer. The most extensive kin network was that of the Foyer family which was present continuously from 1892 onwards. Andrew Foyer began work as a 28-year-old fitter in 1892 and became a foreman in 1915. For Sam Mavor, the prime attributes of the foreman were not solely technical and organizational competence but 'also and chiefly his *character* ... a kindly disposition, even temper, common sense, and ... experience'. The foreman's authority hinged on his 'understanding of the individual mentality of his men, and by considerately using this knowledge in his daily dealings with them, he wins their respect and confidence'.[59] Who better than the head of an extended family to have such intimate knowledge of the workers under his control? Between 1901 and 1915 Foyer senior sponsored two apprenticeships and the employment of his brother, William. In turn, William Foyer also initiated his son's engineering apprenticeship in 1902. The three second-generation Foyers – all skilled engineers – proved equally adept at securing work for a further four cousins and nephews during the difficult inter-war years. In the four decades after 1892 the Foyer family axis grew to a core group of six fitters, spanning two generations. The experience of the Foyer clan demonstrates that family employment networks were cumulative over time, becoming increasingly dense, cohesive and self-policing. The viability of paternalism was, Patrick Joyce insists, not so much about ideological hegemony, but the interpenetration of family, work and community life. Recruitment and family networks bound family and work together, rendering paternalist ideology not just plausible but resonant with the realities of daily life on the shop floor, the intimate 'theatre of paternalism'.[60] To be one of the long-serving 'fathers of the M&C family' offered not just the opportunity to sponsor employment of family, friends and neighbours, but also enhanced the individual's promotion prospects. There is clear evidence that, in this firm at least, promotion to foreman rested on the durability, vitality and reputation of employment networks.

The inter-war period witnessed significant reductions in the scope of the foreman's role. The foreman of the early twentieth century was responsible for the efficient coordination of workflows, including ordering the necessary materials and for the quality of the finished product. Especially in the volume production sectors such as the car industry, production planning, rate fixing, and quality control gradually became the preserve of independent departments and specialized staff. But this was a complex, uneven, and negotiated process. The power and autonomy of the rate-fixer varied markedly between firms. In craft-based heavy engineering, payment-by-results systems were introduced primarily for their divisive and coercive qualities rather than as part of a concerted effort to increase managerial knowledge and control over skilled work. By grafting payment by results onto existing forms of craft administration it tended to supplement rather than challenge the personal powers of the foreman. Even where rate fixers accompanied the introduction of payment by results, their powers and duties were not part of a rationally ordered structure with distinct spheres of bureaucratic responsibilities. Rather, the shop floor remained a shifting constellation of competing sources of authority. For this reason, the manager of Barclay Curle offered would-be innovators the following advice:

> To make the position of rate-fixer tenable, a rank such as will enable him to exercise plenary powers over all departmental staff should be given him. A conscientious pursuit of his duties savours of encroachment on the preserve of others, and while it is possible for the executive of the establishment to adjust any material differences which might crop up, the persistent nagging of some workmen, often, unfortunately, backed by their foremen, tends, in the absence of personal authority, to make the rate-fixer seek other occupation.[61]

As the author ruefully acknowledged, even his firm had been unable to satisfy these strictures: authority relations were not depersonalized by the arrival of rate-fixers on the shop floor, they simply became more complex and contested. Similarly, in the car industry, management's anticipation of the effectiveness of passive resistance by workers reduced the appeal of any concerted Taylorization of production:[62] 'Anyone with any knowledge of the independent and, it must be confessed, awkward spirit, characterizing the workers of say the Northern Midlands, would hesitate before applying the extreme methods of the latest American Scientific Management, well knowing the futility of the task.'

The introduction of quasi-bureaucratic payment systems was not, therefore, necessarily accompanied by the wholesale bureaucratization of workplace authority relations. Indeed, on the contrary, employers routinely acknowledged the incompatibility of personal and bureaucratic authority and the failure to subordinate both grades to impersonal rules. Typically, manufacturers side-stepped such clashes by defining the rate-fixer's role as supplementary to that of the craft foreman. 'All too often', an employers' association official lamented, factory managers 'defer to the judgement of the foreman' on matters of payment and production techniques despite 'the best advice of his clerical staff' in order to preserve supervisory authority intact. In the engine shops of British shipyards, the rate-fixer's role was, at most, supplementary or, more likely, subordinate to that of the craft foreman. This choice reflected the assumption that 'shop foremen naturally offer the best service, but such duties are liable to disrupt "old friendships"'. For those manufacturers who were critical of the traditional craft model of foremanship this sensitivity to shop-floor opinion made craft foremen unreliable vehicles for the introduction of innovative production methods.[63] British employers were sceptical about scientific management, a scepticism that was reflected in their preference for ad hoc forms of work measurement.[64] The negotiated nature of work measurement ensured the continued importance of the foreman alongside the rate-fixer. In Morris Motors, 'the foreman, *with* the rate-fixer, plus stop watch would time the fastest and most reliable operator, a few seconds might be added or subtracted, the price would be arrived at rather than agreed to'.[65]

In the car industry, uneasily poised between craft and mass production from the early twentieth century, the tension between the foreman and the rate-fixer was not fully resolved before 1939. Even where rate fixing had become an established technical function, the craft foreman retained the power to mediate between job measurement and the operator. In the Midlands' car factories the rate-fixer had to consult the foreman before a price was set.[66] One foreman at Morris Commercial Cars, a factory based on short-cycle tasks synchronized by assembly lines, recalled his role in negotiating the relationship between the operator and the rate-fixer in this complex bargain. 'My job was to see that the operator didn't swing the lead – but my job was also to see that the rate-fixer didn't cut the operator's throat.'[67] Supervisors could, for example, ignore unofficial working methods: using hammers to 'rectify' irregular components rather than the much more time-consuming re-machining; using reject tools rescued from the stores.[68] Conversely, although the ability to mediate between rate-fixer and operator was a potent source of supervisory power, to break established patterns of custom and practice was to risk compromising authority. The allocation of tasks was a formidable weapon but had to be used diplomatically. The foreman retained his powers to hire and fire labour, irrespective of the development of personnel departments. During the inter-war depression this was the foreman's greatest power. Arthur Exall recalled the foreman's key role in maintaining the harsh, arbitrary regimes of the inter-war car factories: 'You couldn't talk, you couldn't sing. If you was away from your bench for two or three minutes he was chasing you.... That was their attitude all the time, it was the threat of the sack every time they came to you.'[69] We should be wary of assuming that driving supervision was universal. In Ford, a company that used day wages rather than piecework, American corporate management expressed their disappointment with British foremen – 'the stiff white collars ... who refused to get their hands dirty and drive production'.[70] In sum, the use of the stop watch did not necessarily signify the development of a Taylorized work regime or even the search for the one best way to perform a specific task. Jobs were timed but not necessarily reorganized, just accelerated. No enhancement or centralization of managerial knowledge was necessarily involved in this process. In a certain sense, the foreman's traditional role, straddling the divide between capital and labour and understanding the pressures on both, was confirmed by his mediation in the detail of rate fixing. There were exceptions, however, where the rate-fixer exercised significant power and had eclipsed the craft foreman in costing production and establishing individual earnings. The 'job-pricer' in Alldays Engineers, Coventry, was rarely wrong in his calculations and never reproached by management or workers.[71]

The foreman's control over quality control was also eroded during the inter-war period. As late as the early 1930s, foremen in Alvis checked each crankshaft, tested every oil pump, and passed each assembled component personally. Mass production made this personalized quality control impossible. Detailed inspection of the first production run was the function of pattern viewers. Quality control during full production was conducted by patrol inspectors making selective checks, supplemented by routine, deskilled inspection by semi-skilled personnel – 'gauge merchants' – using pre-set go/no-go gauges.[72] Despite the limited skill and autonomy of routine quality inspection, piecework systems placed enormous power in the inspector's hands. Nobody was paid for scrapped work, and bonus earnings were jeopardized if the inspector delayed passing a batch of work. To come into conflict with inspectors was to make high and stable earnings all but impossible for the pieceworker. In the car factories inspectors could supplement their earnings by exploiting their power to exercise quality control tightly or leniently. Inspectors in William Morris, Oxford, raffled the same sovereign for twenty-three shillings in several sections simultaneously, with operators treating their purchase of a lottery ticket as obligatory, despite their awareness that this was a petty racket.[73]

In both heavy engineering and the car industry, the role and status of the foreman changed significantly between the wars. The rise of the FMBS reduced the salience of trade union membership for supervisors and of the unions' claim to represent their interests. While the institutional landscape had been transformed, this did not signify that the supervisor's role and status were clearly defined. Rather, the foreman now had to articulate his brokerage role in terms not just of capital and labour but also in relation to new managerial technicians. Although the foreman retained formidable powers to hire and fire labour and to allocate and coordinate work, new managerial functions now jostled for power and authority on the shop floor.

Conclusion

Before 1914 the employers' push to sever the links between the foreman and the craft societies opened up a rhetorical space in which distinct, ambiguous and clashing definitions of foremanship were articulated. The issue was not resolved before 1914. Indeed, we suggest that these questions were raised institutionally for the first time after the 1897 engineering dispute. While employers were aware of the strategic importance of the supervisor in industrial relations and in routine workshop operations, there was no universal adoption of the employers' federation's policies. In particular, the FMBS remained a relatively weak institution with limited employer support. Inside the workshops, the power of the craft societies was displayed by the challenges issued to major employers over the selection and status of supervisors. The inter-war years saw the consolidation of the FMBS not as a result of a push by the employers but as a consequence of their victory over the unions in 1922 and their increased use of the foremen's society as a hiring hall. Supervisory authority remained negotiated and complex. To the tensions inherent in the supervisor's role was added the emergence of new payment systems and a significant increase in the numbers of managerial technicians. Foremen's scope for independent decision making remained considerable but it was now hedged by a variety of strengthening operations professions. The foreman's claim for legitimacy and authority could no longer be articulated in terms of craft expertise but also involved operational and managerial effectiveness. In 1939 the nature of supervisory authority was no more settled than it had been in 1914.

Notes

1. The subtitle for the heading of this section is quoted from Amalgamated Engineering Union (AEU), Amalgamated Managers and Foremen's Association, Open Meeting, Newcastle, May 1920, Modern Record Centre, Warwick University (hereafter, MRC), 237/3 /1/F(10)17.
2. Engineering Employers' Federation (hereafter, EEF), Circular Letter, March 1899, MRC 237/3/1/F(10)3.
3. East of Scotland Engineering Employers' Association (hereafter, ESEA), Minutes, 16 November 1897, Glasgow City Archives (hereafter, GCA), TD1059/22/1/1.
4. North West Engineering Trades Employers' Association (hereafter, NWETEA), Executive Committee (hereafter, EC), Minutes, 10 April, 4 October 1899, 6 April 1904, GCA, TD1059/1/1/1; ESEA, Minutes, 13 March 1899, 2 February 1900, GCA, TD1059/22/1/1.
5. NWETEA, EC, Minutes, 27 December 1904, 29 March 1905, GCA, TD1059/1/1/2.
6. NWETEA, EC, Minutes, 20 February 1912, GCA, TD 1059/1/1/3.
7. Biggart to Wilson, North-East Coast Engineering Employers' Association, 22 August 1896, Private Letter Book, GCA, TD1059/22/2/1.
8. J. Zeitlin, 'Between Flexibility and Mass Production: Strategic Ambiguity and Selective Adaptation in the British Engineering Industry, 1830–1914', in *World of Possibilities: Flexibility and Mass Production in Western Industrialization*, ed. C. Sabel and J. Zeitlin (Cambridge, 1997), 241–272.

9. K. Burgess, 'Authority Relations and the Division of Labour in British Industry, with Special Reference to Clydeside, c. 1860–1930', *Social History* 11, no. 2 (1986): 211–233, here 226–228.

10. EEF, 'Notes of Conference', 1913, MRC 237/3/7/17.

11. Maudsley, 'Memo', 1898, MRC 237/3/7/3/M(15)11.

12. FMBS (Foremen's Mutual Benefit Society), *Constitution and Rules* (Glasgow, 1929), 7.

13. EEF, Management Board, Minutes, 31 March 1927, MRC 237/3/9/F(10)17.

14. K. McClelland, 'Time to Work, Time to Live: Some Aspects of Work and the Re-formation of Class in Britain, 1850–1880', in *The Historical Meanings of Work*, ed. P. Joyce (Cambridge, 1987), 180–209, here 192.

15. Biggart, Foremen's Mutual Benefit Society (hereafter, FMBS) to EEF, 1 September 1909, MRC 237/3/1/97, 2.

16. Barclay Curle to Clyde Shipbuilders' Association, 18 November 1902, GCA, TD241/12/1.

17. West of Scotland Foremen Engineers, AGM, 13 November 1915, GCA, TD1115/1/3.

18. NWETEA, EC, Minutes, 28 February 1912, GCA, TD 1059/1/1/3; for managerial and supervisory salaries and wages, see Barclay Curle, 'Salaries of Officials', GCA, TD265/3.

19. J. Melling, '"Non-Commissioned Officers": British Employers and Their Supervisory Workers, 1880–1920', *Social History* 5, no. 2 (1980): 183–221, here 207.

20. Scottish Coppersmiths Employers' Association, Minutes, 30 October 1912, 11 February 1913, GCA, TD1059/12/1.

21. Kilmarnock & District Engineering Employers' Association, Minutes, 7 September, 6 November 1923, GCA, TD1059/18/3.

22. Federated Employers' Associations, Regional Committee, Scotland and Ireland, Minutes, 26 October 1914, GCA, TD1059/20/1.

23. Glasgow & West of Scotland Association of Foremen Engineers and Draughtsmen (hereafter, FED), Minutes, 9 March 1907, GCA, TD1115/1/2.

24. FED, Minutes, 8 January 1898, GCA, TD1115/1/1.

25. East of Scotland Engineering Employers' Association, Minutes, 11 June 1907, GCA, TD1059/22/1/2; for Manchester employers' somewhat greater enthusiasm for FMBS recruitment, see A. McIvor, *Organised Capital: Employers' Associations and Industrial Relations in Northern England* (Cambridge, 1996), 128.

26. Biggart, FMBS to EEF, 1 September 1909, 1–2, MRC 237/3/1/97, 2.

27. 17th Annual Report, FMBS, 1914; West of Scotland Foremen Engineers, 9 March 1907, '10th Annual Supper', GCA, TD1115/1/2.

28. Sir Arthur Lawson, Brocks & Doxey, Manchester, on behalf of the FMBS, to EEF, 30 April 1915, 2, 6, MRC 237/3/1/97, 2.

29. EEF, 'Notes of Conference', MRC 237/1/10/M(15)6.

30. EEF, 'Memo', September 1913, MRC 237/7/1/M(15)11.

31. EEF, 'Memo: Unions, Societies and Associations: Coventry, London', 1920, MRC 237/3/1/97 F(10).

32. Conference Report, Foremen's Mutual Welfare Society (FMWS) and London and District EEA, 29 August 1919, MRC 237/1/17/M7.

33. West Midlands Engineering Employers' Association, Management Board, Minutes, 20 March 1920.

34. Extract from Minutes of Joint Standing Committee for West of England Area, 5 August 1921, MRC 237/3/1/97, 2.

35. Biggart, Secretary, FMBS, to EEF, 18 November 1920, MRC 237/3/1/87, 2.

36. A. McKinlay and J. Zeitlin, 'The Meanings of Managerial Prerogative: Power and Authority in British Engineering, 1897–1939', *Business History* 31, no. 2 (1989): 32–47.

37. *Paths to Peace in Industry: Report of the Committee Appointed by the Glasgow and West of Scotland Association of Foremen Engineers and Draughtsmen to Investigate the Subject of Goodwill in Industry* (Glasgow, 1930), v, 16, 25.

38. FED, AGM, 13 October 1923, GCA, TD1115/1/4.
39. FED, Minutes, 9 March 1933, GCA, TD1115/1/4.
40. FED, 1 March, 2 November 1923, GCA, TD1115/1/4.
41. Biggart, FMBS Secretary, to EEF, 27 July 1921, MRC 237/3/1/97, 2.
42. FMBS membership calculated from MRC 237/3/1/97(1). '
43. See A. McKinlay, 'Maîtres ou employeurs? Travail et rapports d'autorité dans la construction navale: L'exemple des chantiers de la Clyde (1900–1939)', *Le Mouvement Social* (1989): 75–94.
44. J. Melling, 'Employers and the Rise of Supervisory Unionism, 1914–39', in *A History of British Industrial Relations, Vol. II: 1914–1939*, ed. C. Wrigley (Brighton, 1987), 243–283, here 257.
45. Wigan and District Engineering and Foundry Masters' Association to EEF, 15 July 1926, MRC 237/3/1/97, 2.
46. W. MacKay reply in J. McGovern, 'Economy in Shipbuilding: Some Lines of Progress', *Transactions of the Institute of Engineers and Shipbuilders in Scotland* (1926–1927): 824–858, here 844; Wallacec, Clark & Co, 'Report to Barclay Curle', 2 March 1939, Glasgow University, Business Archives, UCS3/1/106.
47. 'Report of Investigation at Mavor & Coulson, 1929–30', National Institute of Industrial Psychology, 29, 47, GCA, uncatalogued deposit.
48. M. Burawoy, *Manufacturing Consent: Changes in the Capitalist Labor Process under Monopoly Capitalism* (Chicago, 1979), 60–62.
49. *The Foreman*, September 1928, 6–7.
50. S. Mavor, 'The Foreman', *M&C Magazine*, October 1926, 95.
51. Ibid., 100.
52. *Engineering*, 23 June 1922.
53. NWETEA, Minutes, 30 January 1926.
54. A. McKinlay and P. Taylor, 'Factory, Family and Community: Mavor & Coulson, c. 1890–1939', *Business History* (forthcoming).
55. Mavor & Coulson, *M&C Magazine*, Christmas 1929, 193.
56. Ibid., Spring 1930.
57. P. Thompson, 'Playing at Being Skilled Men: Factory Culture and Pride in Work Skills among Coventry Car Workers', *Social History* 13, no. 1 (1988): 45–69, here 55.
58. M. Grieco, *Keeping it in the Family: Social Networks and Employment Chance* (London, 1987), 39.
59. Mavor & Coulson, *M&C Magazine*, Spring 1934, 29; ibid., October 1926, 100.
60. P. Joyce, *Work, Society and Politics: The Culture of the Factory in Later Victorian England* (Brighton, 1980), 111–116; R. J. Morris and J. Smyth, 'Paternalism as an Employer Strategy 1800–1960', in *Employer Strategy and the Labour Market*, ed. J. Rubery and F. Wilkinson (Oxford, 1994), 195–225; P. Ackers, 'On Paternalism: Seven Observations on the Uses and Abuses of the Concept in Industrial Relations, Past and Present', *Historical Studies in Industrial Relations* 5 (1998): 173–193.
61. Anonymous, 'The Hard Case of Shipbuilding and Engineering Foremen', *Engineering*, 12 October 1917.
62. A. Reeves and C. Kimber, 'Works Organisation', *Proceedings of the Institute of Automobile Engineers*, no. 12 (1916–1917): 385–399, cited in J. Lowe, 'The Supervisor in the Automobile Industry' (PhD diss., University of Wales, Cardiff, 1995), 375.
63. NWETEA, *Practical Problems in Payment by Results* (Glasgow, 1928), 23, 47.
64. W. Lewchuk, 'Men and Monotony: Fraternalism as a Managerial Strategy at the Ford Motor Company', *Journal of Economic History* 53, no. 4 (1993): 824–856, here 835; L. L. Downs, 'Industrial Politics, Rationalization and Equal Pay: The Bedaux Strikes at Rover Automobile Company', *Social History* 15, no. 1 (1990): 45–73; L. L. Downs, *Manufacturing Inequality: Gender Divisions in the French and British Metal-Working Industries, 1914–1939* (Ithaca, 1995).

65. E. H. Simpson, Operator, Morris Motors, 1930s, personal letter, c. 1982, Making Cars Archive, Oxford City Library (hereafter, OCL).
66. F. Omrod, Foreman, Smethwick Works, 1930s, 'Interview'; J. Broadbent, Foreman, Vauxhall Motors, 'Interview', OCL.
67. G. Baker, Foreman, Morris Commercial Cars, 1930s, interviewed by R. Coopey, 1985; R. Whiting, *The View from Cowley: The Impact of Industrialization upon Oxford, 1918–1939* (Oxford, 1983), 30–31.
68. Baker, 'Interview'.
69. A. Exall, 'Morris Motors in the 1930s', *History Workshop* 6, no. 1 (1978): 52–78, here 65, 74.
70. S. Tolliday, 'The Failure of Mass Production Unionism in the Motor Industry, 1914–39', in *A History of British Industrial Relations, Vol. II: 1914–1939*, ed. C. Wrigley (Brighton, 1987), 298–322, here 304.
71. G. Lewis, Operator, Alldays Engineers, 1916–20, 'Interview'; B. Moore, Car Worker, Oxford, 1930s, 'Interview', OCL.
72. Omrod, 'Interview'.
73. B. Honour, Panel Beater, Morris Motors, Oxford, 1930s, 'Interview', OCL.

CHAPTER 9

PORIONS AND CONDUCTEURS

Supervisory Functions in the Belgian Limburg
Coal-Mining Industry (1917–1939)

Bart Delbroek

When the Belgian Limburg coalfield began to be exploited in the 1920s, it was an entirely new industry in a scarcely populated rural region without any industrial tradition. Confronted with problems of management and organization of labour, employers borrowed from the practices and traditions of the Walloon and French collieries and adapted them to local needs, while at the same time introducing some innovation. After all, the financial means to construct the seven coal mines in Limburg came mainly from French and Walloon industrial groups, such as Schneider-Le Creusot, the Société Générale and the Banque de Bruxelles-Coppée, which controlled a large part of the coal and steel industry in the older Walloon coalfields.[1] Since most mining engineers were recruited from there up to well into the 1950s, technological know-how was based primarily on the expertise gathered in these earlier mines.[2]

At the end of the nineteenth century, Belgian colliery owners had been confronted with a stagnating productivity of their workforce, while the demands of a powerful labour movement increased the pressure on prices.[3] Combined with the availability of technical innovations, this encouraged the search for technological and organizational means that would enhance labour productivity. In this respect the mechanization of the underground works (both in production and transport) and a more intensive production in longer coal faces was considered crucial.[4] Yet practical applications remained limited, and productivity was not improved. A commission of inquiry on working hours deemed a 'complete and radical transformation' of existing production methods necessary.[5]

Notes for this chapter begin on page 212.

The owners of the Limburg collieries were clearly aware of the opportunities that the new coalfield offered in this respect. In 1911 – that is, six years before the company started producing coal – the general manager of the Winterslag coal mine, A. Dufrasne, had already developed the basic principles of an intensive exploitation in a limited number of long coal faces. He argued as follows: 'Acting differently would pose the risk of great disappointment when changing the system that the labour population is getting accustomed to; this would mean losing the immense advantage we have at the moment of being in a new land, without a formed labour population.'[6] The absence of a strong labour movement in the region and the development of extensive paternalist initiatives – which effectively stifled the growth of unions – ensured that employers were not to expect much resistance from the workforce. Because of the specific geological circumstances and the size of the concessions (on average 4,500 hectares) each company had to opt for a concentration of installations in one large colliery. Dufrasne aimed at a daily coal production of between 3,000 and 4,000 tons, with a labour force of 3,000 to 4,000. This level of productivity was unheard of in Belgium in those days.[7]

Such modern, large-scale production required a rigorous work organization based on a strict division of labour and discipline: 'The starting point of the organization … was the introduction of an absolutely rigid discipline on the work floor, requiring of each team the strict obligation of completing the assigned task within the foreseen time frame.'[8] In the same article, F. Allard – a future general manager of the Zwartberg colliery in Limburg, but at the time engineer at the Walloon Maurage mine – stressed the crucial importance of the supervisory staff in this new organization of labour: 'The formation of the supervisory staff, and especially of *chef-porions* and *porions*, constitutes the most arduous and delicate part in the reorganization of work.'[9] Supervisors were responsible for the proper and strict execution of the workload imposed on the miners per shift. The increasing number of rules imposed by the government with regard to coal extraction, industrial relations and safety, also led to more control on the work floor.[10] Traditionally work-floor supervision in mining was difficult because remote production areas were hard to control and production itself was difficult to measure.[11] The mechanization, concentration and rationalization of production in larger units, however, made control somewhat easier.[12] According to Allard, supervisors in the older Belgian coalfields apparently considered all work performed outside the coal shift as merely auxiliary, and they were therefore inclined to shift around the order in which some tasks should be performed.[13] Moreover, they had a tendency to distrust all new developments, and as a consequence they were not eager to adopt methods to which they were not accustomed.[14] Employers in the Limburg coal mines, however, had the immense advantage of having a labour force largely unfamiliar with these established practices.

Finding a Needle in a Haystack, or the Search for Supervisors in the Archives

Intermediaries between management and workforce in the Belgian Limburg coal mines have never been studied before.[15] We know of their ill-famed reputation as revealed, for example, in novels. In *De Put* (The Pit) of 1928, Leo Ladens has one of the coalface workers describing his superiors as 'supercilious people, strangers who often loathed their own language and who wore a purse or even a decoration where their heart should have been'.[16] Although Ladens tended to exaggerate – as a Catholic priest fearing the advent of the 'red danger' he was opposed to the development of a coal-mining industry – the mention of the purse seems to suggest that superiors used harsh authority to make a profit, for themselves or for the company. We do not know how overseers were selected. Nor do we know who these men were. Were they foreigners, as Ladens's quote suggests, or were they recruited internally among Belgian miners? Particular to this new industry is the issue of experience, authority and age, which leads to the basic question of the function and role of mining supervisors, with the ensuing problem of their position in industrial conflicts. I shall study some of these questions with regard to the inter-war years, because during that period the hierarchical system was established, whereas after the war the existing labour organization was refined and adapted to new needs. Then the focus was mostly on schooling (usually by means of the TWI method[17]) and improving safety.

Supervisors of the Limburg collieries are far less visible in the archival sources than one would expect. In his study on the labour market for coal miners, Pluymers pointed out that none of the seven Limburg mines made a strict distinction between unqualified and qualified work. The company rules specified that each employee had to perform all assignments, whether qualified or not.[18] According to Versteegh, miners often had to perform several different jobs during one work period.[19] This implies that in company records, such as wage books or enrolment lists, professions are seldom mentioned, even though supervisors would probably rarely change their function. This, however, made it quite difficult to pinpoint *all* supervisors in a coal mine in a certain period. Luckily, in my research I was able to make use of a file from 1957 containing names and dates of promotion of retired overseers of the Beringen mine.[20] Thus, fifty-four men were traced who had had at least the rank of *porion* (*opzichter* in Dutch), the lowest rank of supervisor, prior to 1940. I looked them up in the so-called *Model 34* registers,[21] and was able to find a date and place of birth for fifty-one men.[22] Considering that the sample is not a cross-sectional one, but a longitudinal reconstruction of individual careers over a period of about twenty years, and since the total number of supervisors (and their ratio to the workforce) changed in the course of those years, it is obvious that these men are hardly representative enough to justify general statements.

To allow a comparison in time and between coal mines, a second record – a wage book from Winterslag for October 1923 to March 1924, containing 159 names of supervisors – seemed promising.[23] Unfortunately, companies started to use *Model 34* only in 1925. Some of these names could be found, but the very high turnover among supervisors in the period makes this highly difficult.[24] For this reason, only some general statements concerning nationality and wages will be made with respect to the second list. I shall therefore consider my small group of supervisors as a first step towards in-depth research on *porions* in the Limburg coal mines.

The Belgian Limburg Coalfield

Unlike the much older Walloon coalfields, a coal-mining industry in Belgian Limburg developed only in the twentieth century. The first core samples were drilled in 1901 and the first coal was produced in 1917. Limburg at the time was a scarcely populated rural area without an industrial or urban employment tradition. In the nineteenth century the region had primarily been an emigration area directed at industries in Liège and Germany. As a consequence, the few roads and railroads were mostly oriented towards these areas. During the pioneering years, the Limburg coal mines tried to be as autonomous as possible with regard to work and recruitment, building their own private railroads and constructing large garden cities. Since the local labour supply was not able to provide for the growing demands of the rapidly expanding companies, many more coal miners had to be found in more distant areas.[25] The first areas of recruitment were the Walloon coalfields, as well as the provinces of Antwerp and Brabant that had traditionally supplied miners for the Walloon coal mines. However, according to employers these men were mostly 'young workers who came to the Campine coalfield trying their skills in a category in which they would not have been accepted in the old coalfields, or bad workers who had run into trouble with their superiors or the judicial authorities'.[26] In several periods of severe or enduring scarcity of labour supply, foreign workers had to be recruited. These were mainly of Polish, Czech and North-Italian origin, often without any experience in coal mining. This diversity of nationalities brought about communication problems, with possible grave consequences regarding safety, especially when inexperienced miners were involved.

The lack of workers was not the only problem mine owners had to solve. From the very beginning they were confronted with very high rates of labour turnover and absenteeism. Between 1926 and 1930 more than two-thirds of the underground workforce of the Beringen colliery left the company within the year.[27] Foreigners turned out to be even more mobile. Almost 30 per cent of immigrant miners in Winterslag and Beringen left within a month.[28] In 1929 the Beringen coal mine examined the number of working days lost each week because of unauthorized absences. An absenteeism of 10 per cent of the underground workforce turned out to be very common, while on Mondays this was easily doubled.[29] The daily uncertainty about the exact number of workers present posed a serious challenge to management. As a result, a certain flexibility in the organization of labour had to be deployed, shifting workers around where needed.

A Rigorous Pecking Order

Although there were some differences and changes over time, all seven Limburg coal mines were organized according to a similar model, largely based on the nineteenth-century industrial traditions of the older Walloon coalfields, which in turn had been influenced by practices in the French coal-mining industry. The labour organization and hierarchy were also based on military experience, and, in theory, each level of supervisors had to obey only one direct superior, while giving orders to at most three or four subordinates.[30]

At the top of the pyramid was the *directeur-gérant* (general manager) who functioned as the representative of the board of directors. He had direct control of everyday life within and around the company. Because he represented the mining company to the outside world, upholding his prestige was important. During the inter-war years these men, who were former engineers, were recruited from one of the company's Walloon collieries. Only after the Second World War did the recruitment of *directeur-gérants* shift to the internal labour market.

Although the *directeur-gérants* had a lot of authority – the result of the stability of their position[31] – most of their tasks were delegated to their direct subordinates: an administrative manager (*directeur administratif*), a chief engineer for the surface works (*directeur des travaux de surface*), and a chief engineer for the exploitation of the underground works (*directeur des travaux de fond*). In this chapter, I focus on the supervisory staff in the underground coal-producing units, since the great diversity of activities and professions in the supporting services both on the surface and underground would make the comment on this general model too complex.

The Limburg coal mines had a complex underground organization, mainly because of concession size and the rapidly increasing mechanization of exploitation. Production predominantly took place by means of pneumatic picks, which – unlike in the case of long-wall coal cutters – could be used in nearly

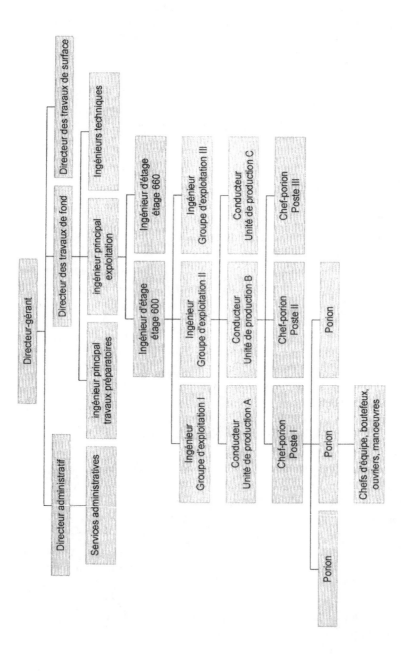

Figure 9.1 *The Organization of the Limburg Mines. Source:* J. Dalemans and L. Suetens, *Handleiding tot de mijnbouwkunde* (Brussels, 1947), 280–281.

all geological circumstances and were easier to use by inexperienced miners.[32] In organizing both production and preparatory works, the chief engineer for the underground works could rely on two *ingénieurs principals*, one for each department. Each floor was controlled by a division engineer or *ingénieur d'étage* or *ingénieur divisionair*. The latter relied on several regular engineers, who each oversaw one particular work-team.[33] The situation was even more complex in the auxiliary operations where, depending on the importance to coal production, mining engineers, technical engineers or even lower-ranked supervisors had the main responsibility. Because of the size of housing in the mines' garden cities – in which engineers were obliged to live, but rent-free – and the accompanying private garden, the exact position of each engineer in this strict chain of command was apparent to everyone, both within the company and to the outside world.

The *porions*, the supervisors on the work floor, were situated directly beneath the level of engineers. Highest in rank were the *conducteurs*.[34] In a 1958 Limburg mining dictionary this function was described as 'the highest degree in the hierarchy of supervisors. He receives his orders from an engineer, passes them on to his *chef-porions* and controls their proper execution'.[35] The *conducteur* was responsible for all operations in one to four galleries during all three shifts,[36] which meant that he regularly had to change shifts himself. To maintain constant control over production and safety, each *conducteur* could use three *chef-porions* (*meester-opzichter* in Dutch), one for each shift. At the lower-end of this chain of command were the *porions* (*opzichters*) who had direct control of the workforce of a section or of an entire coalface, depending on its size and output. They also had to lend a helping hand (i.e. actually performing the work of a miner), especially when higher management was not satisfied with productivity. It would be interesting to study exactly how often this was the case, as it would largely limit the time a *porion* could dedicate to his other tasks, which will be discussed later. Most probably a *porion* would help out a coal hewer at the end of the shift, if it became clear that the latter would not make up his appointed quota. After all, for reasons of safety the coalface needed to maintain a straight line over its entire length.

Porions could easily be recognized by the *meterstok* (yardstick)[37] they were carrying and by a specific headlamp (e.g. with a white or green ring). Each *porion* could have up to twenty-five men underneath him.[38] In important production areas the number of *porions* could be as high as five, not counting the ones in the auxiliary services.[39] In his instruction manual for coal miners (1947), J. Dalemans mentioned the common division of labour in a working place with a front-length of 200 metres, in which twelve supervisors, divided over three shifts were responsible for a total of 167 men (i.e. one *porion* for fourteen miners).[40]

The *porions* had direct control over the workforce. However, in most cases each group of miners also had their own person in command (*chef d'équipe*). This was not only the case at the coalface. These *chefs* were quite common in a lot of supporting services, such as engine drivers or stone hewers. Finally, the *boute-feu* (*schietmeester* or explosives expert) had a special position. In most Limburg coal mines these experts belonged to the surveillance staff, and although under normal circumstances they were subordinate to the *porions*, when carrying out detonations they had absolute responsibility and could have all other nearby activities put on hold. In some cases the same person could perform the tasks of *porion* and *boute-feu*.[41] In the services on the surface and in some underground auxiliary services, such as the electro-mechanical department, the occupations of *chef-porion* and *porion* were known as *chef-brigadier* and *brigadier*.

The everyday functioning of the supervisory staff could of course vary to a certain degree, especially with the ever-increasing complexity of large-scale production. In the late 1920s and the 1930s, the complexity of the chain of command kept pace with increasing mechanization and concentration. For example, in Beringen the function of a *premier porion* (*eerste opzichter*), an extra intermediary between *chef-porion* and *porion*, was introduced during the inter-war years, at first only during the night shift.[42] Similarly a gradual increase in the number of overseers may be noted. According to an enquiry in 1928, the total number of underground supervisors in the then five active mines was 806 with an average of 161 per mine (Table 9.1). At the time 12,566 underground miners were working in the Limburg coalfield, which meant that supervisors constituted 6.4 per cent of the entire underground labour force (and almost sixteen miners for one *porion*).

Table 9.1 *Number of Underground Supervisors in 1928*

	No. of Supervisors			No. of Underground Workforce			%
	Shift 1	Shift 2+3	Total	Shift 1	Shift 2+3	Total	
Beringen	46	120	166	1,221	1,608	2,829	5.9%
Eisden	89	32	121	1,402	798	2,200	5.5%
Waterschei			190			3,139	6.1%
Winterslag	96	108	204	1,660	1,233	2,893	7.1%
Zwartberg		125				1,505	8.3%
Total			806			12,566	6.4%

Source: G. Coppieters, 'Waren wij maar Walen of Kongolezen: Arbeid en lonen. Sociale geschiedenis van de Limburgse mijnen 1917–1985. Deel 2' (research report, Vrije Universiteit Brussel, 1999), 28.

The number of supervisors in the Limburg collieries varied considerably. The large number of supervisors in Winterslag was, most probably, owing to the fact that it had been producing coal since 1917, and had more production areas in use. This mine also had the reputation of being the most rigid and hierarchical of all seven mines, mostly because of its notorious *directeur-gérant*, A. Dufrasne.[43] The high percentage of supervisors in Zwartberg is most remarkable, especially since it was the last of the mines to start exploitation (1925). Maybe the unfavourable geological conditions, which later on led to the construction of five levels, made work-floor supervision more cumbersome. Apparently in Eisden there were only thirty-two supervisors during the second and third shifts, when no coal was cut, which is striking when compared to Beringen and Winterslag. Eisden also employed the highest number of foreign miners, which would lead one to expect a greater need of *porions*. The small number may also have been the consequence of a shortage of supervisors.

In Beringen the number of supervisors had increased to 333 by 1957 (Table 9.2) from a total underground workforce of 4,749, which means that one overseer was responsible for about fourteen miners, while in 1928 this had been seventeen. Just as the *brigadiers* to the *premiers brigadiers*, the *porions* show a ratio of about 1 to 4 to the superiors (grouping the intermediary *premiers porions* and *chef-porions* together). As was mentioned above, giving orders to at most four subordinates was theoretically considered ideal.[44]

Table 9.2 *Number of Underground Supervisors in Beringen on 30 August 1957*

Porions	255
Brigadiers	16
Premiers brigadiers	4
Premiers porions	25
Chef-porions	33
Total	333

Source: 'Hoofdopzichters inlichtingen, 1957', VMM, 51-1-7-G.

Prerequisites for the Job

A complex and strictly hierarchical system had developed during the first years in the Limburg collieries in answer to the specific necessities and characteristics of the new coalfield. Choosing the right people for the right job was of course of crucial importance for higher management, in order to increase productivity and cut costs. It is therefore necessary to inquire what the job's prerequisites were. According to a handwritten document from the 1920s, a *porion* had to answer to the following requirements.[45]

> The supervisors have to be of good conduct without a passion that could lead to a shortage of money. They cannot hold political mandates nor be involved in trading.
>
> Supervisors need a thorough knowledge of the profession in order to exercise their function with authority.
>
> Supervisors have to give orders to the personnel in a resolute and benevolent manner. Any favouritism is strictly forbidden and under no circumstances may family relations or friendships play a role in decision-making.
>
> Supervisors have to be polite towards the workforce and have to be wary of making unjust decisions.
>
> Supervisors need to retain a positive influence on the workforce by encouraging them in their work. They therefore have to be aware of the existing piece wages and inform their superiors whether the wages are either too high or too low, in order to achieve a just compensation for the work carried out.[46]

Not surprisingly a thorough knowledge of the profession was expected. Considering that *porions* (and their superiors even more) had to check up on the work of a diverse group of people, ranging from unqualified helpers to coal hewers, it is obvious that they had to know all the aspects of mining labour. Their subordinates probably would not have accepted their authority had it been it otherwise. The fact that most miners had started out as simple helpers and gradually worked their way up to a more specialized job was supposedly not enough.[47] In an interview with two former coal miners of the Beringen pit, T. Gielis found that a certain degree of flexibility was necessary for becoming a *porion*.[48] The career of one *conducteur* in Beringen, designated as J.C., illustrates the diversity of work experience that was deemed necessary for promotion (see Table 9.3).

Experience and skill were thus considered more important than theoretical knowledge, which would partly explain the lack of incentives for developing specific schooling for supervisors during the 1920s. Nevertheless, with the increasing mechanization of production, this gradually changed. In 1932, J.C. started schooling at the School voor Mijnopzichters, a three-year training programme after working hours, which he finished in 1935. It was then that he became *chef-porion*. The fact that he only started with this training after he had become a *porion* suggests that a combination of work experience and schooling was considered ideal. Boucneau mentions that management seldom promoted coal hewers, especially the productive ones, to the function of *porion*. Experienced coal hewers were scarce, and consequently difficult to replace. Moreover, because of the piece wages, they could often earn higher wages than supervisors.[49] Nevertheless, J.C. had been a coal hewer for about two years, and was a stone hewer – often earning even higher wages – for five years when he was made *porion*. Maybe management urgently needed to replace

Table 9.3 *The Career of J.C.,* Conducteur *in the Beringen Mine*

Year	Age	Function
1919	20	surface – *manoeuvre*
Sep/19	20	shaft excavation
Apr/22	23	coal hewer
1924	25	shaft worker
1927	28	stone hewer
1932	33	*porion* at shaft
1934	35	*premier porion* at shaft
1935	36	*chef-porion* at preparatory works
1940	41	*conducteur* for preparatory works
1951	52	*conducteur* for preparatory works and shafts
1954	55	retirement

Sources: Coppieters, 'Waren wij maar', 163; 'Hoofdopzichters inlichtingen, 1957', VMM, 51-1-7-G.

another *porion,* and J.C. was the most viable choice, or perhaps his qualities as a supervisor took precedence over the loss of an experienced hewer. The fact that he achieved the rank of *conducteur* seems to suggest the latter.

It is astonishing that the above document did not mention work experience as the first requirement for the job. The obligation to refrain from any political mandate was primarily aimed at membership of the coal miners' labour unions, the Christian Centrale der Vrije Mijnwerkers (CVM) and the socialist Mijnwerkerscentrale (MC). During the inter-war years membership of these unions was never higher than 33 per cent of all miners, with an average of 24 per cent during the 1920s.[50] Relations between coal owners and the socialist union in particular were very sour. On more than one occasion union members were sacked, and some Limburg coal mines even refused to participate in the meetings of the conciliation board (Nationale Gemengde Mijncommissie[51]), while others simply ignored its agreements. Nevertheless, this particular prerequisite was not always applied rigorously. For example, on 22 March 1921 in Winterslag a spontaneous strike broke out because a *porion,* who was apparently a member of the socialist Mijnwerkerscentrale was fired by the *conducteur* for not doing his job properly. Some of the *porion*'s colleagues started a strike, which resulted in his reinstatement after a few hours.[52]

Dalemans mentioned that *boute-feux* were expected to be serious and experienced workers with sufficient willpower in order to resist workmen who, for some reason, wanted to use explosives. In no way could a *boute-feu* be biased towards the workforce.[53]

The other requirements mentioned above dealt with the treatment of the workers, which had to be fair and polite, at least in theory. Many miners stated that the circumstances on the shop floor and the criteria for becoming a *porion,* were two different things. Interviews with ex-coalminers and comments by contemporaries all agreed: coal-mine supervisors in Limburg were foul-mouthed, loud and eager to fight.[54] In a letter to Allard, the *directeur-gérant* of Zwartberg, A. Cool of the CVM complained during a strike in 1930 that the 'brutalizing of the workers by some supervisors is worse now than it used to be'.[55] He then gave an example of a *conducteur* who had beaten a boy so badly that the latter bled from the mouth. Cool stressed the fact that no steps whatsoever had been taken against the *conducteur.* In 1936 the CVM once more criticized a *conducteur*'s behaviour. According to his subordinates he was a very brutal man who shouted and cursed like the devil, but was not able to have a sensible conversation.[56] More than once, coal miners mentioned that their supervisors were even illiterate, and that their reports were drafted by one of their subordinates.[57] This kind of behaviour was not limited to the inter-war years. Woijtek, a *porion* of Polish origin, admitted that in the 1960s he had fought with a Turkish miner, in his words after refusing to follow up his orders.[58] Management seems to have accepted and even supported this confrontational behaviour. The local newspaper *Nieuw-Limburg,* heavily sponsored by the regional coal-mine employers' organization, considered this aggressive conduct as absolutely necessary because of the extremely undisciplined workforce.[59] Although in theory favouritism was forbidden, being on friendly turns with superiors could prove to be very useful for workers who, for example, wanted a better spot at the coalface, a job at the surface or a house in the garden city.[60]

Increasing Output: Both Assignment and Benefit

Depending on their workplace, supervisors had a wide array of tasks to perform. Yet some duties were the same for all *porions.* First of all, supervisors played an important role in the daily checking of the presence of workers that mining regulations imposed on employers. When passing through the gate, each miner had to take his copper tag (with his personal work number) from a panel at the entrance. This tag was then traded in for a headlamp, after which miners had to report to their *porion* who filled in the presence list, and gave each miner his assignment for the day. Likewise, they composed the work-teams and possible overtime hours were announced. Maintaining good relationships with supervisors could assure miners of better working conditions or a place in a highly productive work-team, and thus a good wage. In some coal mines workers received a third tag, together with their headlamp, which was handed over to the supervisor when entering the lift-cage.[61] An extra control on the work floor by *porions* in so-called *punteerboeken* (work registries) had to make sure everyone was where they were supposed to be. For reasons of safety, discipline and productivity, engineers severely punished irregularities, even by immediate dismissal.[62] At the end of the shift this process was reversed. By using this system with two or three tags with multiple checkpoints, management thus had a fairly reliable control system.

Secondly, supervisors had a responsibility to sustain proper and safe working conditions. They had to make sure the coal-front maintained a straight line over its entire length, in order to assure proper air circulation and avoid the accumulation of mine gases.[63] Likewise, they had to check on the maintenance of machinery. Special attention was given to the work done by coal hewers, since their remuneration by means of piece wages possibly gave them an incentive for ignoring safety conditions.[64] Every day at the beginning of their shift, supervisors were supposed to make a tour around their entire workplace, determining possible problems and points of attention for the day. This tour was repeated at the end of the shift. During the inter-war years, and to a certain degree also after the war, safety issues nevertheless often came secondary to the main duty of supervisors, i.e. ensuring the planned production. Only after the disaster at the coal mine of Bois du Cazier near Charleroi in 1956, which caused the death of 262 miners, did safety become more predominant.[65]

Sometimes *conducteurs* and *chef-porions* were responsible for measuring the progress of coal and stone hewers, which determined their wages. However, this kind of work was usually performed by specific employees: the *marqueurs*. Several methods were used, varying from a fortnightly proportional division of the total earned wage among all miners in the gallery, to a daily measurement of the individual performance of each hewer.[66]

An important part of a supervisor's job consisted of filling in paperwork and making reports, such as the presence list of the workforce, requests for materials or safety issues. The most important reports were the daily accounts of the work progress in each working area that each *porion* noted in a general report book after their shift. Thus, *conducteurs* and engineers had at a glance an overall picture of the production of coal, tons of cleared stone, number of available men and their output, material used, accidents, etc.[67]

Finally, supervisors were responsible for maintaining discipline in their working area. For this, supervisors had to make sure that

> [they] do not take their breaks at the same time as the workers. During this time they check up on the operations and make sure the break does not take longer than agreed.
> Supervisors particularly superintend those places where many workers are present, in order to maintain a satisfactory discipline and to prevent breaks from getting longer because of chitchat or for whatever other reason.[68]

Likewise, *porions* had to make sure all personnel went directly to their working area when leaving the lift cages, and returned at a designated time at the end of their shift. This meant that they could come up to the surface only after the last of their subordinates. A *chef-porion* on the other hand, came up a while earlier to inform the *chef-porion* of the next shift about the conditions in the workplace, who then in turn briefed his subordinate *porions*.[69]

To ensure discipline, supervisors had a wide array of measures at their disposal. Although dismissal or a few days of unemployment did not happen regularly, threats to use these drastic sanctions was much more common.[70] Since supervisors had to make reports about the performance of each miner, they could easily tamper with these data. This of course gave them another means of coercion, especially when workers on piece rates were concerned.[71] It was the system of *cinquième*, a fine of one-fifth of the daily wage, which was the most common way of punishing a lack of discipline underground. This was even part of the employers' production policies. In 1934 *directeur-gérant* Fontaine of Waterschei, for instance, complained that the handing out of penalties had lost its *feu sacré*.[72] The system of *cinquièmes* was so widespread that in several strikes during the inter-war years, specific demands were made concerning the behaviour of supervisors and their unfair use of these fines.[73] This, of course, made supervisors highly unpopular among the workforce, which for some candidate-overseers appears to have been reason enough to decline the promotion when offered. The prospect of having to order around former workmates did not appeal to everyone.[74]

Having supervisors ensure production levels could not work without providing them with some form of incentive. They therefore received a rather high wage. As a result of the complex occupational structure of the middle management in the Belgian Limburg coal mines, it proved unfeasible to analyse these wages in detail for the entire inter-war period. Moreover, the problems already cited as regards the mention of profession in the sources allow only for some general remarks.

In March 1919 the management of the Winterslag mine informed its counterpart in Beringen that it would raise the wages of *porions* and *chef-porions* by one franc to 19.25 and 21.25 francs respectively. At that time a *porion* in Waterschei – less than 5 kilometres away from Winterslag – earned 18 francs, while a *chef-porion* got 20.25 francs. Workers involved in sinking the shaft were paid between 12.50 and 15 francs.[75] The wage increase for supervisors most probably has to be interpreted in terms of fierce competition between the Limburg coal mines for a small number of experienced coal miners, which Winterslag as the first company to start production would have experienced most acutely.

In the above-mentioned 1923–1924 Winterslag wage book, the wages were set out as below. Even though it has not been possible to define the exact rank of each supervisor, the different levels in wages are clearly observable. Table 9.4 contains the daily wages of some supervisors for each *quinzaine* (a two-week

Table 9.4 *Daily Wages of Supervisors at Winterslag, 1923–1924*

Medal No.	1–15 Oct. 1923	16–31 Oct. 1923	1–15 Nov. 1923	16–30 Nov. 1923	1–15 Dec. 1923	16–31 Dec. 1923	1–15 Jan. 1924	16–31 Jan. 1924	1–15 Feb. 1924	16–29 Feb. 1924	1–15 Mar. 1924
451	46.2	48.5	48.5	48.5	48.5	48.5	48.5	48.5	48.5	48.5	48.5
452	\	\	\	29	33	33	33	\	\	\	\
	\	\	\	\	\	\	\	34.6	\	34.6	34.6
453	38.5	40.4	40.4	40.4	40.4	40.4	40.4	40.4	\	40.4	40.4
454	\	29.2	29.2	34.6	34.6	34.6	34.6	34.6	32.6	\	\
	\	\	\	\	\	\	\	\	27.5	30	30
455	31.5	33.1	33.1	33.1	33.1	\	\	\	\	\	\
	\	\	\	\	26	26	26	\	\	\	\
	\	\	\	\	\	\	38.6	38.6	\	38.6	38.6
456	33	34.6	34.6	34.6	34.6	34.6	34.6	34.6	\	34.6	34.6
11	40.2	42.2	42.2	42.2	42.2	42.2	42.2	42.2	\	42.2	42.2
12	28.3	29.7	29.7	29.7	29.7	29.7	29.7	30.7	34.6	34.6	34.6
13	46.2	48.5	48.5	48.5	48.5	48.5	48.5	48.5	\	48.5	48.5
14	31	32.5	32.5	32.5	32.5	32.5	32.5	32.5	\	32.5	\

Source: 'Salaires des surveillants, 1924', VMM, 51-10-2-E.

wage period) between October 1923 and the first half of March 1924. Like all other employees, each supervisor had his own specific tag number, which was re-assigned to another person in case of discharge. This was clearly the case with the numbers 452, 454 and 455 in the following table. In the latter case, for example, the first supervisor with a daily wage of 33.1 francs was replaced during the first two weeks of December 1923 by another person, who was paid only 26 francs. He in turn left the company in the first *quinzaine* of January 1924. His replacement was apparently more experienced, since he was paid 38.6 francs. The reason for the limited number of entries in the first two weeks of February 1924 is not clear to me. The rapid re-assignment of some tag numbers gives another indication, although very preliminary, of the considerable problems Winterslag had in keeping their staff.[76]

According to the *Annales des Mines de Belgique*, the average wage in 1924 for a supervisor in Limburg was 35.49 francs, but as can be seen from Table 9.4 there could be substantial differentials. These can be explained by differences in rank – a *conducteur* had a higher wage than a *porion* – but also by bonuses for high productivity. According to Table 9.5 supervisors had the highest wages of all categories of workers, but these averages are misleading. As a result of the piece-rate system, experienced and skilful coal hewers and stone hewers could in fact arrive at much higher wages.

A 1943 wage book for supervisors showed that a *premier porion* in Beringen had a basic wage of 84.15 francs, while a *porion* was paid between 69.10 and 75.40 francs. Depending on output, a daily bonus of between 4 and

Table 9.5 *Average Wage Levels in Limburg Mines, 1924*

Category	Daily Wage (francs)
Total surface personnel	20.69
Total personnel	26.40
Coal-face workers	33.43
Supervisors	35.49
Other underground workers	26.25
Total underground personnel	30.36
Qualified surface workers	24.37
Other male surface workers	19.10
Female workers	8.81

Source: J. Lebacqz and A. Delmer, 'L'industrie charbonnière pendant l'année 1924', *Annales des Mines de Belgique* (1925): 255–272, here 265.

11 francs was awarded.[77] By the second half of the 1920s most supervisors received a monthly wage. According to management this created 'a better and more stable situation'.[78] From 1 January 1923 on, moreover, all supervisory functions were allocated a complementary pension. Management also made sure that supervisors, even future ones, could get proper housing in the company's garden cities if they wanted to. Unlike engineers, most supervisors were not obliged to live in company-owned housing.[79] Only the highest levels of middle management, who had to be available for emergencies day and night, lived in company houses.[80]

However, the best incentive for increasing productivity and exercising authority efficiently was the yearly Saint Barbara bonus, paid out to all levels of management. The amount was partly based on company profit, rank and number of years of service, but it was primarily a direct reflection of the output throughout the year of the departments for which the supervisors were responsible. As such, the bonus system was a clear-cut indication of both engineers' and supervisors' chances of promotion. Management measured loyalty in terms of productivity. In the Winterslag colliery, for example, the Saint Barbara bonus of 1935 for a certain *conducteur* was 2,500 francs, while the *chef-porion* for the preparatory works was paid 1,650 francs, and another *chef-porion* 825 francs. One *porion* took home a bonus of 400 francs.

The rest of the workforce was not given a bonus, which caused frictions now and again. One miner wrote: '[W]hy celebrate Saint Barbara? Who has reason to celebrate? Only the ones who get a bonus. The *porions* less, the *chef-porions* more and *conducteurs* even more. Not the worker, he has to celebrate at his own expense.'[81]

Supervisors, then, had to carry out a number of tasks, but were primarily focused on ensuring high productivity. Through an elaborate set of incentives the employers made sure its middle management was properly motivated to get the most out of the workforce. A last and crucial question then remains: who were the men who carried out these functions?

The Origin of *Porions*

Work experience was the primary precondition for promotion to the supervisory staff in a Limburg coal mine. At the beginning, however, this expertise was lacking among the local population. Experienced labour therefore had to come from elsewhere, that is, primarily from the other Belgian coalfields.[82] The main areas of recruitment of the seven coal mines were very diverse. Beringen and Zolder, the most westerly mines, had rather easy access to the provinces of Antwerp and Brabant, areas where the collieries of the Liège coalfield had traditionally recruited a lot of miners. The mines of Zwartberg, Waterschei and Winterslag, all situated within the city of Genk, were fierce competitors on the labour market because of their proximity. Eisden, finally, the most easterly mine, was in an isolated position. Hindered on one side by the river Meuse and the Dutch coal mines, and on the other side by the three coal mines in Genk, it had to depend on foreign miners to a much greater degree than the other mines.[83] Thus, notwithstanding the limited distances between them, all seven Limburg coal mines had to deal with specific circumstances that greatly influenced their labour market opportunities.

A first group of miners consisted of those born in the Walloon provinces who had had careers in Walloon coal mines. Though in the literature it is generally agreed that this group was never more than a small percentage of the workforce,[84] the ones that did opt for the Limburg field 'were very often invested with a position of trust'.[85] A list of the personnel of the Eisden coal mine in 1918, when the pit was still in the phase of digging both shafts, supports this assertion.[86] At the time 29-year-old Antoine Vandevyver was the only *porion* in service at the pit,[87] and despite the Flemish name he was born in Houdeng-Aimeries in the province of Hainault. Most likely he was brought along, together with another large part of the staff, by the shareholders, who also owned coal mines in Wallonia. The Waterschei coal mine recruited several miners from the Liège area, and before 1920 five of these became *conducteurs*, while others acquired leading positions in the supporting services on the surface.[88] In the 1924 list of *porions* in Winterslag, a look at the surnames also gives the impression that a lot of them were not part of the local population. Though several names are clearly of French-speaking origin, it has not been possible to retrieve the origin of these 159 men. Actually, the number of Walloon miners might have been even higher, since many of these were descendants of Flemish immigrants from the nineteenth century.

The small sample of fifty-one supervisors of the Beringen mine shows the following places of birth (Table 9.6). All of them attained at least the rank of *porion* between 1920 and 1939.

Table 9.6 *Place of Birth of Supervisors in Beringen*

Province	No.
Limburg	28
Antwerp	13
Brabant	2
Liège	3
Hainault	5
Total	51

Source: 'Hoofdopzichters inlichtingen, 1957', VMM, 51-1-7-G.

Eight out of fifty-one supervisors were born in Walloon provinces and when taking the dates of entry and promotion into account, all of them attained a function of at least *porion* during the 1920s. Most of them, however, became part of the supervisory staff only in the late 1920s, which seems to suggest that they already formed a second 'generation' of overseers, perhaps replacing the first supervisors after their retirement. This assumption cannot be proven without more research.

A second group of experienced workers were Flemish miners from the provinces of Limburg, Antwerp and Brabant, who had commuted on a daily or weekly basis to the Walloon coalfields. For them the Limburg coal mines were closer to home, and therefore an interesting alternative.[89] Especially for the Beringen mine these regions were an important area of recruitment, as can be seen from the sample: twenty-eight supervisors were born in Limburg, thirteen in Antwerp and two in Brabant. Moreover, in the sample all municipalities in the latter provinces are situated within about 20 kilometres of the Beringen mine, and these supervisors may be considered locals. Beringen, then, could rely above all on a locally recruited supervisory staff, which probably had some advantages as regards communication with the workforce. Considering the many different nationalities in the Limburg coal mines, communication problems have often caused accidents. French was the predominant language among engineers, and they considered it self-evident that middle management also spoke their language. For both Flemish and foreign miners, being able to speak French therefore seems to have been a necessary (and tacit) prerequisite for promotion. As opposed to the Walloon and foreign supervisors, who often spoke no Dutch at all, the locally recruited *porions* had the advantage of speaking both Dutch and French.[90]

The last group of experienced miners were foreigners – that is, from 1923 on, mostly Central and Eastern Europeans. Employers focused their attention especially on Polish nationals, first because they were qualified miners with experience in mining in the German Ruhr area or Silesia.[91] In the Beringen sample, no Polish supervisors were found, but in the list from Winterslag at least thirty-five entries had a Polish or Czech name, which would mean that about 20 per cent of all supervisors was of foreign origin. In a sample of the registration records of the Waterschei colliery – less than two kilometres away – for the period 1929–1930 however, Versteegh found only five Poles recorded as *porion,* which was only 1 per cent of all registrations of Polish nationals.[92] In contrast, she found seventeen new Belgian *porions,* which would mean 6.8 per cent of all Belgian records. This discrepancy might be partly explained by the changing position of foreign miners during the crisis years.[93] By 1934, the situation seems to have 'normalized' again. Twenty-six Poles were part of the supervisory staff, which was 4.1 per cent of all Poles in the company. For Belgians the equivalent figure was 5.5 per cent. Nevertheless, the difference with the very provisional percentage of 1924 is rather large, but might possibly be explained by the replacement of Poles by experienced Belgian supervisors from within the internal labour market. At least, this was what the unions were asking for.[94]

Age and Career of Supervisors

A final question concerns the average age of members of the supervisory staff. Age was of course closely related to work experience, required to become a supervisor, especially because of the lack of schooling for miners during the inter-war years. The record of the Beringen supervisors provides a, very sketchy, indication of the average age for each category of colliery overseers. It needs to be noted that these averages are based on a limited number of cases, and that some dates are provided only by estimation (Table 9.7).

Table 9.7 *Average Age at the Different Steps of a Supervisor's Career, Beringen*

Average Age	1920s	Cases	1930s	Cases
At entry	29.7	21	23.2	28
Promotion to *porion*	29.6	10	29.4	26
Promotion to *premier porion*	38.3	6	35.7	22
Promotion to *chef-porion*	34.3	17	38.9	24
Promotion to *conducteur*	38.6	5	47.0	3

Source: 'Hoofdopzichters inlichtingen, 1957', VMM, 51-1-7-G.

The required experience for becoming a *porion* is well reflected in the cases of the 1930s. On average, *porions* had worked in Beringen for about 6.2 years before being made part of the supervisory staff. Moreover, the data contained only the last date of entry, so I have no information about the possible working years before this average of 23.2. Perhaps experience in mining had already been clocked up in another coal mine, or in Beringen itself. In the 1920s, however, the average of entry into the company is just about the same as the age of promotion to *porion,* both in the 1920s and 1930s, which supports the assumption that experienced miners from other coalfields were immediately offered supervisory jobs.

Subsequent promotion always took many years. It needs to be noted, however, that the average age of 38.3 for promotion to *premier porion* in the 1920s seems odd when compared to the other data. Indeed, if we ignore the relatively great age of one particular case, the average is 34.2. That this is almost exactly the same as the average for *chef-porion* in the 1920s may be explained by the fact that the new function was introduced only gradually, and only for certain activities. On average it took *porions* 4.6 years in the 1920s to climb up the ladder to the level of *premier porion,* while in the following decade it was 6.3 years. The limited number of cases in the former case might explain the difference. *Chef-porions* seem to have become slightly older in the 1930s. Part of the explanation probably comes from the increased use of *premiers porions* on the work floor, which meant that supervisors had to pass an extra level of middle management. The fact that the mechanization and rationalization of the 1930s required men with more experience may have played a role as well. The average age of *conducteurs* differed greatly. Most workers were well into their forties, or even their fifties, when they reached this stage.

Although in the above table the weighted averages for the 1920s and 1930s are 32.6 and 31.7 respectively, sometimes workers were promoted to the supervisory staff at a much younger age. Gielis, for instance, mentions a man who became a *porion* in 1944 at the age of seventeen.[95] Whether this had to do with the specific circumstances of the war is unclear, but it seems likely that this would have had repercussions in the exercise of authority. In later years, the young age of supervisors seems to have been considered a problem. In an interview in the 1980s, a former supervisor commented on the situation: 'Who became supervisor in former days? Someone, who did his job well. And during the last years this was no longer the case. [They] followed mining school, got their qualification. Still a schoolboy, so to speak. When I gave someone a tip on how to do a task a bit more easily, or [if] a 22-year-old said this to a worker ... he'd just laugh at him.'[96] Even though supervisors had followed specific schooling, the emphasis was still on experience and thus on a certain age.

Conclusion

In Limburg mining was organized in seven modern large-scale companies with an increasingly mechanized production, while state regulation became steadily more intrusive in virtually all aspects of coal mining. The initial development of this new coalfield gave employers the opportunity for a radical transformation in the organization of labour, unhampered by old habits. Since the workforce was slow to organize itself in unions, it was in no position to resist these changes. Work-floor supervision in the Limburg coal mines constituted a crucial element in the organization of work, which had to rely on a strict division of labour and a rigid discipline.

Nevertheless, all levels of supervisors, from *porions* to *conducteurs,* had a considerable range of tasks to perform. First of all they were in charge for the daily allocation of labour, which as a consequence of the high degree of absenteeism could prove cumbersome. Sometimes they were also responsible for measuring the progress of hewers, although this task was usually left to specially appointed employees. Likewise, *porions* had to oversee the proper execution of work and the maintenance of safe working conditions. However, safety issues became a predominant issue only in the late 1950s, while in the inter-war years mining regulations were often ignored. The role of supervisors in training the workforce is somewhat unclear. Employers made no efforts to organize schooling until the late 1930s, and training took place primarily in the workplace itself, where new miners were placed alongside more experienced ones in order to learn the job. To what extent supervisors were involved in this, is unclear.

Finally, because of the large staff of engineers, overseers had few responsibilities with regard to technical and organizational innovation. However, during the inter-war years expertise was considered the primary criterion for promotion to the supervisory staff, as is shown by the average ages and provenance of *porions, chef-porions* and *conducteurs* in the sample of the Beringen coal mine. For this reason, most *porions, chef-porions* and *conducteurs* in the 1920s (and to a certain degree also the 1930s) came from the Walloon coalfields. In Winterslag an important proportion of the overseers was Polish or Czech.

All this meant that supervisors had mainly to focus on increasing output. High wages, bonuses and several other incentives were provided to make sure that supervisors were properly motivated to get the most out of the workforce, or in the eyes of this same workforce, even more than that. Thus, *porions* were first of all disciplinary agents. Although they were supposed to communicate with the workforce in a strict but polite way, it was mostly the violent and loud-mouthed workers, with a desire to earn as much as possible, who were selected by employers. This brutalism, however, was by no means limited to the Limburg coalfield, but seems to have been typical of coal-mining supervisors everywhere.

Notes

1. G. Kurgan-Van Hentenrijk and J. Puissant, 'Industrial Relations in the Belgian Coal Indus-try Since the End of the Nineteenth Century', in *Workers, Owners and Politics in Coal Mining: An International Comparison of Industrial Relations*, ed. G. D. Feldman and K. Tenfelde (New York, 1990), 203–270, here 216.

2. As a consequence, French mining jargon became commonplace with all coal miners in the Limburg coalfield. The French influence was also very clear in the prestigious architecture of several company buildings. For example, the first designs of employee housing for the Beringen coal mine were copied from the French mining region of Anzin.

3. J. Gadisseur, 'Output Per Worker and Its Evolution in Belgian Industry, 1846–1910', in *Productivity in the Economies of Europe*, ed. R. Fremdling and P. O'Brien (Stuttgart, 1983), 141–151, here 144.

4. E. Geerkens, *La rationalisation dans l'industrie belge de l'entre-deux-guerres* (Brussels, 2004), 16. Long-wall mining is a method of working coal by which the seam is removed in one operation by means of a long working face or wall. Work proceeds in a continuous line, which may vary in length. The space from which the coal has been removed (the gob, goaf or waste) is allowed to collapse (caving) or is completely or partially filled with stone and debris.

5. Own translation. L. Denoël, *Commission d'enquête sur la durée du travail dans les mines de houille: Les moyens de production et l'effet utile de l'ouvrier dans les houillères belges* (Brussels, 1908), 86.

6. Own translation. A. Dufrasne, 'Organisation du travail au fond et au jour', Rijksarchief Hasselt (hereafter, RH), Winterslag, 119, Genk, 14 November 1911, 1.

7. This kind of productivity of about one ton per worker (underground and surface) was achieved only in 1934 (996 kg): Geerkens, *La rationalisation*, 21.

8. Own translation. F. Allard, 'De l'emploi des moyens modernes de production dans les charbonnages belges', *Bulletin technique de l' Union des ingénieurs sortis des Écoles spéciales de Louvain*, no. 55 (1928): 23–65, here 43.

9. Own translation. Ibid., 44.

10. P. Lefebvre, *L'invention de la grande entreprise: Travail, hiérarchie, marché. France, fin XVIIIe–début XXe siècle* (Paris, 2003), 173–176; J. Melling, 'Safety, Supervision and the Politics of Productivity in the British Coalmining Industry, 1900–1960', in *Management, Labour and Industrial Politics in Modern Europe: The Quest for Productivity Growth During the Twentieth Century*, ed. J. Melling and A. McKinlay (Cheltenham, 1996), 145–173, here 146.

11. D. Reid, *The Miners of Decazeville: A Genealogy of Deindustrialisation* (Cambridge, 1985), 29.

12. J. Winterton and R. Winterton, 'Production, Politics and Technological Development: British Coal Mining in the Twentieth Century', in *Management, Labour and Industrial Politics in Modern Europe*, 122–144, here 125–127.

13. Geerkens, *La rationalisation*, 325.

14. Allard, 'De l'emploi des moyens', 44.

15. Only two master's theses, focusing on the issue of schooling, have paid some attention to supervisors: J. Boucneau, 'Hier porions vormen? Een historisch-pedagogisch onderzoek naar de behoefte aan en het ontstaan van mijnbouwonderwijs in het Kempisch Bekken, 1901–1954' (MA thesis, Katholieke Universiteit Leuven, 1987); J. Col, 'Van mijnwerker tot ploegbaas: Recrutering, onthaal, aanpassing en vorming' (MA thesis, Hoger Instituut van de Arbeid, 1962).

16. Own translation. L. Ladens, *De Put* (Tongeren, 1928), 41.

17. TWI (training-within-industry) was first developed in the United States during the Second World War and was later taken over in the Belgian mining industry as a fast way of training new, foreign miners.

18. B. Pluymers, 'De Limburgse mijnwerkers (1917–1939): Ontstaan en consolidatie van de arbeidsmarkt voor mijnarbeid' (research report, Limburgs Universitair Centrum, 1996), 58.
19. A. P. Versteegh, *De onvermijdelijke afkomst? De opname van Polen in het Duits, Belgisch en Nederlands mijnbedrijf in de periode 1920–1930* (Hilversum, 1994), 210–213.
20. 'Hoofdopzichters inlichtingen, 1957', Archief Vlaams Mijnmuseum (hereafter, VMM), 51-1-7-G. Since the file was compiled with the purpose of determining an additional pension for supervisors, only those who were active in Beringen until their retirement were included.
21. Yearly records compiled by each coal mine for the Voorzorgskas der Kempen, the regional pension fund for coal miners.
22. When coming across different men with the same name, in most cases checking with workplace (underground or surface) or wage sufficed to be left with one possibility.
23. 'Salaires des surveillants, 1924', VMM, 51-10-2-E.
24. For each supervisor the number of his work tag is mentioned. When quitting his job, this number would be reassigned to another supervisor, most likely his replacement. In the half-year period of this particular wage book only 94 different numbers are recorded against 159 names. For some numbers as many as 5 different names are written down.
25. The number of coal miners in the Limburg coalfield increased rapidly from 3,199 in 1920 to 9,851 in 1925 and 23,484 in 1930.
26. Own translation. 'Note sur les rendements des charbonnages de Campine, Waterschei, 3 October 1929, 1–2', RH, Waterschei, 139.
27. Pluymers, 'De Limburgse mijnwerkers', 49–50.
28. Ibid., 55; M. Van Haegendoren and B. Pluymers, 'Belgisch-Limburgse mijnwerkers in de jaren twintig: Willige slachtoffers van het kapitaal of een "blauwe-maandag compagnie"?' *Tijdschrift voor Sociale Geschiedenis* 24, no. 1 (1998): 31–55, here 43–47.
29. 'Absences Beringen, 1929', VMM, 51-10-2-E.
30. H. Verdinne, *Le problème de l'organisation scientifique du travail dans les mines* (Brussels, 1947), 34.
31. Several of the *directeur-gérants* stayed for about twenty years, and A. Dufrasne was in charge of the coal mine at Winterslag for an astonishing thirty-six years (1912–1948).
32. Geerkens, *La rationalisation*, 317–318. The following part is largely based on J. Dalemans and L. Suetens, *Handleiding tot de mijnbouwkunde* (Brussels, 1947), 282–283.
33. In the Limburg collieries the number of production levels varied between three and seven.
34. Like all the mining jargon in the Limburg coalfields, the French expressions for supervisory functions were taken over from the Walloon pits, and as such the Dutch words *hoofd-opzichter* or *meester-opzichter* were never generally adopted. Besides, the French and Dutch terms do not seem to cover entirely the same meaning, which caused a certain degree of confusion. For example, *afdelingsopzichter* was used both in the meaning of *conducteur* and *chef-porion*. See Boucneau, 'Hier porions vormen', 27; H. Crompvoets and H. H. A. Van De Wijngaard, *Woordenboek van de Limburgse dialecten. 2: Niet-agrarische vakterminologieën. 5: Mijnwerker* (Assen, 1989), 58.
35. G. Defoin, *555 termen uit de vaktaal der mijnarbeiders van Belgisch-Limburg* (Zonhoven, 1958), 23.
36. Work in the Limburg coal mines was organized in three eight-hour shifts with a focus on one type of work. In the first shift (6 AM to 2 PM) the coal was cut, while in the second one (2 PM to 10 PM) the conveyor belts were moved closer to the coalface. During the nightshift, dug-out areas were secured with backfill or more commonly caved in and preparations were made for the coal-shift of the next day. In practice the work often varied according to the specific circumstances and the ongoing mechanization of coal production and transport. This cyclical organization of labour was first introduced in 1924 by the Winterslag coal mine, replacing the traditional cutting of coal in two shifts with a simultaneous filling. This continuous system certainly accounts for part of the complexity of the production process and the labour organization. See G. Coppieters, 'Waren wij maar Walen of

Kongolezen: Arbeid en lonen. Sociale geschiedenis van de Limburgse mijnen 1917–1985. Deel 2' (research report, Vrije Universiteit Brussel, 1999), 62–66; Geerkens, *La rationalisation*, 327.

37. Supervisors used the yardstick for measuring the progress of coal and stone hewers, and as an instrument for checking the condition of the roof in the production areas. In his study on labour relations in the nineteenth-century British coal-mining industry, Jaffe describes the yardstick as a symbol of the viewer's authority or tyranny: J. Jaffe, *The Struggle for Market Power: Industrial Relations in the British Coal Industry, 1800–1840* (Cambridge, 1991), 62.

38. Dalemans and Suetens, *Handleiding*, 282.

39. L. Roppe, *De steenkool en haar problemen* (Hasselt, 1948), 16.

40. In the three shifts these numbers were respectively 4, 3 and 5 supervisors for a workforce of 77, 45 and 57. The rather high proportion of supervisors during the third shift (10 PM to 6 AM) reflects the higher number of different activities (backfilling, caving-in, supporting), and the importance of safety issues when performing these. See Dalemans and Suetens, *Handleiding*, 36.

41. Verdinne, *Le problème*, 282.

42. Coppieters, 'Waren wij maar', 163.

43. Ibid., 144.

44. Verdinne, *Le problème*, 34.

45. Only after the Second World War did the selection of supervisors take place according to strict criteria, based on age and seniority, health, absenteeism, qualifications and studies, and advice from hierarchical superiors. Coppieters, 'Waren wij maar', 161.

46. 'Le choix des surveillants: quelques notes sur la conduite des travaux souterrains', Verzameling Luc Minten (hereafter, VLM).

47. Pluymers, 'De Limburgse mijnwerkers', 57. When from the late 1930s specific schooling for future supervisors was gradually developed, a few years of experience were still considered necessary. That practice remained decisive even then is illustrated by the fact that in 1950 only about one-fifth of the *porions* in Beringen had a qualification from the mining school for supervisors.

48. T. Gielis, 'Van vader op zoon? De keuze van de mijnwerkerszoon voor de mijn in Beringen (1945–1989)' (MA thesis, Katholieke Universiteit Leuven, 2005), 51.

49. Boucneau, 'Hier porions vormen', 27.

50. G. Van Meulder, 'Arbeidsverhoudingen en syndicalisme: Sociale geschiedenis van de Limburgse mijnen 1917–1985. Deel 1' (research report, Vrije Universiteit Brussel, 1999), 21.

51. This national negotiation board, in which employers, unions and government were represented, was established in 1920 primarily in order to contain social unrest in the mining industry by means of collective agreements.

52. Van Meulder, 'Arbeidsverhoudingen', B.4–4.

53. Dalemans and Suetens, *Handleiding*, 56.

54. T. De Rijck and G. Van Meulder, *De ereburgers: Een sociale geschiedenis van de Limburgse mijnwerkers* (Berchem, 2000), 132–133. This kind of behaviour was, however, in no way limited to the Belgian Limburg coal mines, but seemed to be part of coal mining in general. See, for example, Melling, 'Safety, Supervision', 158. Cooper-Richet stated that the harsh authority of *porions* was based on the fact that their professional skills were not transferable to other industrial sectors, and as such they had no career opportunities outside the coal industry. As a consequence *porions* were inclined to be very loyal to their company: D. Cooper-Richet, 'Les porions', *Travail* (1987): 50–53.

55. 'Werkstaking Zwartberg 1929–1930. Brief van August Cool, namens de CVM aan Allard, Winterslag, 26 maart 1930', Provinciaal Archief Hasselt (hereafter, PAH), 232.

56. Coppieters, 'Waren wij maar', 156.

57. De Rijck and Van Meulder, *De ereburgers*, 132. The same was true for France: S. Vandecas-teele-Schweitzer, 'Comment peut-on être contremaître?' in *L'usine et le bureau: Itinéraires sociaux et professionnels dans l'entreprise XIXe et XXe siècles*, ed Y. Lequin and S. Vandecas-teele (Lyon, 1990), 93–108, here 97–98.

58. Gielis, 'Van vader op zoon', 73. Although violence was never completely eliminated from the work floor, the more rigorous selection procedure of supervisors after the Second World War probably made it less likely.

59. Coppieters, 'Waren wij maar', 159; see also Van Haegendoren and Pluymers, 'Belgisch-Limburgse mijnwerkers', 31–55.

60. De Rijck and Van Meulder, *De ereburgers*, 132.

61. Dalemans and Suetens, *Handleiding*, 284–285.

62. Coppieters, 'Waren wij maar', 69.

63. In Winterslag, maintaining a straight coalface was also enforced by giving coalface work-ers a bonus of 5 francs (1924) when they complied with this requirement. Geerkens, *La rationalisation*, 328.

64. Dalemans and Suetens, *Handleiding*, 286.

65. Several consultation organs were introduced that promoted research and regulation con-cerning safety and health issues. The national government issued stricter preconditions for miners under the age of twenty-one.

66. Dalemans and Suetens, *Handleiding*, 287–288.

67. Ibid., 289.

68. 'Le choix des surveillants: quelques notes sur la conduite des travaux souterrains', VLM.

69. Dalemans and Suetens, *Handleiding*, 289.

70. Coppieters, 'Waren wij maar', 156.

71. De Rijck and Van Meulder, *De ereburgers*, 136.

72. Coppieters, 'Waren wij maar', 157.

73. L. Minten, 'De stakingen in de Limburgse steenkoolmijnen tijdens het interbellum' (MA thesis, Katholieke Universiteit Leuven, 1984), 117.

74. Gielis, 'Van vader op zoon', 46.

75. 'Salaire: augmentation du 1er avril 1919, 1919', VMM, 51-10-2-E.

76. 'Salaires des surveillants, 1924', VMM, 51-10-2-E.

77. 'Salaire des surveillants EST, 1943', VMM, 51-10-2-E.

78. Own translation. 'Réunion Association Charbonnière de la Campine, 8 April 1925', VLM, as quoted in Coppieters, 'Waren wij maar', 164.

79. In a 1956 enquiry in the coal mine of Beringen, it seemed that most *chef-porions* and *premiers porions* were house owners and did not want to move into company housing. 'Hoofd-opzichters inlichtingen, 1957', VMM, 51-1-7-G.

80. R. Biasi, 'Migranten in de mijnbouw: Een onderzoek naar de leefwereld van de Italiaanse mijnwerkers in Eisden na de tweede wereldoorlog' (research report, Limburgs Universitair Centrum, 1996), 48.

81. Gielis, 'Van vader op zoon', 75.

82. Dalemans and Suetens, *Handleiding*, 5.

83. Between 1922 (the first year of exploitation) and 1930, the proportion of foreigners in the total workforce rose from 20 to about 50 per cent.

84. At 15 per cent the coal mine of Eisden had by far the highest percentage. Pluymers, 'De Limburgse mijnwerkers', 26. The faster work rhythm, the language and the relative isolation were reasons why Walloon miners loathed working in Limburg. P. Gruselin, *Le bassin minier de la Campine* (Brussels, 1925), 31; B. Van Doorslaer, 'Het Kempisch steenkoolbekken 1901–1940: Bijdrage tot haar geschiedenis en haar problematiek' (MA thesis, Rijksuniversiteit Gent, 1976), 175; F. Caestecker, 'Vervanging of verdringing van de buitenlandse mijnwerkers in Limburg: De emancipatie van de Limburgse mijnwerkers', *Limburg: Het Oude Land van Loon* 77 (1998): 309–326, here 312.

85. Own translation. Gruselin, *Le bassin minier,* 31.
86. 'Personnel: directeur, ingénieurs & employés, 1918', Museum van de Mijnwerkerswoning Eisden (MMW).
87. This can be explained by the fact that Foraky, the company responsible for the excavation of the shafts, had its own specialized personnel.
88. N. Paesen, 'De André Dumont-mijn van Waterschei (1907–1940): Bijdrage tot de mijn-werkers-problematiek' (MA thesis, Katholieke Universiteit Leuven, 1986), 66.
89. Van Haegendoren and Pluymers, 'Belgisch-Limburgse mijnwerkers', 40–41.
90. De Rijck and Van Meulder, *De ereburgers,* 188–191.
91. F. Caestecker, 'Het vreemdelingenbeleid in de tussenoorlogse periode in België, 1922–1939', *Belgisch Tijdschrift voor Nieuwste Geschiedenis* 15, no. 3–4 (1984): 461–486; F. Caestecker, 'Centraaleuropese mijnwerkers in België', in *Geschiedenis van het eigen volk: De vreemdeling in België van de prehistorie tot nu,* ed. A. Morelli (Louvain, 1993), 165–174.
92. Versteegh, *De onvermijdelijke afkomst,* 207–224.
93. The years between 1930 and 1935 showed a strong decline in the number of foreign miners in the labour force. F. Caestecker, 'Vakbonden en etnische minderheid, een ambigue ver-houding: Immigratie in de Belgische mijnbekkens, 1900–1940', *Brood en Rozen: Tijdschrift voor de Geschiedenis van Sociale Bewegingen* 16, no. 1 (1997): 51–64; I. Goddeeris, *De Poolse migratie in België, 1945–1950: Politieke mobilisatie en sociale differentiatie* (Amsterdam, 2005). On the other hand, job changes within a company were not mentioned in the regis-tration records. Polish miners who became *porion* afterwards thus remain invisible.
94. Caestecker, 'Vervanging of verdringing', 321; Caestecker, 'Vakbonden en etnische mind-erheid', 51–64; A. Morelli, 'Ambiguités et contradictions des rapports entre syndicats et étrangers: Le cas des Italiens', *Brood en Rozen: Tijdschrift voor de Geschiedenis van Sociale Bewegingen* 16, no. 1 (1997): 65–71.
95. Gielis, 'Van vader op zoon', 45.
96. De Rijck and Van Meulder, *De ereburgers,* 135.

POSTSCRIPT

Patricia Van den Eeckhout

Overall, the contributions to this volume illustrate the multiple faces of the foreman in Western European industry. He was not a one-dimensional figure, embodying either an iron fist or fatherly wisdom, but a multifaceted character combining experience and technical expertise with educational and organizational qualities. The foreman as a savage brute, portrayed among others by Richard Edwards, undoubtedly existed, but in the chapters assembled in this volume he hardly crosses our path. It appears, however, that in the Limburg mines, characterized by a highly volatile workforce and absenteeism, foremen were portrayed as more brutal than in other sectors dealt with in this book. This suggests a connection between the character of authority relations and the matter of whether the workforce was accustomed to shop-floor discipline or not. In the absence of the latter form of experience, human relations seemed much harsher. The Limburg case also illustrates that even if modern administrations tried to 'depersonalize' the relationship between foreman and worker for reasons of efficiency, they did not necessarily succeed in removing abusive language, threats, arbitrariness and protection.

The composition of the workforce could also influence the level of supervision deemed necessary: in late nineteenth-century France, urban workshops, and Parisian ones in particular, were less in need of foremen than were those areas with less experienced workers. This might lead to the conclusion that in sectors attracting workers who were less accustomed to industrial routines, the disciplinary character of the foreman's job was more developed. In the supervision of a more stable and experienced workforce, it may have been more efficient to establish and maintain the reciprocal ties that bound foreman and work-group together, as the chapter on the English mining and printing sectors of the 1830s shows.

The composition of the workforce was not the only factor to influence the character of shop-floor relations. The disciplinary side of a foreman's job was more obvious in the cases of the Belgian miners, the Catalan weavers, and the

Notes for this section begin on page 224.

Ghent and Catalan spinners who performed supervisory functions: in all of these cases supervisors and foremen benefited financially from coercing workers.

In the other industrial sectors studied in this volume, the disciplinary aspects of foremen's tasks appeared to be less salient. That could be the result of the fact that in craft-based sectors, such as engineering and heavy manufacturing, the disciplining of the workforce was not the sole responsibility of the supervisor, but was part of the workers' socialization process. Craft discipline was embedded in a workshop culture, shared by workers and foremen. The authority of the latter was a complex mixture of experience, expertise, coercion and paternalism, and as a result the association of foremen with mere compulsion was less pronounced. Whether that kind of workshop culture reigned in the Ghent artisanal enterprises is not clear, but we do know that in these cases also, imposing discipline was only one of the foreman's duties. Being reliable and a good organizer, and having expert knowledge seemed to be even more important assets: these qualities were as vital for the workers who were supervised as for their employers.

The contributions dealing with British engineering, heavy manufacturing and car industries confirm the view of scientific management's slow and piecemeal introduction in British industry, but they also reveal that the undermining of the foreman's position as a result of this process was less pronounced than older literature suggests. The expansion of a technical staff did not lead to a drastic and unambiguous erosion of his prerogatives. Overall, the transformation of the foreman's power and autonomy was a far more complex process than hitherto assumed. How long that process (or at least how it was perceived) might have taken is illustrated by David Collinson's ethnographic study of Slavs, a fictive name for a plant producing heavy trucks in the North of England in the late 1970s. Collinson mentions the impressions of a foreman named Stan, who had been thirty-eight years with Slavs and twenty years as a foreman: 'Perhaps in danger of romanticizing the past, Stan defines the dramatic organizational changes at Slavs in terms of increasing impersonality, bureaucracy and the erosion of foremen's discretion and authority. According to Stan, the "American system" has increased wastage, costs, inefficiency and boredom, where "nobody will believe you unless it's in black and white". The old managerial style depended on trust and verbal forms of communication, but this has been replaced by inflexible bureaucratic systems.'[1] Pronounced at the end of the 1970s, this statement echoes comments of a few decades earlier.

Supervisors in Russia, Japan, China and India

In our survey of the literature on supervision in American and European industry we encountered a wide variation in forms of labour management:

from the independent contractor recruiting labour for different firms to the salaried foreman who spends his whole career with one employer. In the course of the nineteenth century, systems of indirect labour management operating with semi-independent internal contractors tended to be replaced by directly employed foremen who had less autonomy than their predecessors. The literature on supervision in industry elsewhere in the world is not abundant. Case studies on St. Petersburg, Shanghai, Bombay and Japan regarding industrial relations in the first decades of the twentieth century suggest that, with the exception of St. Petersburg, indirect labour management was very important even beyond the First World War.

Employers in these regions resorted to the services of contractors when labour was scarce, when their demands were highly variable, when they lacked information or connections or when labour had to be recruited at long distance. In the way these contractors functioned there were sometimes quite a few similarities with their counterparts in Western Europe and the United States. Often contractors not only recruited but also managed labour and operated as internal contractors, who worked with the employers' infrastructure. As such, they were responsible for the whole production process: they hired, trained and supervised labour and had to cope autonomously with all the organizational and technical problems. The system was a solution for employers who lacked technological and organizational know-how and appreciated that these middlemen kept productions costs low.

At first sight, labour relations in the industries of St. Petersburg, Shanghai, Bombay and Japan were more often characterized by clientelism, nepotism and bribery than in Western Europe and the United States. However, it would be premature to underscore the contrast, in the first decades of the twentieth century, between Western firms with emerging personnel departments and formalized and 'objectified' criteria for hiring, evaluating and firing employees, and the practices in other parts of the world. The chapters in this volume dealing with that period suggest that interpersonal relations and networks still coloured the rapport between supervisors and workers. The study of labour relations in smaller firms and other sectors than mining, engineering, heavy manufacturing and car industries would undoubtedly reveal that 'archaic' practices were still part of the day-to-day management of labour. Walter Licht, for instance, emphasizes 'the oscillating, recurring, and uneven nature of personnel practices' after studying some twenty Philadelphian firms between 1850 and 1950.[2] Roger Horowitz's account of foremen's arbitrary practices in the meatpacking industry of the post-1930 period is but one other example of the persistence of a 'pre-modern' approach to personnel policies.[3]

'The Little Whip'

According to Steve Smith's description of foremen in pre-war St. Petersburg,[4] the foreman as a tyrannical character using driving methods seems to have dominated the scene. As in the industrialized West he hired and fired, allocated work, set rates and imposed labour discipline, but he did it with such violence and disrespect that, as a result, a substantial number of economic strikes on the eve of the First World War were related to authority issues. Before that, the 1905 revolution led to an explosion of protest against inhumane treatment by supervisory personnel.[5] Female workers were victims of sexual harassment, but when forewomen were in charge bullying and abuse were not necessarily absent.[6] However, in industries relying on craft labour, cooperation was friendlier and welcoming rituals were organized so as to secure goodwill on both sides.[7] Workers of all types tried to survive by developing patron-client relations with their foremen. Nepotism and corruption, mentioned in some of the American literature on foremen and contractors, were widespread in Russian cities. Family relations, bribery or the fact that foreman and worker came from the same region, bought the latter a ticket to work. Some foremen made a handsome income from the 'gifts' they received. Informing on co-workers was another way of ingratiating oneself with the overseer.[8] In the trade-union and social-democratic press, foremen were presented as class traitors and agents of capital. In contrast with Great Britain, the idea of incorporating foremen and assistant foremen in workers' unions was rejected.[9]

Oyakata, Middlemen and Jobbers

While the importance of internal contracting remains unclear where St. Petersburg is concerned,[10] there is no doubt that in countries such as Japan, India and China forms of indirect labour management were an essential part of industrial life before the First World War and even beyond. In Japan the engineering and metalworking industries knew the system of the *oyakata*, an intermediary who either operated as an external subcontractor who worked for various companies or someone who functioned as an internal contractor for one particular company. By the early 1900s the latter type of *oyakata* became more important.[11] But the large-scale government-run factories, developed between the 1860s and the 1880s, adopted a direct-employment system and an elaborate system of supervision. According to Hiroshi Hazama, it resembled policing rather than labour management. For leaving work without notice, for example, workers were tied to a wooden post.[12]

  Privately run factories were initially of a smaller scale. The *oyakata* system was a response to their fluctuating demand for trained workers. At the basis of the development of the system lay problems in labour recruitment and the fact that higher management lacked practical understanding of the work process and had no authority over workers.[13] The *oyakata* acquired a contract by competitive bidding, trained and hired labour, determined work methods, supervised the work process, paid his crew and kept the rest as his profit although he was expected to share part of it with his men as drinking money. Even workers directly employed by private firms were under the *oyakata*'s control. The *oyakata* pocketed a large part of job contract wages: in fact workers had to give the *oyakata* a commission for services rendered. On the other hand, the *oyakata* provided informal benefits and care to his crew and he was more or less responsible for procuring jobs for its members.[14] Since the *oyakata* felt no particular loyalty to a firm, he moved easily from one company to another, taking his crew with him, thus contributing to the high level of turnover.[15]

Around 1900, the increasing mechanization in large metalworking companies enhanced the need for a more specialized workforce (instead of the training in manual skills provided by the *oyakata*) and a more direct control of the labour process. Efforts were made to integrate the *oyakata* into the company as foremen. For the workers, paternalist company initiatives compensated to some extent for the informal benefits offered by the *oyakata*, while specific welfare policies were designed for the latter so that they would stay and identify with the company.[16] Koji Taira concludes that 'management's direct grasp of the work force transferred to management three functions of the traditional *oyakata*: training, pay, and the provision of job and income security'.[17]

While the *oyakata* recruited and managed labour, the middlemen operating in the Japanese textile industry only took care of recruitment. Employers made use of their services when the local labour market proved inadequate to satisfy the growing demand for workers. By the 1890s the use of these intermediaries was widespread. They recruited young, unmarried women in distant areas and they were paid a commission for each worker who signed up. These textile workers were subsequently imprisoned in dormitories (widely used by the 1890s), in order to reduce the high level of labour turnover and absenteeism and thus the loss of workers that the employer had paid a commission for.[18]

In the Shanghai cotton mills, the functions of foreman and labour contractor were often combined.[19] The foreman hired and fired and in order to secure a job, workers needed connections or they had to resort to bribery. However, this was not a one-way relationship. The bond between workers and foremen was based on reciprocity: foremen offered work, protection and mediation with higher management while workers showed loyalty and enhanced the prestige of their patron. When the management of some firms tried to introduce direct hiring in the 1920s, workers went on strike because they resented the loss of power of those they regarded as their protectors. When a foreman died or left, workers felt insecure because of the disappearance of ties based on kinship, common geographical origin or 'gifts'.[20] Sometimes solidarity between foremen and workers went as far as going on strike to back up each other's position. These clientelist relationships were limited to the Chinese-owned enterprises because in the British-owned and Japanese-owned mills foremen were usually foreign. Japanese and British foremen made use of interpreters, while their Chinese and Japanese supervisors, 'Number Ones', assigned and supervised work. In the 1920s, hiring in Shanghai's Chinese mills came under control of labour racketeers and foremen and forewomen with gang connections.[21]

Tim Wright observes that until the 1920s and 1930s Chinese mines also operated with contract labour. Contractors supplied and supervised the labour force and often provided tools and materials. The larger the scale of the operations, the greater was the need to subcontract management functions. A lack of trained supervisors, the inability of foreign owners to speak Chinese and the aversion of the Chinese upper class towards manual labour, were all factors leading to the widespread use of the system. Its gradual demise was caused, among other things, by the fact that workers increasingly opposed it.[22]

R. Chandavarkar remarks with some irony that the jobber, who operated as an intermediary between employers and workers, has been portrayed as 'an institution peculiarly suited to the specificities of Indian culture and conditions'.[23] In fact the Indian jobber can be considered a variant of the (internal) contractors we discussed for other countries. Chandavarkar stresses that the jobber's function and power and his relationship with employers and workers varied considerably according to the sector.[24] In general the jobber ensured a steady supply of labour in the face of fluctuating demand, but his role and influence reached beyond the labour market. While he was usually promoted from the shop floor, thanks to the patronage of friends or relatives, it was the neighbourhood network on which he relied that supplied him with the casual labour he required. Some jobbers established commercial and social ties with potential workers by procuring services such as credit, advice, boarding for single workers or arbitration in disputes. The combination of these spheres of influence made the jobber a powerful man, but also raised the pressure to meet his followers' expectations. Both on the shop floor and in the neighbourhood, competing patrons were a threat to his position.[25] In the Bombay cotton mills the jobbers' role was particularly important given the extensive use of casual labour. Jobbers hired and fired workers and when they quit they often took their crew with them. Jobbers also disciplined labour, played an important role in the distribution of work, raw materials and machinery and in the administration of fines. Some jobbers fulfilled technical functions. The jobber's power largely depended on the bargaining position of the workers he supervised. Groups like skilled weavers, who were in a favourable position in this respect, experienced a more lenient control from their jobber than their unskilled colleagues.[26]

Research Perspectives

In the conclusion of his ethnographic study of work organization in a domestic appliance factory, Oswald Jones remarks that 'we do not know in enough useful detail what management is, what it is like to manage'.[27] If such is the complaint of researchers who can resort to participant observation, then how desperate must the historians of labour and shop-floor relations be. Even if historians are unable to duplicate the ethnographers' methods in the archives, they might be inspired by the ethnographic imagination, 'a way of getting at some of this cultural complexity, a way to reflect on experience in ways that go beyond easy categories and distinctions'.[28]

While this collection of essays has certainly increased our knowledge of the foreman's functions, his job profile and what workers and employers expected from him, we can paraphrase Jones's observation and conclude: we do not know in enough useful detail what supervising is, what it is like to supervise. Not only do we lack information on the foreman's daily routines and reactions in crisis situations, but we also need to find out more about his relations with his superiors and with the local networks of which he was a part. The foreman still remains too much of a cardboard character, reduced to the 'objective' functions he was performing: hiring, instructing, sanctioning and firing.

Most striking in the lacuna of our knowledge of foremen in the industries of Western Europe is the intertwining of authority with gender and ethnic relations. We might have succeeded in making fore*men* more visible, but we were unable to bring forewomen to life. In fact, we know hardly anything about them. Our knowledge of how gender constructed the relations between the male supervisor and the men or women he was directing, is not that much better. 'Gender is central to any examination of the routine reproduction of the contradictory conditions and effects of controls, resistances and subjectivities in organizations', Collinson remarks.[29] In general, we seem to be somewhat better informed on how the construction of masculinity interfered with the relation between male workers and their supervisors, than on the relationship of the latter with their female subordinates. However, Steve Meyer points to the selectiveness in the study of working-class masculinity. Researchers show a preference for the more respectable rather than the rougher expressions of 'manliness'. He is convinced that 'the tendency to heroicize working-class struggles has limited a thorough examination of the more savage, violent, and sexist forms of gendered behavior at the workplace'.[30] Histories of immigrant labour in European industries undoubtedly contain numerous mentions of experiences with foremen, but a systematic approach of how ethnic relations shaped shop-floor management is still lacking.

How we might proceed in writing these histories of European experiences is suggested in Geert De Neve's plea for more 'thick description' in the literature on labour and labour relations in India:

> Studies of 'labour relations' could well dispense with their teleological contents and open up to incorporate a study of everyday relations, interactions and discourses which bring alive many workplaces – small or large – throughout India. It is suggested that the study of labour relations on the subcontinent would vastly benefit from a more intricate study of work arrangements and social relations on the shop floor, thereby enhancing our understanding of the way in which structural class positions were reproduced as well as challenged through everyday interactions at work.[31]

Notes

1. D. L. Collinson, *Managing the Shopfloor: Subjectivity, Masculinity and Workplace Culture* (New York, 1992), 168–169.
2. W. Licht, 'Studying Work: Personnel Policies in Philadelphia Firms, 1850–1950', in *Masters to Managers: Historical and Comparative Perspectives on American Employers*, ed. S. Jacoby (New York, 1991), 43–73.
3. R. Horowitz, *'Negro and White, Unite and Fight': A Social History of Industrial Unionism in Meatpacking, 1930–1990* (Champaign, 1997).
4. 'The little whip' was a nickname for the foreman used in the socialist propaganda in pre-war Russia: S. Smith, 'Workers against Foremen in St. Petersburg, 1905–1917', in *Making Workers Soviet: Power, Class, and Identity*, ed. L. H. Siegelbaum and R. G. Suny (Ithaca, 1994), 113–137, here 128.
5. Smith, 'Workers against Foremen', 113–121; G. D. Surh, *1905 in St. Petersburg: Labor, Society, and Revolution* (Palo Alto, 1989), 150, 181, 194.
6. Smith, 'Workers against Foremen', 120–121.
7. Ibid., 123–125.
8. Ibid., 117, 125–127.
9. Ibid., 127–128.
10. Ibid., 116, note 12.
11. A. Gordon, *The Evolution of Labor Relations in Japan Heavy Industry, 1853–1955* (Cambridge, 1985), 36–38; C. Littler, *The Development of the Labour Process in Capitalist Societies* (London, 1982), 146–160; K. Taira, 'Factory Labour and the Industrial Revolution in Japan', in *The Cambridge Economic History of Europe*, 7 vols., ed. P. Mathias and M. M. Postan (Cambridge, 1978), vol. 7, part 2, 166–214.
12. H. Hazama, *The History of Labour Management in Japan* (Basingstoke, 1997), 111–121.
13. Gordon, *Evolution of Labor Relations*, 38–40.
14. Ibid., 38–43, 57; Hazama, *History of Labour Management*, 25, 137–140, 151.
15. K. Thelen, *How Institutions Evolve: The Political Economy of Skills in Germany, Britain, the United States, and Japan* (Cambridge, 2004), 158–159.

16. Gordon, *Evolution of Labor Relations*, 51–62, 70.
17. Taira, 'Factory Labour', 207.
18. J. Hunter, *Women and the Labour Market in Japan's Industrialising Economy* (London, 2003), 72–74, 103–109; Taira, 'Factory Labour', 180–187, 199–205.
19. S. Smith, 'Workers and Supervisors: St Petersburg 1905–1917 and Shanghai 1895–1927', *Past and Present*, no. 139 (1993): 131–177.
20. See also S. Smith, *Like Cattle and Horses: Nationalism and Labor in Shanghai, 1895–1927* (Durham, 2002), 20–37.
21. M. W. Frazier, *The Making of the Chinese Industrial Workplace: State, Revolution, and Labor Management* (Cambridge, 2002), 33–35.
22. T. Wright, '"A Method of Evading Management": Contract Labor in Chinese Coal Mines before 1937', *Comparative Studies in Society and History* 23 (1981): 656–678.
23. R. Chandavarkar, *The Origins of Industrial Capitalism in India: Business Strategies and the Working Classes in Bombay, 1900–1940* (Cambridge, 1994), 100.
24. Ibid., 101. See also the practices of the suppliers and supervisors of labour in the Calcutta jute mills: D. Chakrabarty, *Rethinking Working-Class History: Bengal 1890–1940* (Guildford, 2000), 94–114.
25. Chandavarkar, *Origins of Industrial Capitalism*, 195–200.
26. Ibid., 295–307. See also R. Chandavarkar, 'The War on the Shopfloor', in *Coolies, Capital and Colonialism: Studies in Indian Labour History*, ed. R. P. Behal and M. Van der Linden (Cambridge, 2007), 265–278.
27. O. Jones, 'Scientific Management, Culture and Control: A First-Hand Account of Taylorism in Practice', *Human Relations* 53, no. 5 (2000): 631–653, here 649.
28. N. Dolby and G. Dimitriadis, 'Learning to Labor in New Times: An Introduction', in *Learning to Labor in New Times*, ed. N. Dolby, G. Dimitriadis and P. E. Willis (London, 2004), 1–16, here 5.
29. Collinson, *Managing the Shopfloor*, 34.
30. S. Meyer, 'Rough Manhood: The Aggressive and Confrontational Shop Culture of U.S. Auto Workers During World War II', *Journal of Social History* 36, no. 1 (2002): 125–147, here 125.
31. G. De Neve, *The Everyday Politics of Labour: Working Lives in India's Informal Economy* (Oxford, 2005), 135–136.

CONTRIBUTORS

Cristina Borderías is professor at the department of Modern History at the University of Barcelona and director of the research group Work, Institutions and Gender. Her publications include *Entre Líneas. Trabajo e identidad femenina en la España Contemporànea: La Compañía Telefónica Nacional de España* (Barcelona, 1993); 'Women's Work and Household Economic Strategies in Industrializing Catalonia', *Social History* 29, no. 3 (2004): 373–383; 'A Gendered View of Family in Mid-Nineteenth Century Barcelona', *Histoire et Mesure* 18, no. 1–2 (2003): 113–146; and 'Salarios y subsistencia de las trabajadoras y trabajadores de La España Industrial, 1849–1868', *Barcelona Quaderns d'Història* 11 (2006): 223–238.

Jérôme Bourdieu is research fellow at the Institut National de la Recherche Agronomique (France). His research fields are labour and income distribution. He has recently published, with B. Reynaud, 'Factory Discipline, Health and Externalities in the Reduction of Working Time in Nineteenth-Century France', *Socio-Economic Review* 4, no. 1 (2006): 93–118; and, with L. Kesztenbaum, 'Vieux, riches et bien portants.: Une application de la base TRA aux liens entre mortalite et richesse', *Annales de démographie historique*, no. 1 (2004): 79–105.

Richard Coopey teaches history at the University of Wales, Aberystwyth, and is a visiting research associate in the Business History Unit, London School of Economics. He has published widely on a range of economic, technological and business history topics, including *Banking and Finance in Britain since 1850* (London, 2007); with D. O'Connell and D. Porter, *Mail Order Retailing in Britain: A Business and Social History* (Oxford, 2006); with D. Clarke, *3i: Fifty Years Investing in Industry* (Oxford, 1995); and edited *Information Technology Policy History: International Perspectives* (Oxford, 2005). Currently researching the technologies and politics of water, he is director of the

Aberystwyth Water History Project and co-founder and past president of the International Water History Association.

Bart Delbroek studied history and international and European law at the Vrije Universiteit Brussel. His master's thesis in history was on the anti-nuclear movement in Flanders from 1973 to 1986. Funded by FWO-Vlaanderen, he is currently preparing a PhD on the daily functioning of the labour market for coal miners in Belgian Limburg (1901–1966) at the same university. On the history of the *livret*, he published 'Werkboekjes in de 20e eeuw: De charmes van een vergeten bron', *Brood & Rozen: Tijdschrift voor de geschiedenis van sociale bewegingen*, no. 2 (2006): 7–27.

James A. Jaffe is professor of history at the University of Wisconsin-Whitewater. He has written widely in the field of British labour history, including *The Struggle for Market Power* (Cambridge, 1991) and *Striking a Bargain* (Manchester, 2000). An edited and annotated version of the diaries of Francis Place was published by the Royal Historical Society in 2007. Currently, his interests include the cultural foundations of workplace industrial relations, the transplantation of British modes of alternative dispute resolution to India and other areas of the empire, and the study of the creation of identities during the era of British industrialization. He has held fellowships from the National Science Foundation (US), the National Endowment for the Humanities (US), among others, and is a Fellow of the Royal Historical Society.

Alan McKinlay is professor of management at the University of St Andrews. He has published extensively on labour and business history, contemporary management and work organization, and organization theory. With Ken Starkey he co-edited *Foucault, Management and Organisation Theory* (London, 1998). He is a member of the editorial board of *Management and Organizational History*. His current research includes the long-term impact of team-working initiatives on workplace trade unionism and the interaction of strategy, work organization and performance in commercial television.

Joseph Melling is professor of history and medical history at the University of Exeter. He was educated at Bradford, Glasgow Universities and has been employed at Glasgow, Cambridge, Liverpool and Exeter Universities. He has published widely in labour history, urban history and medical history, including, with Bill Forsythe, *The Politics of Madness* (London, 2006) and, with Alan Booth, *Managing the Modern Workplace* (Aldershot, 2008). He is presently researching the history of occupational health in Britain, United States and Africa while completing a book on supervisors in the United Kingdom since 1850.

Gilles Postel-Vinay is director of studies at the École des Hautes Études en Sciences Sociales and senior research fellow at the Institut National de la Recherche Agronomique (France). His main publications include *La rente foncière dans le capitalisme agricole* (Paris, 1974); with J.-M. Moriceau, *Ferme, entreprise, famille* (Paris, 1992); *La terre et l' argent* (Paris, 1998); with J.-M. Chanut, J. Heffer and J. Mairesse, *L'industrie française au milieu du XIXe siècle: Les enquêtes de la statistique générale de la France* (Paris, 2000); with P. Hoffman and J.-L. Rosenthal, *Priceless Markets: Credit in Paris, 1660–1870* (Chicago, 2000) and a French version *Des marchés sans prix: Une économie politique du crédit à Paris, 1660–1870* (Paris, 2001); with P. Hoffman and J.-L. Rosenthal, *Surviving Large Losses* (Cambridge, MA, 2007).

Peter Scholliers is professor of history at the Vrije Universiteit Brussel. He teaches and studies the social history of Europe since 1800, and particularly the history of labour, food and material culture. He published *Food, Drink and Identity: Cooking, Eating and Drinking in Europe since the Middle Ages* (Oxford, 2001); with Leonard Schwarz, *Experiencing Wages: Social and Cultural Aspects of Wage Forms in Europe since 1500* (Oxford, 2003), and, with Carmen Sarasua and Leen Van Molle, *Land, Shops and Kitchens: Technology and the Food Chain in Twentieth-Century Europe* (Turnhout, 2005). In the field of labour history, he currently directs research on wage forms and wage systems in Belgium around 1900, and on the labour market of Belgian miners in the twentieth century. Previously, he was involved in a study of the standard of living of Ghent cotton workers, *Wages, Manufacturers and Workers in the 19th-Century Factory* (Oxford, 1996).

Patricia Van den Eeckhout is professor of history and discourse analysis at the Vrije Universiteit Brussel. She has published on the history of social housing policy, working-class family income, consumption, advertising in retailing, leisure and labour relations ('Giving Notice: the Legitimate Way of Quitting and Firing, Ghent, 1877–1896', in *Experiencing Wages: Social and Cultural Aspects of Wage Forms in Europe since 1500* [Oxford, 2003]); social statistics ('Statistics and Social Policy in Inter-war Belgium: The 1928–1929 Inquiry into the Family Budgets of Blue-Collar and White-Collar Workers', *Histoire et Mesure* 19, no. 1–2 [2004]: 95–132); and the historiography of social history ('The Quest for Social History in Belgium, 1948–1998', *Archiv für Sozialgeschichte* [2000]: 217–232). In 1999 she edited a reference book on the sources of Belgian history with G. Vanthemsche, *Bronnen voor de studie van het hedendaagse België*. A new edition is due to be published in 2009. She is currently doing research on workshop regulations and the use of space in Belgian working-class housing.

INDEX